ATLA Monograph Series
edited by Dr. Kenneth E. Rowe

1. Ronald L. Grimes. *The Divine Imagination: William Blake's Major Prophetic Visions.* 1972.
2. George D. Kelsey. *Social Ethics Among Southern Baptists, 1917–1969.* 1973.
3. Hilda Adam Kring. *The Harmonists: A Folk-Cultural Approach.* 1973.
4. J. Steven O'Malley. *Pilgrimage of Faith: The Legacy of the Otterbeins.* 1973.
5. Charles Edwin Jones. *Perfectionist Persuasion: The Holiness Movement and American Methodism. 1867–1936.* 1974.
6. Donald E. Byrne, Jr. *No Foot of Land: Folklore of American Methodist Itinerants.* 1975.
7. Milton C. Sernett. *Black Religion and American Evangelicalism: White Protestants, Plantation Missions, and the Flowering of Negro Christianity, 1787–1865.* 1975.
8. Eva Fleischner. *Judaism in German Christian Theology since 1945: Christianity and Israel Considered in Terms of Mission.* 1975.
9. Walter James Lowe. *Mystery & The Unconscious: A Study in the Thought of Paul Ricoeur.* 1977.
10. Norris Magnuson. *Salvation in the Slums: Evangelical Social Work, 1865–1920.* 1977.
11. William Sherman Minor. *Creativity in Henry Nelson Wieman.* 1977.
12. Thomas Virgil Peterson. *Ham and Japheth: The Mythic World of Whites in the Antebellum South.* 1978.
13. Randall K. Burkett. *Garveyism as a Religious Movement: The Institutionalization of a Black Civil Religion.* 1978.
14. Roger G. Betsworth. *The Radical Movement of the 1960's.* 1980.
15. Alice Cowan Cochran. *Miners, Merchants, and Missionaries: The Roles of Missionaries and Pioneer Churches in the Colorado Gold Rush and Its Aftermath, 1858–1870.* 1980.
16. Irene Lawrence. *Linguistics and Theology: The Significance of Noam Chomsky for Theological Construction.* 1980.
17. Richard E. Williams. *Called and Chosen: The Story of Mother Rebecca Jackson and the Philadelphia Shakers.* 1981.
18. Arthur C. Repp, Sr. *Luther's Catechism Comes to America: Theological Effects on the Issues of the Small Catechism Prepared In or For America Prior to 1850.* 1982.
19. Lewis V. Baldwin. *"Invisible" Strands in African Methodism.* 1983.
20. David W. Gill. *The Word of God in the Ethics of Jacques Ellul.* 1984.
21. Robert Booth Fowler. *Religion and Politics in America.* 1985.
22. Page Putnam Miller. *A Claim to New Roles.* 1985.

23. C. Howard Smith. *Scandinavian Hymnody from the Reformation to the Present.* 1987.
24. Bernard T. Adeney. *Just War, Political Realism, and Faith.* 1988.
25. Paul Wesley Chilcote. *John Wesley and the Women Preachers of Early Methodism.* 1991.
26. Samuel J. Rogal. *A General Introduction of Hymnody and Congregational Song.* 1991.
27. Howard A. Barnes. *Horace Bushnell and the Virtuous Republic.* 1991.
28. Sondra A. O'Neale. *Jupiter Hammon and the Biblical Beginnings of African-American Literature.* 1993.
29. Kathleen P. Deignan. *Christ Spirit: The Eschatology of Shaker Christianity.* 1992.
30. D. Elwood Dunn. *A History of the Episcopal Church in Liberia, 1821–1980.* 1992.
31. Terrance L. Tiessen. *Irenaeus on the Salvation of the Unevangelized.* 1993.
32. James E. McGoldrick. *Baptist Successionism: A Crucial Question in Baptist History.* 1994.
33. Murray A. Rubinstein. *The Origins of the Anglo-American Missionary Enterprise in China, 1807–1840.* 1995.
34. Thomas M. Tanner. *What Ministers Know: A Qualitative Study of Pastors as Information Professionals.* 1994.
35. Jack A. Johnson-Hill. *I-Sight: The World of Rastafari: An Interpretive Sociological Account of Rastafarian Ethics.* 1995.
36. Richard James Severson. *Time, Death, and Eternity: Reflecting on Augustine's "Confessions" in Light of Heidegger's "Being and Time."* 1995.
37. Robert F. Scholz. *Press toward the Mark: History of the United Lutheran Synod of New York and New England, 1830–1930.* 1995.
38. Sam Hamstra, Jr. and Arie J. Griffioen. *Reformed Confessionalism in Nineteenth-Century America: Essays on the Thought of John Williamson Nevin.* 1995.
39. Robert A. Hecht. *An Unordinary Man: A Life of Father John LaFarge, S.J.* 1996.
40. Moses N. Moore. *Orishatukeh Faduma: Liberal Theology and Evangelical Pan-Africanism, 1857–1946.* 1996.
41. William Lawrence. *Sundays in New York: Pulpit Theology at the Crest of the Protestant Mainstream.* 1996.
42. Bruce M. Stephens *The Prism of Time and Eternity: Images of Christ in American Protestant Thought from Jonathan Edwards to Horace Bushnell,* 1996.
43. Eleanor Bustin Mattes. *Myth for Moderns: Erwin Ramsdell Goodenough and Religious Studies in America, 1938–1955.* 1997.
44. Nathan D. Showalter. *The End of a Crusade: The Student Volunteer Movement for Foreign Missions and the Great War.* 1997.

The End of a Crusade

*The Student Volunteer Movement
for Foreign Missions and
the Great War*

Nathan D. Showalter

ATLA Monograph Series, No. 44

The Scarecrow Press, Inc.
Lanham, Md., & London
1998

SCARECROW PRESS, INC.

Published in United States of America
by Scarecrow Press, Inc.
4720 Boston Way
Lanham, Maryland 20706
4 Pleydell Gardens, Folkestone
Kent CT202DN, England

British Library Cataloguing in Publication Information Available

Library of Congress Cataloging-in-Publication Data

Showalter, Nathan D., 1949–
     The end of a crusade : the Student Volunteer Movement for Foreign
Missions and the Great War / Nathan D. Showalter.
          p.   cm. — (ATLA monograph series ; no. 44)
     Includes bibliographical references and index.
     ISBN 0-8108-3340-9 (alk. paper)
     1. Student Volunteer Movement for Foreign Missions—History—20th
century.   2. World War, 1914–1918—Religious aspects.   I.   Title.
II. Series.
BV2360.S8S56   1998
266′.023′0601—dc21   97-20169
                                                                                    CIP

ISBN 0-8108-3340-9 (cloth : alk. paper)

♾ ™The paper used in this publication meets the minimum requirements of
American National Standard for Information Sciences—Permanence of
Paper for Printed Library Materials, ANSI Z39.48–1984.
Manufactured in the United States of America.

Contents

Editor's Foreword

Since 1972, the American Theological Library Association has under-taken responsibility for a modest monograph series in the field of religious studies. Our aim in this series is to publish two studies of quality each year. Titles are selected from studies in a wide range of religious and theological disciplines. We are pleased to publish Nathan D. Showalter's *The End of a Crusade: The Student Volunteer Movement for Foreign Missions and the Great War*.

Kenneth E. Rowe
Series Editor

Preface

The subject of missions has never been foreign to me. I grew up in a family that was involved in home missions in Appalachia. I took my first overseas mission assignment in Nairobi, Kenya, when I was fresh out of college—partially in response to the Vietnam War and the requirement that I, as a conscientious objector, perform an alternative to military service. After returning from East Africa, I became interested in the Student Volunteer Movement for Foreign Missions (SVM) while studying the history of Christian missions with Ralph D. Winter at Fuller Theological Seminary's School of World Mission in California. Several years later I experienced a modern reincarnation of the SVM quadrennial when I represented Mennonite mission agencies at an Inter-Varsity Christian Fellowship convention in Urbana, Illinois, in 1979. At Lancaster (Pennsylvania) Theological Seminary, Professor Elizabeth C. Nordbeck whetted my appetite for further study in American religious history and introduced me to William R. Hutchison.

This book began to take shape during two years of study with Professor Hutchison, who engaged us in reading and responding to the chapters of his (now published) history of Protestant thought and foreign missions. Throughout this project, Professor Hutchison has remained a patient, perceptive, and collegial ally and critic. Friendly but vigorous criticism came also from members of the Harvard New World Colloquium, helping to shape my early thinking and writing on John R. Mott and the volunteer movement. During my years in Cambridge, Professor Lamin Sanneh, from the Gambia in West Africa, worked gently to remove the Western intellectual blinders that often kept me from seeing the deeper meanings of the story of the spread of the Christian faith. He and his wife, Sandra, in opening their hearts and their home to migratory

scholars like myself, may symbolize something of the mature reciproc-
ity of the Christian world mission.

Theron F. Schlabach of Goshen College provided valuable suggestions for the revision of my dissertation, and Gloria Cooper helped with
the proofreading. Kenneth Rowe saw the potential of the manuscript and
steered me safely through the publication process. Less visible in these
pages, but more important to their completion, was the unwavering support of my wife, Christina, and the tolerance of our son, Eli.

To the source and end of mission—and the final critic of our efforts
to probe the deeper meanings of the human story—*soli Deo gloria*.

Lunar New Year, 1996

Introduction

The volunteer movement at the end of thirty-three years is strong and vital and never more so. Why has it gone from strength to strength all these years and what has been the secret of its productive power? The true answer to this penetrating question will point the way to the larger achievements which lie before the student missionary uprising. In the first place, its personnel has been made up of those who are young and vigorous, whose minds are educated and whose lives are consecrated to the service of God and man. Its members have been fired with undying enthusiasm and have ever been responsive to new and larger visions and plans. Their eyes have been fixed on the coming day and they have never lost the first flush of optimistic hope.

—John R. Mott, 1920

When these sentimental old world-wreckers were young, the world was such a different place. . . . Life for them was bright and pleasant. Like all normal youngsters, they had their little tin-pot ideals, their sweet little enthusiasms, their nice little sets of beliefs. Christianity had emerged from the blow dealt by Darwin, emerged rather in the shape of social dogma. Man was a noble and perfectible creature. Women were angels. . . . Right was downing might. The nobility and the divine mission of the race were factors that led our fathers to work wholeheartedly for a millennium, which they caught a glimpse of just around the turn of the century.

—John F. Carter Jr., 1920

During the latter years of the nineteenth century, a group of American students came to believe that by the end of the century the Christian message could be proclaimed to the entire world. The Student Volunteer Movement for Foreign Missions (SVM), born at a Young Men's Christian

Association conference at Dwight L. Moody's New England convention center in 1886, popularized for several subsequent generations of students the watchword, "The evangelization of the world in this generation."[1] This was not just a spiritual mission. As the nations of Africa and Asia accepted the Christian faith, they would also come to share the blessings of Western science and culture. The Student Volunteer Movement recruited thousands of North American students for missionary service. By 1900 it had forged links with students in Europe, Asia, Australia, and Africa in a world federation designed to build enthusiasm for the evangelization crusade among students everywhere.

The Student Volunteer Movement did not stand alone. It never existed as a separate, fully independent organization. From the beginning, it was organized as a complementary part of the larger Protestant Christian student movement.[2] That movement had different national expressions and varied markedly from country to country. In the United States, the SVM—with its national office on Madison Avenue in New York City—functioned as the missionary department of the college Young Men's Christian Association (YMCA) and Young Women's Christian Association (YWCA). In Great Britain, the Student Volunteer Missionary Union (SVMU) became the missionary arm of the Student Christian Movement (SCM) to which it had earlier given birth. In countries such as France and Italy, on the other hand, where the Protestant student Christian movement was not strong, the student volunteer concept remained weak or was nonexistent. Few students signed on as volunteers in Germany, where the crusade for world evangelization often carried overtones of Anglo-Saxon imperialism.

Where the SVM was vigorously supported by the larger student Christian movement, as in the United States, Canada, and Great Britain, it flourished. In the heyday of the student associations (YMCA and YWCA) in the United States, one out of a hundred American college and university students attended the SVM conventions held every four years.[3] Through campus programs and conventions the SVM challenged college and university students to consider a career in foreign missions service.

In North America, students who signed a pledge to become foreign missionaries were called volunteers.[4] These recruits were enrolled in campus missions study courses, through a local volunteer band, and in regional and national missions activities, through SVM unions. The volunteer became a missionary candidate when accepted for overseas service by a mission board. The volunteer movement attempted to provide enough missionary candidates to meet the needs of the major Protestant mission boards in North America. Before 1925, the SVM was successful in doing this, providing a pool of volunteers from which came one-half to three-quarters of the North American Protestant missionaries sent overseas.

John King Fairbank has pointed out that "the end of the open land frontier in the 1880s coincided with the rise of the Student Volunteer Movement" in the United States.[5] An expression of a larger Protestant missions movement that began in the late eighteenth century, the volunteer movement flourished in the Anglo-Saxon student world during the so-called imperialist era—the heyday of European colonialism and American expansionism. William R. Hutchison suggests that America's mission, described occasionally by Puritans as an "errand into the wilderness," had become for nineteenth-century Protestants an "errand to the world."[6] In the Student Volunteer Movement, the errand was an Anglo-Saxon one. During the years when the SVM minded its numbers, three countries—the United States, Canada, and Great Britain—produced 95 percent of all "sailed volunteers," those sent to the mission field.[7] And for the SVM the errand had become more aggressive. It was described to the first volunteers, the Mount Hermon Hundred, as "a war of conquest," and so they often characterized their spiritual mission.[8]

World's Student Christian Federation

John R. Mott was the best known of the founders of the Student Volunteer Movement. While in Europe on an around-the-world tour in the mid-1890s, he helped to launch an international association of student movements called the World's Student Christian Federation (WSCF). If not the first truly worldwide organization, the WSCF was the first in which members from every continent were brought together in a democratic partnership. As it worked to unite Christian movements around the world, the federation also enlisted students in the cause of "extending the kingdom of God throughout the whole world." The founders conceived the WSCF as an international missionary extension of the Student Volunteer Movement. It gradually became a broader union of student Christian movements, many of which had their genesis in the volunteer movement. After World War I, Mott reported that there were fifty-eight thousand students in ten federation countries enrolled in mission study circles and that volunteers from throughout the federation were supplying well over half of the world's Protestant missionary force.[9]

The WSCF not only united the student missionary forces of the Western world, it also sent workers to encourage fledgling movements in the emerging institutions of higher learning in Asia and Africa. In 1895 the nascent federation commissioned Mott to establish and enlist national student movements in India, Japan, and China. At a time when Western-style colleges and universities were beginning to appear in Asia, the idea of a student Christian movement was welcomed by both missionary educators and students curious about or newly initiated into the Christian faith. By 1897, when he and his wife returned from their trip around the world, Mott had succeeded in founding national student Christian movements in India, Japan, and China and in Ceylon (Sri Lanka) as well. He forged relationships that soon led to the participation of these movements in the new World's Student Christian Federation. By the time the federation met in Tokyo in 1907, student movements in twenty-five countries sent delegates.

By the turn of the century, student activists began to realize that they would have to work harder to complete the task of world evangelization within their lifetime. There were more Protestant missionaries serving overseas than ever before.[10] But this growing Western Christian presence abroad resulted in a clearer picture of the world the missionaries wished to evangelize, a world far more complex culturally and religiously than the first volunteers had realized. At the same time, missionaries found it harder to agree on what evangelization meant. By the time of the great Edinburgh Missionary Conference of 1910, both the world that remained to be evangelized and the task of evangelization appeared more formidable than they had two decades earlier.[11]

To the American leaders of the student missions movement, the larger and more complex task required the launching of new organizations and the mobilization of larger resources. Between 1900 and the outbreak of World War I, several new organizations were started to assist in the task of world evangelization. The Young People's Missionary Education Movement (later the Missionary Education Movement) was founded in 1902 to educate and enlist young people outside of colleges and universities. In 1906, the Laymen's Missionary Movement was organized to raise the funds needed to support the armies of missionaries being recruited. A new Men and Religion Forward Movement organized a year-long series of rallies and follow-up institutes in 1911–12 that focused on practical expressions of Christian mission, both spiritual and social, at home and overseas. The following year, a Men and Religion Forward team carried the campaign to more than half a dozen countries in Asia,

Africa, and Europe. In America, at least, hopes were still high in 1914 that the world would soon be won for Christ.

Changes in American Higher Education

The half century between the Civil War and World War I was a time of remarkable change and growth in American higher education. From 1870 to 1900, while the country's population nearly doubled (from 40 million to 76 million), the number of college students increased almost fivefold from 52,000 to 238,000. The percentage of college-aged youth in college or university went from less than 2 percent in 1870 to more than 12 percent in 1930. Harvard's student body, for example, quadrupled, from one thousand in 1869 to four thousand in 1909; its faculty grew tenfold, from sixty to six hundred. Fueled by the growth in public high schools and the growing numbers of women seeking higher education, this surge in attendance provided the human capital for what the volunteer movement leaders often called the "student uprising" for missions and for world evangelization.[12]

Significantly, the sources of funding for this growth in higher education were not the Christian communities and denominations that had largely financed the cost of advanced education in America before the Civil War. With the Morrill Act of 1862, the federal government took an increasingly active role in higher education through the provision of both land and money. More important than government support was the role of big business and the newly wealthy industrialists. Banker and railroad investor Johns Hopkins left $3.5 million to the university that bears his name and an equal amount to establish a teaching hospital in Baltimore. Steamship and railroad magnate Cornelius Vanderbilt gave $1 million to establish a "Harvard of the South," the first of many generous endowments for the school named in his honor. John D. Rockefeller, whose son became a patron of John R. Mott and the student movements with which he was associated, provided gifts that eventually totaled some $45 million to found and fund a Baptist institution that became the University of Chicago. The old colleges prospered along with the new. In the half century before World War I, Harvard's endowment rocketed from $2.5 million to more than $20 million. In the two decades before 1900, private donors gave $140 million to American colleges and universities (25).

This "new money" was concerned more with science than with faith, more with organizational efficiency or a donor's memory than with orthodoxy. The new breed of teachers and college administrators were typically less Christian than the old, and college presidents were less often "men of the cloth" and sometimes even religiously indifferent or agnostic. By the time World War I started, the American college and university context was significantly less Christian and evangelical than it had been when the Student Volunteer Movement was founded in 1886. Before the war, while the campus context was not for the most part opposed to the religious expansionism of the SVM, it was an environment in which the very foundations of the missionary appeal were being attacked by what Walter Lippman termed the "acids of modernity."

The change in philosophy and values that took place on American campuses between the Civil War and World War I was of fundamental importance to the future of Christian student movements like the Student Volunteer Movement. According to Mark A. Noll, American colleges were generally Christian in outlook at the end of the Civil War, most having been recently founded by a member of the clergy or by a single Protestant denomination. Almost all were strongly influenced by Christian ideals of order, society, and citizenship and required of all students a course in moral philosophy or mental science, often taught by the college president. This was an effort to integrate all knowledge into a comprehensive whole, and it offered "comprehensive exhortations to live morally in society, to support religion, to put public good above selfish interests, and to work for the coming of God's kingdom in America" (19).

By the beginning of World War I, this academic synthesis had crumbled, and the old science was largely replaced by a new one. The new science was popularly associated with Darwinism, a complex of ideas that permeated American culture at three different levels: as a scientific method, as a scientific or social result, and as a philosophical system. "At each level," Noll writes, "Darwinism both undercut the antebellum scientific world of American higher education and offered the glowing prospect of unprecedented scientific progress" (27). Where the old science assumed that inductive investigation would lead finally to God, the new science was frankly agnostic. Francis Bacon was dethroned in favor of Charles Darwin, a scientist willing to follow the data even when it challenged the most fundamental Christian beliefs.

With regard to scientific result, the principle of natural selection seemed to deny the essential spirit of moral philosophy and appeared to be incongruous with a world controlled by a benevolent creator. When this scientific result was given a social application, the religious concept of sin was subdued by an inevitable progress, and religion itself began to be seen as part of an evolutionary process rather than as a word from God. As a philosophy, Darwinism provided a comprehensive, non-biblical explanation of the world, its progress, and its future. According to Herbert Spencer's *Systematic Philosophy* (1862–93), humankind was progressing from the simple to the complex, from inferior to superior patterns of life, and from the primitive to the sophisticated, all under the governance not of the divine hand but of a natural and random selection process in which the weak die and the strong inherit the earth.

Some of Darwin's more radical interpreters were strongly antagonistic to traditional Christian orthodoxy and to evangelical piety. In its popular expressions, however, Darwinism was not entirely out of tune with the missionary spirit that flourished in America and Europe before World War I. If Western colonial hegemony illustrated for Social Darwinism the superiority of Western civilization, then missionary successes might provide a similar validation of the truth of Christianity. If social progress was achieved through struggle, then the civilizing work of Christian missions could have strategic importance for world progress.

The world was thought to be engaged in a struggle for mastery among the races and religions, and this, as John R. Mott wrote in 1910, was a struggle in which the Christian faith could either succeed or fail. The credibility of the Christian message both at home and abroad was at stake. To preserve the purity of Christianity, a worldwide plan for spiritual conquest was needed. If the Christian mission succeeded, then the church at home would be strengthened, and those who were now losing their faith could be won back. The future of Christianity itself was invested in the missionary enterprise. If the missionary propaganda should fail to conquer the non-Christian religions of Asia and Africa, the mission and power of Christianity would be shaken to its foundations. This was the decisive hour, Mott thought, not only for Christian missions but for Christianity itself.

The Great War

A few years after Mott penned these thoughts, the missionary enterprise of Christianity was shaken to its foundations. The struggle for mastery that brought the quake, however, was vastly different from the one Mott described in 1910. Far from being a struggle between Christian and non-Christian nations, World War I was a bitter and devastating conflict that erupted among the most civilized of the Western Christian nations. In the astringent words of a modern playwright, "Britain owned the world and Germany wanted it."13 When the American Congress formally joined the conflict on Good Friday in 1917, it was in the spirit of a crusade, a holy war. Religious leaders—Catholic, Protestant, and Jewish—joined in a litany of support for the war. Those who did not, mainly the historical peace churches—the Quakers and the Mennonites—and the new Jehovah's Witnesses, were often insulted and harassed, and some of their members went to prison. Shailer Mathews, the Social Gospel and Modernist scholar from the University of Chicago, spoke for many Christian leaders when he declared that it was unchristian for an American not to participate in this war. A conscientious objector could be spared persecution, Mathews thought, "provided that he does not speak with a German accent." Evangelist Billy Sunday, on the other side of the theological spectrum, lent his support, and his theatrics, to "Hang the Kaiser" rallies. "Christianity and patriotism are synonymous terms," he said, "and hell and traitors are synonymous."14

Germany, for a century America's tutor, theological mentor, and ally in the crusade for world evangelization, had now become the enemy. Although missionaries continued to sail from the United States during the war, their mission of spiritual conquest had to play second fiddle to the new national passion for putting the Huns in their place and making the world safe for democracy. The war against "this unholy and blasphemous power"15 in Europe took precedence over the task of Christianizing the nations beyond. The Christian nations had a few old scores to settle in Europe, it seemed, before they could return to the missionary battlefields of Asia and Africa. This was a decisive hour for Christian missions, but the outcomes were not those expected by John Mott and the leaders of the Student Volunteer Movement.

Chapter One

Thunderclap out
of a Clear Sky

It was nearer last year than it was the year before; it is nearer this year than it was last year; it is nearer now, today, than it was on the first day of the present year, and, with an advancing step, that has never gone backward, through all these years, the prophecy is safe and beautiful that we are marching swiftly into the vast open of universal peace.

—New York newspaper editorial,
several years before the war

Never was a war begun which was less desired by the Christian people of the nations involved. . . . Yet the great nations are at each other's throats. In spite of the Hague conference and peace movements of growing power, Europe has been drenched with blood.

—George Irving, 1914

"For the vast majority of students, the outbreak of war was a thunderclap out of a clear sky," World's Student Christian Federation leader and historian Ruth Rouse recalled.[1] Though there had been signs of an impending catastrophe, the students and their leaders were blind to the portents. American Student Volunteer Movement leader and evangelist George Sherwood Eddy described the shock of a war that "exploded like a mine," affecting at its greatest extent two-thirds of the human race. The war was like a searchlight "turned upon our civilization and its defects."[2]

European students had firmly believed that war could never come again, least of all a war exploding from the heart of Christendom and throwing its shadow over the entire world. After a century of peace in Europe and the birth of scores of national and international Christian associations whose purpose was the salvation of a pagan world beyond the West, war in Europe, the missionary homeland, was unthinkable. Christian

9

students were committed to peace and to an international federation that transcended national loyalties. Even if they had discussed war, they would not have considered the unimaginable—a conflict in which European federation members would be fighting each other. Student volunteers were unprepared for the apparent clash between the ideals of earthly and heavenly kingdoms, a clash that replaced the missionary crusade with a military one and threatened to destroy the Christian federation itself.

Tissington Tatlow, leader of the British Student Christian Movement, reflected, "it is a curious thing how blind people can be, even when they are recognized leaders." Federation leaders were as oblivious as the students to the coming of war. It should have been different, Rouse thought. In the nineteen years of its existence, the WSCF had already weathered at least fourteen conflicts, some serious enough to limit participation in international student conferences.[3] But those "local" wars did not prepare the student leaders for the magnitude or the ferocity of the conflict that spread through Europe in 1914 and by Easter 1917 had come to affect most of the rest of the world. A robust optimism nurtured in an era of relative peace seemed to obscure the realities that led to war. "The war took us by surprise," Tatlow wrote; "few of us had thought about the question of Christianity and war."

The leaders of the volunteer movement and the student federation, their eyes focused on a distant horizon, failed to see the impending tragedy at hand. When the unimaginable happened, they rushed to support their own governments while still trying to keep alive the memory of shattered federation ideals. Peace education efforts lasted while the United States was neutral but quickly gave way to the inflated rhetoric of war. The generation that wished to save the world gave the world to war.

With the memory of their own Civil War fading, Americans were no less shocked by the war than the Europeans. In the last decades of the nineteenth century, Protestants were birthing new and more complex organizations, raising larger budgets than ever before, and launching daringly ambitious crusades, such as the SVM campaign to evangelize the world in this generation. It was "the time of all times," John R. Mott said. If the church sent her armies to battle, the world would see victories eclipsing all those of the past.[4]

American Protestants in the early years of the twentieth century were newly awakened to social problems and the need for social justice at home. An aroused social conscience did not at first diminish their zeal for the evangelization of non-Christians abroad; instead, it entrusted to the missionaries a larger gospel. As the Social Gospel movement came to full flower in the first decade of the new century, there seemed greater hope than ever before of bringing about a genuine expression of the kingdom of God on earth and of sharing the fruits of that transcendent kingdom with the entire world. War, especially a conflict among Western Christian nations, was an inexcusable sacrilege in the face of these plans for the Christian conquest of the world.

Some Great Calamity

In a book prepared for the World Missionary Conference in Edinburgh in 1910, John R. Mott, the most prominent SVM leader, recognized a growing turbulence in the world, coming primarily from outside the West. There were unmistakable signs "of the awakening of great peoples from their long sleep" (3). In the whole of human history, Mott believed, there had never been a time when changes so profound had affected such a large part of the world. Fully three-quarters of the world's population, he reckoned, were caught up in a process of economic, social, educational, and religious change.

More than a third of Mott's book described the changes that he and other Western observers perceived to be taking place in non-Western and non-Christian societies. These changes meant crisis in the non-Christian world, but that crisis was an opportunity for Christian missions from the West. Non-Christian nations were being shaken to their foundations by far-reaching movements—national, racial, social, economic, and religious. In all of Christian history, this was a moment of unparalleled opportunity on the "world-wide battlefield of Christianity" (69–95).

Mott acknowledged problems at home but felt it was not necessary "to propagate the blemishes and errors of our Western Christianity." He urged missionaries not to "dispense poison with the bread of life." The shortcomings of Western Christianity did not compel a major change in the strategy of the missionary campaign. Mott gave scant attention to the problems of nationalism, racism, and materialism on the domestic front. He made passing reference to the debate that would soon become a full-blown Fundamentalist-Modernist controversy, paralyzing entire denominations and mission programs. Although this "doubt and hesitation" weakened the missionary message, it merited less than a paragraph in Mott's analysis of the "home base" of foreign missions (158–59).

Western colonialism received a similarly brief mention. "It would be difficult also to exaggerate the evil effect produced by unrighteous aggressions on the part of Western nations upon non-Christian nations and peoples," he wrote (157). But that was all. Mott was well aware of social and political movements dedicated to the overthrow of colonial rule. He apparently did not see these movements as having a significant bearing on the Western missionary enterprise or on the identity of the church in a colonial context.

Mott missed obvious signs of tension in the West and failed to reckon with the possibility of violent fragmentation among the very nations that nurtured the crusade for Christian world conquest. But he did give a warning, noting the possibility of grave consequences to the Western church, "some great calamity," if it failed to perform its missionary duty (233).

The calamity came four years later. But in 1910, Mott's warning was lost in the larger challenge to engage the enemy "over there." The real battle was between the forces of Western Christianity and non-Western paganism. The non-Christian world was in crisis, Mott believed, and the West had a sufficient faith to offer to the world. The missionary problem was "ensuring a vitality equal to the imperial expansion of the missionary program" (235). This was "the decisive hour of Christian missions." The adequacy of Christianity as a world religion was on trial (238–39).

Mott's words were prophetic, but in a way that he did not anticipate. Christianity was soon to face a profound crisis, a crisis from within. Mott failed to gauge the forces of nationalism and militarism that were increasingly visible throughout the Europe in which he often traveled. He occasionally noted, but largely misjudged, the importance of the racist tendencies in the Christian nations in which he sought to recruit missionary forces for Christian conquest. When Mott reflected on the conflicts between workers and their employers in the industrialized nations, he did not judge these important in the world crisis that demanded more Western missionaries along with the export of industry and science. He seemed not to notice the economic disparities between rich and poor in the West that were undermining the integrity of the Christian church and its mission to the world as well as the stability of the Christian societies sending out missionaries. Mott failed to see the extent to which the Protestant missionary crusade had come to depend on the power and the glory of Western civilization.

By 1914, Mott could not ignore the crisis in Europe. "We are living at the most dangerous time in the history of the world," he wrote in a book published just as the war broke. He now admitted that the greatest obstacle to the spread of Christianity was the unchristian impact of Western civilization itself. He catalogued in considerable detail the evils that were being visited on the "weaker nations" by the West, including colonial exploitation and misrule, racism, commercial abuses, and the influences of decadent or immoral Western culture and ideologies. He noted the way in which Christian countries had aggressively exported drugs and alcohol, charging that the "so-called Christian nations have been responsible not only for drugging China with opium but for debauching Africa with alcohol. Mott wanted European and American Christians to understand that the problems created by Western civilization in Africa and Asia were a fundamental threat to the credibility of the Christian message and to the success of the missionary enterprise.[5]

At the level of religious encounter, Mott was becoming aware for the first time of the impact of Western secularism on non-Christian religions and cultures. "The blaze of modern science," he said with reference to Japan, "has dissolved faith in Buddhism and its ethical restraints have been thrown off" (116). Mott, who only a few years earlier would have found it hard to see virtue in non-Christian religions, now acknowledged that "these ancient systems served to hold society together" (117).

In 1914 Mott reversed the formula he had used at the time of the 1910 Edinburgh conference. Then, he had seen Christianity's conquest of non-Christian religions as the test that would determine its credibility at home: "The only faith which will conquer Europe and America is the faith heroic and vigorous enough to subdue the peoples of the non-Christian world." Four years later, he declared that Christianity's effectiveness as a missionary force rested on an authentic application at home.[6]

Mott's insights came too late. By the time he gave these words of warning to student volunteers and to the larger Christian public in America, Europe was already at war. At a time when the public consciences of Germany, Britain, and France might still have been disciplined to resist the slide toward war, he and other leaders of the Student Volunteer Movement in North America and Europe were busy waging a war of spiritual conquest with an enemy on foreign soil. When war was fast approaching, Mott, despite his worries about Western behavior, saw "the tides of pure Christianity" rising as never before, ready to unite the Christian forces for a final sweep to victory. "I would rather live the next ten years than any time of which I have ever read, or than in any time of which I can dream," Mott told a YMCA audience in 1913. "Believe me, it is the time of times."[7]

After Mott went to Europe and witnessed the mounting destruction, both physical and spiritual, he admitted that he was haunted day and night by the thought of what Christians might have done to avert the tragedy.[8] The signs of tragedy were visible, but the SVM and federation leaders saw them too late. Distracted by the successes of a civilization that had seemed to give succor to the missionary crusade, they failed to see how far Western nations had drifted from the kingdom of God they proclaimed.

Christian students fighting one another was a specter that would have been unthinkable two years earlier, when the general committee of the World's Student Christian Federation had planned a meeting in the Austro-Hungarian empire. The war that erupted in and beyond that empire was a painful reminder of the Student Volunteer Movement's themes of uprising and conquest. The language of war, always prominent in the student missionary movement, suddenly lost its metaphorical detachment. The battle and blood were real. Christian soldiers were indeed marching to war, not against the powers of a heathen world beyond but against Christian neighbors, against each other. The metaphors of the battle for world evangelization found their reality in a Christian civil war that did not finally end until 1945.

At the outset of the war, a chapter of the Student Volunteer Movement was active in nearly every belligerent nation. The SVM, along with the larger federation of student Christian movements of which it was a part, found itself in a difficult and delicate position. Student Christian organizations were expected to support national military programs. At the same time, they could not ignore the international aims of the federation. From their earliest days, the SVM and the WSCF had viewed themselves as a force for world peace. Mott believed that the missionary message was the greatest mediating influence in situations of ethnic and national conflict. The federation had been founded as a way of extending the missionary impulse and drawing the nations together. In a 1908 address to the annual meeting of the Lake Mohonk Conference on International Arbitration, Mott noted that the federation had held three world conferences of students and professors before the first Hague peace conference. He offered the student movement as a "moral equivalent of war."[9]

When war broke out in Europe, the federation proved powerless to resist. Any voices of protest in Europe were lost in the rush of Christians to support their governments' positions. Americans had more time to think and debate. Senior SVM leaders—men such as John R. Mott, Robert P. Wilder, and Robert E. Speer—now a generation older than the students fighting the war, hoped at the beginning of the conflict to prevent the war's doing serious damage to the international student and missionary movements. Since American neutrality seemed to serve such a purpose, there was strong feeling among the older volunteers and the college association leaders that the United States ought to stay out of the conflict.

The Christian student movement in the United States had a strong affinity with the broadly based, loosely organized peace movement. During the first years of the war, D. Willard Lyon, secretary of the YMCA's foreign department, published *The Christian Equivalent of War*. The book, whose title was a deliberate play on William James's famous phrase, "the moral equivalent of war," was designed to help students and YMCA discussion groups to grapple with the ethical issues of war. Lyon's reading list included materials from the World Peace Foundation, the New York Peace Society, the Church Peace Union, and the American Association for International Conciliation. He urged students to read Andrew Carnegie's "A League of Peace" and David Starr Jordan on how war leads to the "survival of the unfit." Although he stopped short of a clear-cut pacifist position, Lyon's references marshaled a wide range of arguments—historical, economic, moral, and religious—against war. He did not offer the students a single text in defense of military preparedness or of the just-war position. After reviewing the destructive effects of war, along with a token consideration of its possible "moral good," Lyon offered the quest to establish the kingdom of God on earth as "a social equivalent for war."[10] Beyond educational efforts such as these, little seems to have been done by the student movements to ally themselves organizationally with the American peace movement.

As the national will turned toward war, American SVM leaders went along without a protest, accepting the war with a kind of resigned sadness. For all their dreams of a world in which peace would reign and their efforts to take a message of peace to the non-Western world, the Student Volunteer Movement and the associated movements of the federation had given little thought to how war could be prevented. Theirs was a war of spiritual conquest, and they had no contingency plans for dealing with civil war in the Christian homelands. Although the federation had created international structures for uniting Christian students in many parts of the world, it had never challenged future leaders to consider their role as world rather than national citizens in the event of a serious breakdown of the international order. While the federation made much of a commitment to Christianizing international relations, it had created no practical program—other than its role in the international missionary enterprise—to further that process. The crusade for world evangelization produced leaders with an apparent knowledge of the world to be conquered but a shallow understanding of the crisis in their own world. Men of robust confidence, the volunteer movement founders were intoxicated by the extravagance of their own words and deceived by the achievements of their world.

Chapter Two

Crusade or Catastrophe?

It is clarifying and stimulating to realize that waging the war and spreading Christianity are not separate undertakings, but that the tearing down process of the one and the building up process of the other have the same goal. . . . which is the dissemination through all the world of the democratic spirit and teaching of Jesus Christ.
— J. Lovell Murray, 1918

We have to face the fact that large numbers of men who would have gone to the mission field or into other positions of Christian leadership are being killed, and we have to face the fact also that many women who might have gone into such work will be prevented from doing so by the necessity of earning money to take the place of men who have been killed.
— Ruth Rouse, circa 1916

The faith of men in the ultimate goodness of God is shaken and we want men — men who understand and know. Not politicians, padres and generals of the conventional type, who can explain it all and put us on our feet again. Where is God? Doesn't he care?
— Member of the British Student Christian Movement, 1917

Though caught off guard, students and their mentors were quickly caught up in the drama of making war. It soon became clear that this war was unlike any other. It was total war. No previous European conflict had demanded such complete participation by the nation. The young — students included — were drafted to the front to fill the ranks of armies that soon numbered in the millions. Civilians at home scrambled to support these massive armies with food, supplies, and the weapons of war. Every person, every institution was expected to play a part. These were not just "nations at war" but "nations in arms."[1] And they called for help from their African and Asian colonies. The first total war became the first world war.

This new war posed a dilemma for Christians involved in the crusade for world evangelization. They were working to unite the world under the cross. In recent times Protestant missionaries had made much of the "gospel of the kingdom of God." The missionary enterprise would usher in a new era in human history as God's kingdom was established on earth. Swords would be exchanged for plowshares in a world without war. How could the church, at this critical moment in history, justify a war among Christian nations? And how could Christians justify a total war that increasingly blurred the line between soldier and civilian, both at home and at the front?

During the war the response to these questions seemed conditioned by age and by proximity to the front. For the elders, the war quickly be-came a crusade—the war to end war, a war to make the world safe for democracy. The young who fought saw it from a different angle—from where earth and fire and blood mingled.

Total Mobilization

The Great War revolutionized the methods and scope of military re-cruitment. Military drafts took student missionary movement members and leaders suddenly and in astonishing numbers from campus to bat-tlefield. In France, all students, including those in theological schools, were drafted. By the end of November 1914, all but one of the male members of the Paris Christian movement had been called into active service. In Great Britain, members of the Student Christian Movement (SCM) volunteered for service at a higher rate than the general student population, 60 percent of which was in uniform by Christmas 1914. The German Christian students were no less involved. Sixty percent of the German Christian Student Alliance were already fighting when the school year began, and by the end of the 1914–15 academic year, the movement reported that all able male members were in the armed ser-vices. Even in neutral countries like the Netherlands and Switzerland, as many as half of the male students were involved in the defense of the na-tional borders and were spending six months of the year in military ser-vice.

Although the war was not being fought on their soil, North American students did not watch the conflict from the sidelines. When war broke out in 1914, Canada was immediately drawn into the conflict on the side of Great Britain, and the United States two and a half years later. Students and student volunteers were among the first segment of the population to be recruited or conscripted for the cause. Already in the 1914–15 school year, nearly half of Canada's students were either at the front or in training. By the time the United States joined the war in April 1917, the Canadian Student YMCA reported that between fifteen thousand and twenty thousand undergraduates and wartime graduates had entered the Canadian army. Within a year after the U.S. declaration of war—during which time voluntary enlistments were discouraged and only students over the age of twenty-one were drafted—more than one-fourth of American students entered the army, many as volunteers. Student YMCA leaders reported that the colleges were decimated by the enlistments.

By the beginning of the 1917–18 school year, U.S. colleges and universities fell even more dramatically under the spell of war. The American government created a Students' Army Training Corps designed to turn every college or university of size into a military training camp. All male students were to be in uniform, under military discipline, and receiving soldier's pay. The curriculum was directed by the War Department, with an exacting schedule arranged for nearly every hour of the day. Fraternities were mostly disbanded, and fraternity houses converted into barracks. Athletics were limited to certain restricted hours, and mainly to intramural competition. Under this regimen 90 percent of American students were preparing for active duty.[2]

As the war progressed, the number and percentage of students in uniform increased until, especially in Europe, virtually all able-bodied male students were engaged in the war. Before the war there would have been about four thousand students at Cambridge. In 1917, John Mott's son found only four hundred: foreigners, women, and male British students unable to pass the military examinations. This war permitted no reservation. No longer an affair of princes or kings, the Great War was the first war of modern nation-states. It became a battle for the soul of a civilization, a battle being played out in the lives of the generation who fought in the trenches of Flanders. These young soldiers became sacrificial pawns in a stalemate of armies in which generals and politicians were learning—at the expense of the men in the trenches—the gruesome art of modern warfare. The full story of the war would be told only in the years after they had come marching home. But even during the war the young began to interpret the conflict in terms remarkably different from those of their elders.

Christianity in Crisis

To the older adult leaders of the student movement, the war did not seem
an event that would change the future of the missionary enterprise. Herman Rutgers of the Netherlands wrote that the war had produced a disillusioned outcry against "international unions" that they were "utter
failures" and that they might as well be dissolved. Not so with the federation, he insisted. "Its greatest task lies before it," and "it gives great
hope for the future." John R. Mott was also optimistic about the future
of the federation. "This movement more than any other," he wrote in November 1914, "has preserved its spiritual solidarity in the midst of the
awful strain of this worldwide upheaval." British leader Neville Talbot,
chairman of the Swanwick SCM conference in 1914, was no less san-
guine. He felt that the war helped to clarify the goals of the movement:
vital personal faith, a just social order, and an international Christian fellowship to unite all nations. Talbot insisted that the federation was still
the most inclusive organization in the world.[3]

As the war continued, pacifist sentiment in the United States seemed
to wither with neutrality. For the first part of the war, the student Ys
echoed the sentiments and slogans of a peace movement that had grown
to sizable proportions before the war. After the United States entered the
war, most pacifists quickly adjusted their position to one of support for
war as a means to peace, a final crusade to rid the world of war. Student
Volunteer Movement leaders who had recently favored neutrality now
echoed Woodrow Wilson's idealistic sentiment that America's participation in this war would "make the world safe for democracy." It did not
take long for them to see the opportunities the first world war presented.
The war to end all wars soon became, in the words of Eldon G. Ernst, "a
religious battle with millennial dimensions, a crusade for the salvation
of the world."[4] Although few SVM leaders would have used the imagery
of Fundamentalist revival preacher Billy Sunday who described the war
as "hell against heaven," there was little hesitation to use the media and
movement gatherings to drum up support for the war.

In a wartime address to student leaders, Presbyterian missions executive and longtime SVM leader Robert E. Speer described the war as an
expression of missionary values. The nation had taken the ethical aims
of the war from the missionary enterprise, Speer said. "There ought not
to be any doubt or misgiving in our minds as to what these aims are that
justify us in what we are doing now and what we are prepared to do without limit until this task has been fulfilled," Speer told the students gathered

at Northfield, Massachusetts, in June 1918. America was at war to put an end to war, to resist aggressive autocracy, and to oppose the idea that any nation can set itself above moral law or that power is an end in itself. Speer saw the war as a struggle for a new human order of righteousness, justice, and brotherhood.

These aims, Speer contended, were simply political expressions of the impulses that had started the missionary enterprise and that continued to give it momentum. The missionary movement existed as an instrument of peace and international goodwill, as an agency of righteousness and of human service, and as a spiritual and moral force building toward some form of international organization that would someday help bring the nations together. For a hundred years the Protestant missionary movement had been doing exactly what the war was now declared to accomplish. Speer went on to challenge the students with the urgency of the missionary call, even in wartime. Though the war was a "necessary business," it was essentially negative and destructive—this "thunder of guns, the massing of bodies of men." Only the missionary enterprise could release the "creative and constructive spiritual powers" needed to build a new world.

If this moment of opportunity were allowed to pass, Speer believed, "God will punish us for a hundred years." The world needed unselfish missionary outreach more than ever before. Any weakening of the spiritual outreach of the church would be a diminishing of the nation's struggle to win the war. Thousands of young Americans were going on a foreign mission to northern France, and thousands of these should be ready when the war was over, Speer said, to go forth on foreign missions of peace to Asia, Africa, and Latin America.[5]

One of the most articulate leaders of the volunteer movement, Speer had missed the deeper meaning of the war. He seemed not to see that this European war was undermining the moral authority of the Western missionary enterprise. Publicly at least, he seemed oblivious to the spiritual impact of war on the men at the front.

The SVM did hear some voices of caution from the older generation. Walter Rauschenbusch, a Social Gospel spokesman influential in the SVM, could not see the conflict as a Christian crusade. Instead, it was a great calamity, a "catastrophic stage in the coming of the kingdom of God."[6] But his voice was clearly in the minority. Sherwood Eddy admitted much later that the war produced "its many hymns of hate, its reprisals, atrocities, and mass destruction." Gradually the conviction deepened in the minds of many, Eddy said, that "Christianity will indeed have failed if it does not stop war." But that was a conclusion reached after the war was over. While at war, most Protestants saw America's cause as a divinely sanctioned crusade. For those committed to the missionary cause, it could even be interpreted as an expression of obedience to the Great Commission.[7] Many could agree with Robert E. Speer that "the war was the greatest proclamation of foreign missions which we have ever heard."[8]

The young were not so sure. The British student movement and the Student Volunteer Missionary Union, one of the first to be directly affected by the war, responded with an immediate call to the movement's ideals. In a statement issued in September 1914 to all Christian unions in Great Britain and Ireland, the British student movement leaders said that these ideals were urgently needed at a time when the hypocrisy of Christian nations was being exposed by the "awful horror of a fratricidal war."[9] This statement was issued when it appeared that the war might be largely an affair for professional soldiers. Then came the German invasion of Belgium. Within days, thousands of students were called into action on behalf of king and country.

The meaning of war became immediately more personal. Most British Christian students chose to fight, believing that Germany's violation of her treaty with Belgium gave Britain no choice but to honor her commitment to the people of Belgium. A small minority of students held that under no circumstances should a follower of Christ go to war. Beyond the question of personal response to war, but growing out of these divergent responses, was the question of how the movement should respond to the war. The SCM in Britain "was urged to become a recruiting agency by some, and begged to turn itself into a pacifist society by others." In the first editorial to appear in the periodical of the British movement after the declaration of war by Great Britain, students were reminded that there was a bond between British and German, Austrian and Hungarian students that transcended those even of an international association like the federation. The bond of "fellowship in Christ" transcends all others and must remain unbroken. When conscription came in Britain, Christian students responded differently to the national claim. "At the headquarters of the movement," Tatlow recalled, "men bid goodbye to one another with affection as one went to the front and the other went to prison, each knowing that the other was honestly trying to do what he believed was right for him" (515–16).

Some British students were keenly disappointed that the forces of Christianity seemed powerless to stop the outbreak of war or to bring it to an early end. Tatlow reported in 1915 that students had expected the church to have "something clear and commanding" to say about the war and were disappointed that all the church could do was to second the demands of the state.[10] On the other hand, British students declared "that it is the business of the church, at all costs, to uphold the ideal of the kingdom of God," and they considered "that the church has put the major part of her strength into upholding national ideals."[11]

At the beginning of the war a few Christian students were able to see some good in soldiering. One German student wrote that the war was "a special God-given opportunity to become purified and strengthened." The fight was not person against person but against evil itself. By fighting honorably for God, soldiers could demonstrate that theirs was the cause of right and truth.[12]

Other young soldiers found it difficult to maintain such spiritual detachment from the brutal facts of a war in which battle losses were often numbered in the tens of thousands. The loss of life among French students was high, and the French Protestant student movement was badly battered by the war. Although an enemy had invaded their homeland and their duty to fight seemed clear, Christian students were plagued by the moral ambiguities of the war. When the gap between the ideals of faith and the reality of soldiering could no longer be bridged, some French soldiers refused to tolerate talk of piety and patriotism.[13] The Dutch had a cynical name for combat soldiers—"the pigs at the front." From many who lived through the indescribable horrors of the trenches came the despairing cry, "Never again!"

As the war dragged on with small gains on either side and staggering losses of life for both, it became increasingly difficult for Christian soldiers to see the glory of the war or to maintain the vision given it by sermons and newspaper editorials at home. In a letter to movement leaders written midway through the war, a German Christian student declared, "There is no such thing as a 'holy war'; every war is fiendish." War had not produced any positive religious values but instead had annihilated them. "War is a triumph of the devil and not a means of grace," he concluded.[14]

There were, of course, some gains for the student missionary movement during the war. In France, a volunteer was recruited who would assume international responsibilities in the postwar federation. Suzanne de Dietrich lamented that there were no women in the French volunteer movement, but she saw the war as an opportunity for them to take their rightful place. "We have not yet found *our place* in the evangelization of the world, and we must find it now or never." In a letter to Mott she suggested that the spiritual battles to be fought after the war would require even more courage than the present engagement. In response to Mott's recent challenge to French students that more would be demanded of France after the war, Dietrich had a word of advice: "Don't forget the women!" Women intellectuals of the Latin countries in Europe should unite in forging a battle plan for the larger responsibilities that they would need to carry after the war, she suggested.[15]

The senior volunteers easily saw in the war elements of the battle for world evangelization to which they had given their lives. It was a tragic interruption, but not a meaningless one, for it would set the stage for greater achievements in the future. The young—those who survived— watched their comrades being sacrificed in the indecipherable strategies of generals who were learning the science of modern war. After the first few weeks of dramatic troop movements, the war settled into an entrenched four-year clash of men, metal, and poison gas across a constantly exploding wasteland. There was more gore than glory in this war. For the older leaders it was a crusade, for the young, a catastrophe.

Marching as to War

If judged by the recruitment of volunteers during the war, the student missionary crusade was still in good health, at least in North America. And North America provided some three-quarters of all volunteers tracked by the movements associated with the World's Student Christian Fellowship. Because of the geography of the war, the activities of the North American SVM continued with much less interruption than those of the European chapters.[16]

There was a slight decline in participation levels at the beginning of the war and again when the United States entered the war (see fig. 2.1). But the level of SVM activities during the war suggested a movement that was still robust. In the year after the war ended, the number of student volunteer enrollments rose dramatically, surging nearly to the prewar level. The number of missionaries leaving for foreign fields rose to a record high. In spite of severe interruptions of the volunteer program during the war, the SVM maintained its strength as an influential part of the college Associations and a vigouous recruiting agency for Protestant missions.[17]

The recruitment of British missionary candidates from among students and their deployment was much more adversely affected by the war. The SVMU reported that missionary interest and involvement was an early casualty of the war, at least among men. The number of new volunteers was cut nearly in half during the first year of the war and dropped even more precipitously during the following years (see fig. 2.2). By the end, annual recruits among men were less than one-tenth what they had been before the war. During the first year, women volunteers increased from 91 to 130 but then dropped during the last years of the conflict, though not as much as the number of men. The number of volunteers during the 1918–19 year was 61, the lowest on record, and no student volunteers sailed to the mission field that year.[18]

Wartime Volunteer Program

During the war, student Christian movements were forced to carry on with reduced numbers and to cancel or greatly reduce the normal program of activities. In most countries, budgets were cut, staff posts were left unfilled, and conferences and training events were postponed

Figure 2.1

Volunteers during the War, North America

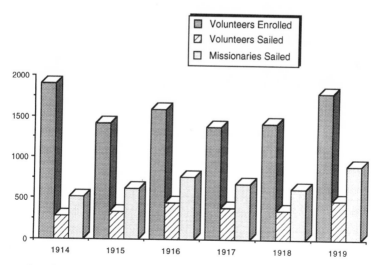

Based on statistics from William H. Beahm, "Factors in the Development of the Student Volunteer Movement for Foreign Missions," Ph.D. diss.,

Figure 2.2

Student Volunteers during the War, Great Britain and Ireland

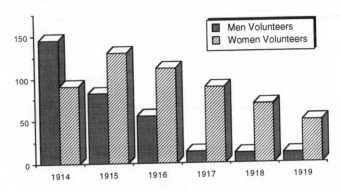

Compiled from *Reports of Student Christian Movements, 1916-1917* (New York: WSCF, 1918): 74; and *The SCM in 1919-20* (London: SCM, 1920): 27.

or canceled. The post of SVMU traveling secretary in Britain was left vacant, never again to be filled. The SVMU did not lose its momentum entirely. Study groups were organized around topics like "Christianity and War" and "The War and Missions." The 1914–15 annual meeting of the SVMU in Cambridge, England, was attended by four hundred undergraduates, nearly half of Oxford's current enrollment. The wartime atmosphere—the pressure to pass examinations more quickly along with the required drills in the Officers' Training Corps—was not conducive to the reflection and spiritual disciplines traditionally associated with the Christian Union, and organized religious activities on campus suffered. At the same time, students were more interested in religious questions than ever before. But they seemed to be less interested in the church.[19]

In Germany, the war brought about a great expansion of the German Christian Student Alliance, mainly because the provision of services to soldiers that in other countries was being done by the YMCA was given over to the leadership of the student alliance. The alliance leaders took the initiative to send regular mailings to some forty thousand students serving in the army. In addition to the movement paper, the alliance also sent the young soldiers two new wartime publications and other Christian literature. Staff carried on personal correspondence with about four thousand students in uniform. The German movement developed mobile libraries of Christian books to travel along with the troops. These were sometimes made available to German prisoners of war in other countries.[20]

Herman C. Rutgers, general secretary of the Dutch Student Christian Movement, visited Germany in 1915 and reported that the German movement had added new staff and offices in order to cope with increased responsibilities. In spite of the stress caused by this rapid growth, the German Christian Student Alliance, a small and rather narrow organization before the war, was reported by Rutgers to have gained unprecedented prestige in the German university world, "a position such as it never had before."[21]

Any of the usual student conferences and training events were out of the question among the belligerent nations in Europe. In Britain, the 1916 quadrennial student conference had to be postponed. In its place students, leaders, and friends of the movement met for a retreat on the theme of missions. In North America the 1918 SVM convention was replaced by a smaller conference of students and leaders from the United States and Canada, the purpose being to consider the future missionary policy of the student movement.

Swanwick

For many British students, the war made a mockery of schemes for world evangelization. The church's failure to prevent the war produced doubt in the minds of many students about the Christian message itself. Even before the war the number of British volunteers leaving for the field had remained constant, whereas the student movement's membership had been growing steadily. Movement leaders identified "a certain failure in spiritual imagination" and recognized that for many Christian students, domestic social needs were increasingly competing with missionary claims for their service. In the face of wartime realities and the needs of the SVMU, a decision was made to hold a special missionary retreat in place of the regular quadrennial student convention that would have taken place in 1916.

Meeting in Swanwick in the midst of war, a group of about seventy students, leaders, and friends of the movement seemed to experience fresh spiritual vision of the uniqueness of Christ and the reality of human need as the motivating core of the missionary message. It began with penitence, "a deep conviction that we had erred and strayed." The reports of the conference were permeated with a kind of mystical transcendence of the tragic realities of the war that was threatening the credibility of the cause they had met to discuss. Participants reported that in a rediscovery of the tragedy and consequences of sin, they had found in a new way the reality and strength of the love of God. "We were led to a deeper understanding of vocation in the consciousness that God has a place for each one of us in the work of winning the world for his kingdom," wrote one of the participants. If God and his kingdom were at the center, then there would be enough workers for both domestic and international programs.[22]

As significant as the conference seemed at the time, it apparently did not have lasting results. The SVMU continued to struggle with the challenge of the missionary vocation in a country whose youth were increasingly unwilling to carry abroad a religion that they thought had failed at home. As the war came to an end, movement leaders found it increasingly difficult to awaken interest in missionary service. Not long after the Armistice was signed, the SCM general committee appointed a commission to make a thorough reappraisal of the student missions movement. Its analysis and recommendations were less transcendent and more pragmatic than those of the Swanwick conference. They projected a diminishing influence for the SVMU in the British student world.

Northfield

Before the war the quadrennial convention of the Student Volunteer Movement had become the largest and most influential gathering of students in North America. Attendance at the conventions had grown from 680 delegates at the first SVM convention in Cleveland in 1891 to more than five thousand at the seventh convention held in Kansas City, Kansas, just before the war. As 1918 approached, the war made it impossible to plan for the usual SVM quadrennial convention. Instead, a much smaller three-day conference was held at Northfield, Massachusetts, attended by about four hundred students and an almost equal number of other delegates, including mission board representatives and faculty members.[23]

In some ways, the message of the conference seemed to have been little changed by the war. "We heard of the strength of the enemies of the cross of Christ," a Canadian professor wrote. "The surging advance of the Mohammedan wave in Africa, the cancer of sin-ridden India, the dreary wastes of sin and ignorance in China, the resourcefulness of selfishness and vice in Japan were impressed on the delegates by a mass of information which left the imagination dazed. When to this was added the failure and viciousness of some of the priests in South America who bear the name of Christ, the effect was appalling. It was a vision of the world's need."[24]

He might have been writing about any previous SVM convention. There was no evidence that the world was embroiled in a war begun and directed by Christian nations or that Christian students were at that moment confronting each other in a bloody conflict whose casualties were already numbered in the millions. There was no hint of the war's having had a chastening effect on the missionary cause. The conference gave no attention to the failings of Christianity—or at least to the failings of Western civilization.

Another Canadian report carried the headline "North American Students Mobilizing for Christian World Democracy." There was a clear relationship, the reporter said, between the spread of Christianity and the modern movement of individual and national freedom. "No one of us doubts but that in this struggle for world democracy, we are in line with God's great purposes for the world." The Northfield conference was a call "to make the peoples of this world not only free, but Christian." Underlying every address was the world's need for an adequate religion. The present crusade would bring millions more into the embrace of "Christian World Democracy."[25]

An American reporter gave a somewhat different impression of the conference, observing that the program differed considerably from previous conventions in that there was a noticeable absence of appeals for foreign missionary service. Instead, there was an emphasis on "the social duties of Christians at home and abroad—the necessity of Christianizing our own life so as to make it, in some degree, a fair representation of Christ's program." In what may have been a hint of penitence for the war, the editors admitted that there certainly was no room for complacency about "the national and international life of so-called Christian nations." But the war was breaking down racial barriers, this observer thought. Northfield delegates were witnessing "the beginnings of the practice of world brotherhood" as men of all races contributed to this new "fraternity in arms."[26] At the same time there was a lament that no students of color were present at the conference, and that there was such a "disproportionately small number of women speakers" (232).

The impact of the war may have been most visible in the ambitious follow-through program drafted by the Northfield conference. The war work campaign seemed to have produced a new sense of unity and larger expectations in a movement not accustomed to thinking small.[27] "All were eager for a new call under which our several armies, with full moral and legal freedom, might voluntarily unite for conquest" (190).

The plans declared by the conference were bold:

1. to enlist two hundred thousand students in study and discussion of Christian principles based on the life and teaching of Jesus Christ, the present world situation in relation to the kingdom of God, and the need for the application of those principles in the interracial and social life of North America;
2. to call students to a decision to live these principles at whatever cost on the campus, in the nation, and in the world;
3. to enlist a sufficient number of qualified men and women for the foreign missionary program of the church; and
4. to secure at least one-half million dollars during the academic year 1918–19 for the foreign missionary program of the church and secure such funds as may be necessary to meet the need arising from the war situation in 1918.[28]

In order to carry out this ambitious program, the SVM executives added two new staff members and devised "great schemes" (192) for bringing the challenge to students throughout North America. Clearly, the war had created a climate favorable to expansive plans and budgets. "We are not and cannot be satisfied, in this war for the kingdom, to go back to the *status quo ante*," the conference declaration stated (190). The war had brought to Northfield a new knowledge, a new zeal, and a new prospect of success. The war had breathed new life into the Student Volunteer Movement, and the student armies were now ready to complete the evangelization of the world—or so the generals of this army believed.

In a study book rushed for completion the month after the Northfield conference, J. Lovell Murray, educational secretary for the SVM, reported that four-fifths of the world's population had to some degree been affected by the war and that the conflict had already cost the belligerents more than $100 billion, five times more than had been spent on all wars in the previous century. The United States was at that time spending $39 million every day for war purposes, including $15 million daily in loans to the Allies, from an annual budget originally set at $39 billion. According to another analysis, the daily cost of the war for all parties was

$130 million in 1918. Three and a half years of war had increased public debt by more than $100 billion for the twelve leading belligerent nations.[29]

But these were only the financial costs. There were forty million men under arms, Lovell reported, "away from their productive pursuits and engaged actively in a fierce work of destruction." More than eight million had already died in the conflict, and this number did not include civilians and those who had died of disease. Some estimates put the number of civilian casualties at one million, with another three million having already starved to death by the beginning of 1918. There were seven million men in prisoner-of-war camps, with an equal number in hospitals, he said. At least two and a half million men had been permanently handicapped by the war.

Such facts were, on the one hand, a call to the recognition that there was something profoundly wrong with Christian civilization. This was a war of Christian against Christian. Of the twenty-three nations then at war, only four could be called non-Christian, said Murray. Before the United States and Romania had entered the war, forty-six million Protestants were on one side of the conflict, and forty-five million on the other. There were sixty-two million Roman Catholics fighting against sixty-three million members of the same church. Christian nations, declared the SVM leader, were at fault in allowing this war to happen—and for allowing war itself to survive.

On the other hand, the awful facts of this war were a call to action, especially to a renewed engagement in the missionary task. But the war now stood as a formidable challenge to the missionary ideal. Evidently there had been in the soul of Christian civilization "some deep-seated and penetrative disease." In view of the war in Europe, was the Christian religion really worth giving away to other nations? Was there enough "genuineness and vitality" in either the religious or the democratic ideal for success to be expected? Had the war made a sham of the missionary proclamation?[30]

These were large and ominous questions that would have been given scant consideration by the Student Volunteer Movement before the war. Christianity had been assumed to be the superior religion, and it was taken to be self-evident that Christian civilization would change for the better the societies in which missionaries were working. Student Volunteer Movement leaders had for a decade acknowledged the shortcomings of the West; they were now quick to advocate a more aggressive Christian mission as a cure for the ills caused by an expansive

Western civilization. The spotlight was turned away from the frontiers—where Christianity and Western civilization were encountering other religions and cultures—and focused instead on the heartlands of Christian faith and of Western civilization. The Christian nations now called for help from those nations to whom they had lately sent missionaries. Nearly a quarter-of-a-million Chinese laborers and thousands of African troops were brought to France to assist in this European civil war. They became witnesses to the unprecedented carnage of war assisted by science.

With attention shifted away from the challenge of foreign gods or hostile pagan prophets, the Protestant missionary movement for the first time was forced to come to terms with the meaning of a war that was being fought largely among Christians and witnessed by much of the non-Christian world. In the clamorous call to the new crusade, troubling questions raised by the war were nearly lost. But for the Student Volunteer Movement and the student Christian associations of which it was part, the wartime propaganda could not completely dispel a sense that the military crusade was dealing a telling blow to the missionary crusade.

Chapter Three

Confronting Nationalism

> Does Christianity have no power to control the nations that are known as Christians? Is it not possible to make peace by uniting Christian hearts throughout the world? Is it because Christianity is not united enough that at present it is at war? Is it not a reproach to Christianity that it has no power to avoid the present war?
> —A letter from six Japanese Christian leaders, circa 1915

Just after the war broke out in August 1914, Tissington Tatlow, general secretary of the British Student Christian Movement wrote to Gerhard Niedermeyer, general secretary of the German Christian Student Alliance, "We can honestly say to one another that war is the enemy of the things which your movement and our movement care for most. We are involved in a struggle which is not of our making, and which we heartily wish had not come to pass." Tatlow expressed the desire of the British students that the war end quickly so that they and the Germans would be free "to give our strength to working together in the World's Student Christian Federation for the coming of the kingdom of God."[1]

Niedermeyer replied immediately, noting that "there is no German nor German Christian who is not ready to give his life blood and all his possessions for this just war." There would always be wars and rumors of wars, he said, and Christians should pray not so much for peace as for justice and for God's will to be done. But Niedermeyer did wonder what would become of the student federation in light of the reports he was reading in the French movement's paper of a "war of revenge against Germany." And he expressed dismay at Britain's betrayal of "the white race for the Mongolian."[2]

In a war distinguished by an extraordinary lack of charity and by mean-spirited pulpit attacks on the enemy, the student Christian and missionary movements maintained a remarkable level of goodwill and respect across the lines of propaganda and hate that were erected between the warring parties. There were, as in this exchange between Tatlow and Niedermeyer, occasional echoes of the nationalistic and cultural passions that had led to the war. And yet federation leaders like Herman Rutgers tried to keep communication flowing between students of both the Allied forces and the Central Powers.

"Sometimes [Rutgers] infuriated us by his defense of the German conduct of the war," Tatlow recalled, "but we learned later that he defended us to the Germans. In the end, his activities were too much for our Intelligence Department at the War Office and his visits to England were prohibited, but he always behaved as a gentleman and a Christian" (521). When British students and their leaders gathered for a special wartime conference in January 1915, there was agreement that taken as a whole, war was "the devil's work" (526). But most were also in agreement that German militarism was the real cause of the war.

When, early in the war, John Mott traveled behind the lines on both sides of the conflict, he found that people became impatient with his neutrality. When he presented arguments of the German Christians to a group of dons at Christ College, Oxford, their eagerness to hear the other side soon turned to irritation at the substance of the German claims. In Germany, Mott encountered a similar impatience with his attempts to represent the British point of view. In the early part of the war, Mott worked among the burgeoning numbers of prisoners of war on both sides. He tried to provide a positive moral, spiritual, and physical service to the fighting men of Europe.

The objectivity of the student journals occasionally gave way to partisan reporting. In 1915, the British student journal responded to a German student publication attack on England for alleged atrocities during the Boer War. The English response quoted an earlier German military history of the South African war in which the British were largely exonerated of any charges of brutality. The British reporter wondered whether the more recent German writer was "as ill-informed on the other matters about which he writes as he is on the subject of the war in South Africa."[3]

In general, student movement reports and periodicals during the war years were remarkably free of the warmongering that dominated much of the national and Christian press of the belligerent nations. The British journal continued to carry articles about student Christian work in Germany, and Tatlow claimed that "news of progress in the German student movement has been received with as much goodwill and satisfaction as news of progress anywhere else."[4] Although federation members were now fighting in opposing armies, there were continuing expressions of faith that "the bonds that unite us cannot be severed by the most powerful explosives or the most deadly firearms." It was the task of the WSCF, many believed, to prove that Christian unity could surpass "all national differences and prejudices even in times of war and misunderstanding."[5] Federation members were urged to respect the honesty and sincerity of their fellow members on the opposing side and to try to understand something of their point of view. "The whole British position as to the causes and the origin of the war is just as incredible to the Germans as the German position is to the Britisher," the federation newsletter noted.[6]

In neutral Sweden the student Christian movement, in consultation with Archbishop Nathan Söderblom, designed a questionnaire on the effects of the war on religious life and the role of the churches in reconciliation. Responses to the questionnaire came from church leaders and theologians in Germany (fifteen replies), Britain (five replies), and France (three replies) and were published in 1915 as *The Struggle behind the Frontiers*. Archbishop Söderblom, a friend of the student movement who worked tirelessly during the war to maintain contact with church leaders "on both sides of the great divide," wrote the preface to the volume.[7]

American students were urged to guard against bitterness, rancor, or hatred toward political enemies. "We do hate war and all its trappings, but we will not be forced to hate those whom we must fight," one student leader wrote.[8] In J. Lovell Murray's book, the SVM's most ambitious wartime publication, North American students were given examples of "hymns of hate" that were said to be currently in use among Christians in both Germany and France. This cult of hate was gaining adherents by the hour in the United States and Canada, the writer said. Students were urged to firmly reject the "preaching of hate" and to pray "that the wounds in the body of mankind should heal clean."[9]

As American sentiment against Germany was building irresistibly toward the declaration of war, Professor Harry F. Ward of Boston University's School of Theology challenged American volunteers to consider whether German student volunteers might not at that moment be praying God that their armies win. Perhaps the German students were echoing the words of Americans: "We must win this war or our faith is gone and our religion is bankrupt." He noted that "our religious life seems to be taking almost entirely at this time the punitive attitude." Recalling a biblical story, he wondered whether Americans at war would stand with the sinning woman or with the self-righteous Pharisees. "Shall we ever find that common goal which we and our German fellow students can seek together above and beyond the mere winning of the war?" he asked.[10]

"He is no true friend of America who tries to arouse hate in the hearts of American citizens," Edward I. Bosworth told students in an article published about the time the United States entered the war. For some time America had seen threatening signs of civil war, Bosworth said, a civil industrial war. "There has been shooting in the streets and American lives have been sacrificed." With these conditions likely to be present after the war, perhaps in an intensified form, Bosworth feared that a campaign of hate against a foreign foe would later backfire with tremendous force in class warfare at home.[11]

One volunteer did not need to wait until after the war to feel the back-fire of wartime chauvinism. On February 18, 1918, Robert E. Speer addressed an intercollegiate YMCA rally at Columbia University on the subject "World democracy and America's obligation to her neighbors." Under the slogan "Win the War and Win the World," the rally was the first of three consecutive meetings at Columbia, part of the ambitious nationwide plan launched at the SVM conference at Northfield in January, to enroll two hundred thousand students in "an educational campaign for world democracy."[12] In his address Speer outlined five elements of the "world problem" that lay behind the current conflict and that needed to be resolved if the future were to be different from the past. He illustrated these problems with examples from several belligerent nations, including the United States. German racial attitudes were used to illustrate the racial element of the world problem, as were American attitudes toward the Japanese and American Indians. Students were challenged to look to Christ and the missionary cause as the only adequate solution to the world problem.

In a letter to the *New York Times* several days later, Henry Bedinger Mitchell, a Columbia University mathematics professor, attacked Speer. In spite of its eloquence and power, Speer's speech had been "insidiously corrupting, both to the will and the intelligence, because it breathed throughout the spirit of pacifism and minimized the infamies that Germany has perpetrated." Mitchell said that Speer's argument "was the stock one of pro-German agitators in this country—that Germany had only done what all other nations had done, or would do if they had the power." Speer was too easy on the Germans, Mitchell thought, and too hard on the Americans.[13]

The Mitchell letter unleashed what historian John F. Piper Jr. described as "a storm of criticism raining down on Speer and the Association." In a two-week period, the *Times* printed ten letters and three editorials "soundly chastising Speer for his pacifism, and denying the right of any man to speak words which might detract from the nation's glory in time of war."[14]

"There is not now and there never has been any uncertainty whatever in my attitude toward our war with Germany," Speer replied to his critics in a statement reported in the *Times* on February 26. Speer affirmed his belief that this was "a righteous and necessary war" and that it was the American duty to carry it forward with courage and devotion until a just end was reached. "I hate war," Speer admitted, "but I believe that this is a war against war and that it must be waged in order that war may be destroyed."

Speer was unwilling, however, to yield to a superficial patriotism. It was not required of a patriot to affirm the nation's "impeccability," either past or present. Anyone who demands a loyalty that denies facts or tolerates in America "what he is warring against elsewhere," Speer insisted, comes perilously close to the "insidious disloyalty" to which one of the writers had referred. The nation's task was "to replace an order of selfishness and wrong and division with an order of brotherhood and righteousness and unity." The war with Germany was only part of this task, he believed. Even in wartime there must be a willingness to look inward and to refuse to tolerate in ourselves anything that stands in the way of this new order. We must not tolerate in ourselves the policies, prejudices, or passions that we decry in our foe. Real loyalty, Speer thought, is making our own hearts pure and our own hands clean so that we may be worthy of being used to achieve victory and peace.[15]

The editor of the *Times* was not impressed. He asserted that Speer really was a kind of pacifist and should be publicly repudiated by the YMCA. Although there were indeed other problems in the world, the editor thought, the war was the only important one at the moment. To divert attention from the war, as Speer had done, was to risk being labeled a pacifist. It was a label Speer deserved, the editor concluded.[16]

The story did not end there. After his hometown paper picked up the story, Speer responded to the controversy by making a public statement in the chapel of the First Presbyterian Church of Englewood, New Jersey. Speer assured his neighbors that he definitely was not a pacifist. He had given the same address on four other occasions in different parts of the country without arousing criticism. The mayor was not satisfied. He wrote to the local paper, insisting that what the American people needed was not the "preaching of pacifism under whatever guise" or "reminders of past national shortcomings" but "an uncompromising and undistracted attention to the immediate task of defeating German propaganda and German arms."[17]

The American SVM and association members were not always as fair as Speer in dealing with the causes and claims of the war. When set in a context of the prevailing American chauvinism, however, their addresses and writings appear remarkably restrained, even balanced. In the magazines of the association and the volunteer movements, there was little warmongering. Militarism was nearly always criticized, and the heroics of war were usually placed alongside its horror and destruction. In spite of this balance, student missionary movement leaders made little effort to distance the missionary cause from that of the nation at war. On the contrary, they often blended the two into one grand crusade to save the world from tyranny and to extend democracy and the kingdom of God.

Of the SVM leaders, Speer was the most cautious in his public statements about the relationship between the war and missions. The missionary enterprise was needed more in this war than at any time in the history of the world, Speer said, because it asserted that all people and all races are one. The missionary cause demonstrated clear thinking about the positive purpose of race and race relations. The missionary message offered an authentic internationalism needed by the church and the world. "Whatever else we may surrender, let us not surrender the missionary enterprise," Speer wrote. "We can hold this fast today with no betrayal of our own nationalistic loyalty."[18]

But could the national cause in wartime be embraced without betraying the missionary enterprise? How could the credibility of a supranational kingdom of God—the cause for which missionaries worked—be maintained when Christians were fighting Christians?

"I have never heard deeper and more sincere prayers," student worker Ruth Rouse wrote during the war, "than those offered by French students for the German student Christian movement and for German students." Harry Emerson Fosdick, a New York pastor and one of the most widely read authors in the student Christian press on both sides of the Atlantic, noted the popularity of "hymns of hate" then in circulation on both sides of the conflict but condemned them as inconsistent with Christian principles. If we had been born in Germany, he said, we would be doing the same as the Germans. "We must win the war," he declared, but the victory must be one without bitterness. Fosdick urged the students to pray not only for their own nation but for their enemies as well:

O God, bless Germany! At war with her people, we hate them not at all, and underneath the cruel divisions that force on us this sorry business of mutual destruction we acknowledge before Thee those underlying unities that yet will be there and will be beautiful when war is over. Our enemies, too, are sons of God and brothers for whose sake Christ died. We acknowledge before Thee our part in the world's iniquity that rolls this burden on Thy heart and crucifies the Son of God afresh. We dare not stand in Thy sight and accuse Germany as though she alone were guilty of our international disgrace. We all are guilty. We confess with shame that the present horror is the natural fruit of sins in which we all have shared. We beseech Thee against those things in Germany and in us that make war possible. And especially we lift up our prayer for every good impulse in every German heart, for all misgivings among Germany's people that cast doubt upon the policies of frightfulness and terror, for all the forces of a forward-looking democracy within her, and for every German Christian on his knees who is asking Thee for the dawn of peace and brotherhood. Save to the great service of the world, we beseech Thee, the wonderful qualities of the people whom we fight; let them not perish from the earth, burned in retributory fire. We need their strength to be our admiration and our help, as it now is our despair. O God, bring us all, Thy wayward people, to such a penitence and shame at having made Thy world by sin so sad a place, that we may learn brotherhood with that same diligence which now we give to war.[19]

But penitence and shame were hardly the characteristic response to the war. While the Student Volunteer Movement did avoid extreme expressions of nationalism, it could not escape the clutches of total war. Its leaders yielded to the temptation of equating the national and the missionary causes, of declaring the war to be an expression of the missionary spirit that would further missionary aims. Given the unprecedented pressure of the government, the military, and the press, it was not surprising that SVM leaders yielded. Courage, or even modesty, on that point might have been more becoming. The war effort gained little from the extravagant missionary endorsement. After the war, this identification of the national with the missionary crusades left the missionary cause vulnerable at a time when an uncompromised internationalism would have been its greatest asset. For the Student Volunteer Movement, the equating of military and missionary objectives may have been the most damaging development of the war.

Chapter Four

The Death of the Watchword

It must be a rude shock to the faith of the church in the mission field to see nations which profess the law of Christ engaged in fratricidal strife.

—J. H. Oldham, August 1914

To teach all nations to observe the ideals which Jesus entrusted to his disciples is no superficial undertaking which can be completed by a few thousand men in a single generation.

—Kenneth Scott Latourette, 1919

Mission leaders were not slow to recognize that the European conflict would have a devastating effect on the missionary apologetic. The day after Britain declared war on Germany, J. H. Oldham of the Edinburgh Continuation Committee—a group vested with responsibility for furthering the vision of the 1910 ecumenical missionary conference—wrote to committee chairman John R. Mott. Distributing responsibility for the war was not as important, he said, as acknowledging "the fundamental fact that Christian Europe has departed so far from God and rejected so completely the rule of Christ that a catastrophe of this kind is possible." Unless Europeans and Americans could see how completely God had been forgotten and denied in national life, Oldham feared that the world's progress would be set back for generations.[1]

Immediately, Oldham began to realize the profound effect this war would have on the younger churches in the field—watching Christian nations engaged "in fratricidal strife"—and within a few days he and other British mission leaders launched an appeal for funds to aid the continental mission societies whose work had already been badly disrupted. They quickly drafted a public statement under the title "The War and Missions: British Appeal for German Missions" and circulated it to

41

mission society representatives around the world. They hoped that "substantial help rendered to Continental missions would be a practical demonstration of the reality and power of the love which is able to transcend differences of nation and race."

Whether face saving or genuinely compassionate, the gesture could not hide how deeply racial issues were ingrained, not only in political policies and prejudices but in missionary thinking as well. Mott's response to Oldham two weeks later was a measure of how much his own views of missions were unconsciously colored by national and racial perceptions. Oldham's letter and appeal for German missions had made a deep impression on him, Mott said, convincing him that "some special effort should be made to safeguard the large interests not only of our Anglo-Saxon missions, but also those of the Continent."[2]

The War and the Missionary Program

The war damaged the entire missionary enterprise. Missionary sailings were delayed by the conflict, and some candidates never reached their intended field of service (see fig. 4.1). So many candidates were killed or disabled in combat that in 1917 John Mott reported the number of missionary candidates had been halved. He noted that one-third of German missionary candidates had already been killed. Some of the brightest student volunteers of France and England had lost their lives in the first three years of the was—"not a few here and there, but hundreds. You cannot mow men down with machine guns as you mow down wheat, without cutting into the missionary operations of this generation and the next," Mott said after his first wartime tour in Europe. For those who survived, the psychological and spiritual impact of the war was enormous. Mott reported that a "great stumbling block" had been thrown across the path of some of the most thoughtful youth who might have been candidates for missionary service.[3]

There were delays or complete stoppages of funds and materials intended for the mission fields. Hundreds of mission schools and colleges were closed for lack of funds. Developing Christian congregations in Africa and Asia were fragmented when missionary leaders were repatriated or called into military service. Mails containing vital missionary communications were intercepted or lost. Fluctuating international exchange rates placed strains on mission fund raising and administration. In the longer term, the war represented an enormous sidetracking of funds that might otherwise have gone into mission work. "You cannot

Figure 4.1

Wartime Missionary Deployments, Great Britain and the United States

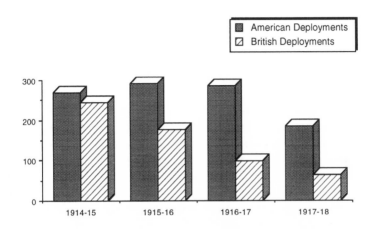

Based on statistics from "Missionary Forces in 1914 and 1918,"
International Review of Missions 8 (1919): 479-90.

spend each hour in the works of destruction and demolition more than the Presbyterian boards, North and South, men's and women's boards united, spent in the entire last year and not have it eat into the economic base of Christendom," John Mott wrote. Each day, he said, we are spending twice as much to destroy than is spent in a year by all the missionary societies—Protestant and Catholic—in their efforts to save.[4]

Mission work was interrupted or permanently halted by the war. During the war, German missionaries were interned as enemy aliens in some British colonies, and by the end of the war more than a thousand German workers had been expelled from their places of work and prevented from returning by the treaty of Versailles. Mission work in Turkey and the Balkans was all but wiped out by the war. Many missionaries in the field became so involved in work with soldiers and in providing relief to victims of the war that the normal work of evangelization and social service was almost completely set aside for the duration of the war. Cooperative efforts in missionary work suffered dramatic setbacks because of the war, and many projects were halted indefinitely by a war that engaged—

or at least distracted from their normal lives—more than half of the human race.[5]

In financial terms, the demands of war seemed to bolster American support for the foreign missionary enterprise. Giving for missions, measured either in total receipts or in per capita giving, continued to grow during the war years. Between 1914 and 1918, receipts of the fifteen largest Protestant denominations showed a combined increase of 35 percent. In an astonishing postwar display of generosity, Americans increased their giving for missions by an unprecedented 80 percent in the two years after the war ended. The foreign service arm of the North American associations, mentioned in chapter 2, showed even more vigor, more than doubling its financial commitment to overseas work during the war and matching the increase of other Protestant agencies for the two years after the war.

Some of the changes the war brought to the missionary program were immediate and obvious. Intellectual and spiritual consequences were not as readily gauged by mission leaders. But even while the guns of August still sounded, it was clear that the missionary message would be challenged by this war. The idea of world evangelization had been the organizing purpose of the Student Volunteer Movement, and the slogan "The evangelization of the world in this generation" had been the primary recruiting appeal during the first two decades of the movement's growth. The watchword gained its widest currency between the turn of the century—when John R. Mott published a book that took the watchword as its title—and the Edinburgh Missionary Conference of 1910.[6] The war undermined all the essential meanings of the watchword.

Evangelization: A Larger Gospel

The traditional Protestant gospel was addressed to individuals, but modern wars were caused and fought by nations. If Christians were to respond to the problem of war, they would have to confront the racial, political, and economic problems of nations. In responding to the war, the student missionary message took on a more strongly social cast. Problems of race and economic justice took center stage, and the gospel became infused with the rhetoric of the American crusade to make the world safe for democracy.

Walter Rauschenbusch, a leading proponent of the Social Gospel, had addressed the college associations before the war, making a prophetic appeal for economic democracy. Rauschenbusch's presence on the platform symbolized the growing interest within the student movement in the social implications of the Christian message. Already in 1906, the Ys had begun studying *The Political and Social Significance of the Life and Teachings of Jesus,* a book by a Cornell professor of economics and politics, Jeremiah W. Jenks. Although not a systematic statement of the Social Gospel, this textbook for students encouraged a progressive view of social reality in which the nation would mature along with the individual, until war would be abolished and a world parliament established that would help ensure the reign of peace and justice among the nations.[7]

Already appealing before the war, the Social Gospel was further popularized during the war years in courses especially designed for student Ys. A unified college voluntary study course, created during the war under the direction of the Sunday School Council and the Council of North American Student Movements, included a text for college seniors, written by Walter Rauschenbusch and entitled *The Social Principles of Jesus* (1916). It was an attempt, said Rauschenbusch in the introduction, "to formulate in simple propositions the fundamental convictions of Jesus about the social and ethical relations and duties of men." Through daily Bible studies, students were led to encounter the personality and teachings of Jesus. The readings and study questions emphasized three of Jesus' convictions: the sacredness of human life, the solidarity of the international human family, and the obligation of the strong to stand up for those whose life was impaired or whose place within the human family was being denied. These convictions aligned Jesus with "the democratic social spirit" of the day. Rauschenbusch believed that the "best forces of modern life" were largely the product of the spirit of Jesus, "diffused and organized in the Western world."

Jesus had set before the human family a new social ideal, the reign of God on earth, and a new social order in which God's will would be done. Fused with the new understandings of the social sciences, this social ideal was now leading to the development of social Christianity. To this new Social Gospel, Rauschenbusch called American college students active in the SVM and YMCA study groups. Their commitment to social Christianity would help to bring the enormous organized forces of the Christian church to bear on the social tasks of American communities, to help create "the nobler America which we see by faith."[8]

Even when most optimistic, Rauschenbusch's Social Gospel did not lose touch with the problem of evil. He was keenly aware of the war and its impact on every dimension of American life as well as growing social and environmental problems, and he gave the college students a Social Gospel that was tuned to tragedy as well as to triumph. Social Christianity had to be tempered, he believed, by Jesus' deep sense of sin and evil in the world. Human nature was frail and persons of evil will powerful. Social regeneration would involve conflict as well as growth. "The way to the kingdom of God always has been and always will be a *via dolorosa* [way of suffering]. The cross is no accident, but a law of social progress" (193).

Rauschenbusch recognized that human ambition tends toward tyranny and oppression and that human societies only rarely escape to find freedom and progress. Jesus taught that ambition should be not suppressed but rather "yoked to the service of society." Rauschenbusch called students to subscribe to a new social order in which leaders would earn power and honor by advancing the welfare of society rather than protecting their own selfish interests.

Rauschenbusch taught that the kingdom of God was already present in the world, overlapping and interpenetrating existing organizations and institutions, sometimes raising them to new levels of integrity and resisting them when they were evil, "quietly revolutionizing the old social order and changing it into the new" (196). In his final challenge to the students, he acknowledged that the kingdom of God also suffers terrible reverses and that the world was in the midst of just such a reverse. Still hopeful in the midst of a war whose end he did not live to see, Rauschenbusch concluded that "after a time it may become apparent that a master hand has turned the situation and laid the basis of victory on the wrecks of defeat" (197).

When wedded to the traditional ministries of the YMCA—physical, mental, and spiritual—the Social Gospel gave the Y its distinctive fourfold program approach. Before the war, the college Associations had developed a new blend of revivalism and the Social Gospel called social evangelism. During the war, labor leader and social activist Raymond Robins led campus campaigns focusing on contemporary social issues and calling students to a personal commitment to Christ and to social Christianity. In just one year during the war, Robins led social evangelism campaigns on forty-two American campuses, with hundreds of students signing commitment cards for personal and social action. After the war, Sherwood Eddy developed this social evangelism concept further, using the campaign approach to challenge the basic foundations of the social order (see chapter 9).[9]

The war reinforced the place of the new gospel in the missionary crusade. "You cannot have a social Christianity in China and an individualistic Christianity at home," Union Seminary professor William Adams Brown argued during the war. Missionaries could not challenge with integrity the treatment of Chinese girls in cotton factories or ask that religion be taught in the schools if, at home, America was making national selfishness the controlling principle of its foreign policy or if labor-management disputes were being treated as private quarrels that had nothing to do with Christian faith. The "missionary consciousness" demanded that Christian principles be applied in all human relationships, beginning with those closest to home.[10]

This was a message that rang true for many students. After the war, radical students were more inclined to put their own civilization on trial than to continue the crusade to save the rest of the world. They warmed to a gospel that turned America's attention away from problems in the mission field and forced the nation instead to look at problems the war had revealed in the West.

By the end of the war, even a conservative SVM leader like Robert E. Speer began to give high priority to the social agenda. As chairman of the Federal Council's General War-Time Commission of the Churches, Speer was asked to speak on the war and the religious outlook. Of the great tasks facing the church after the war, he said, none was more important than "the building of a Christian social order at home." It was clear that the war had conveyed a new message to Speer, a man whose personal and professional life had been dedicated to missions. "The church must preach with new power the significance of Christian principles in all our social relationships." Democracy must be applied in industry as well as in the political process. The churches, Speer wrote, must also deal with the race problem, perhaps the greatest of all human problems of the day.[11]

The Missionary Gospel and Race Relations

Before the war, an awakening social conscience in the college Ys had already put the race problem on their home missions agenda. By the time the war was over, race relations was demanding attention in student discussions of foreign missions as well. YMCA and YWCA work among African Americans began in the 1890s; by 1916, there were forty-six Negro Associations with more than ten thousand members and fifty-five secretaries. During and after the war, the black association work expanded rapidly, nearly tripling in size by 1924. Colleges were included in the YMCA's work with black youth. In 1916, Channing H. Tobias, an

African American staff worker with the college Y, reported that
Associations had been organized on more than one hundred of the one hundred forty state colleges, industrial schools, and denominational colleges
where black students were enrolled. The International Committee employed three full-time Negro secretaries for the work with these students,
now numbering more than seven thousand.

The college Y was quite advanced in its efforts to build interracial understanding and working relationships, especially in the South. Tobias
reported that in addition to carrying out various social work activities in
their own communities, African American students were active in the
southern Race Relationships Movement. Initiated by the YMCA, this
movement sponsored a study of conditions affecting the two races in the
South and encouraged white students to participate in study courses
based on the findings of books such as W. D. Weatherford's *Negro Life
in the South*.[12] Tobias estimated that fifteen thousand southern white students had taken part in these study groups. In 1914 the first ever interracial student conference was held in Atlanta. It was followed by growing
efforts to include black students in association and SVM gatherings.

The war tended to exacerbate racial hostilities in the United States,
not only between whites and blacks but also between whites and other
minority races. At the 1918 SVM conference in Northfield, Weatherford,
a white YMCA worker among black students, told the students and volunteers that they needed a "spirit of evangelism" to counteract the bru-
talizing influence of war. War was dragging down moral standards,
Weatherford said, and bringing a growing spirit of hatred in the colleges.
There must be a new attitude toward other races, he said. The student
who talked about "Japs" or "niggers" could not have the spirit of Jesus
Christ. The message of evangelism, Weatherford believed, would build
a sense of racial solidarity among college men and women.[13]

The Ku Klux Klan revived during the war, its original antiblack aims
now expanded to include anti-Catholicism and anti-Semitism. The
racism aggravated by the war was also acknowledged to be one of the
underlying causes of the European conflict. By the end of the decade,
race relations had become a popular topic of student discussion throughout the United States. The small but growing black presence in association and volunteer-movement activities brought new perspectives on
cross-cultural missions and soon began to cause accommodation problems at conventions in a still segregated America. By 1924, student concern with race relations would upstage the subject of foreign missions at
the quadrennial missionary convention.[14]

The Missionary Gospel and Democracy

During the war the missionary message increasingly became associated with the secular mission President Woodrow Wilson had declared for the United States in entering the war: to make the world safe for democracy. According to Clifton J. Phillips the Student Volunteer Movement had long tended "to confuse the Christianization of the world with the expansion of American or Western civilization."[15] At least for a time the war propaganda removed from the minds of students and leaders any doubts about this alliance. American students were sent out on a righteous mission to destroy war, militarism (or Prussianism), and autocracy—the "arch enemies of democracy." The war was often described in terms that made it seem an extension of the missionary crusade.[16] Christian civilization is based on democracy, students were told, and democracy is sustained by Christian faith. "We believe in democracy," Robert E. Speer wrote in 1918, "because we are Christians."[17]

Democracy and missions had never shared so intimate an association. Volunteers were told in 1918 that the war and Christian missions shared the same goal. It was Jesus Christ himself who had brought the ideals of democracy into the world, J. Lovell Murray, the educational secretary of the American volunteer movement, asserted, and these ideals were at the heart of the divine purpose for humanity. Now they were under attack. The war could stop the attack, but it remained for the missionary enterprise to carry out the "constructive counterpart" to the war, which was "the dissemination through all the world of the democratic spirit and teaching of Jesus Christ." If men in Europe could give their "last full measure of devotion" to this war, how much more should they be willing to give in the battle for world evangelization?[18]

The Missionary Gospel and the Problem of War

While the war undermined the optimism of the Social Gospel, it nonetheless confirmed its critique of the social sins of the West. And the war itself was the most massive and compelling social problem confronting the student Christian movements in their defense of the missionary cause. Why had the churches failed to prevent war? Had they not applied the social teachings of Jesus? Or did Christianity lack the moral authority to control the gods of war? Some students responded to the problem of war by working more vigorously to apply Christ's teachings to the search for permanent peace. Others became skeptical about the church's fitness for such tasks.

Of contemporary observers who wrote about World War I, no friend of the student movements was more articulate in describing the problem of modern war than Harry Emerson Fosdick. In a book published just after the United States declared war on Germany, Fosdick responded to a charge popular in North America as well as in Europe that the Great War was a tragic monument to the failure of Christianity. He pointed out that Christianity was only one of a number of social institutions sharing the blame for not preventing this tragedy; among the others were education, commerce, international law, and social idealism. Fosdick realized that the war had dealt social optimism a fatal blow and that faith itself was at risk. But still there was hope. Only in a world of growing intimacy, he thought, could such an appalling conflict take place. A world war was the price to be paid for the growing internationalism and interdependence that would, in spite of colossal failures such as this, lead to an ultimate federation of nations. A growing intimacy among the nations allowed "seven-eighths of mankind to be engaged in the same war." For American Protestants, the dreams of the old century died hard. The nineteenth century had made the world into a neighborhood; the twentieth century might yet make it into a brotherhood. "We are fighting the war on the way up," said Fosdick, "not on the way down."[19]

Fosdick observed that this was the first war in history that led people to judge Christianity a failure. Until the twentieth century, the Christian church had lived more or less congenially with war. Alleviating its worst horrors, curbing its excesses, offering sanctuary to the enemy and encouraging compromise and truce, the church had been able to justify war and even call its members to a crusading slaughter of the unbeliever. "Christianity and war lived in peace together as did Christianity and slavery," Fosdick said. As had happened with slavery in the previous century, Christians were now coming to see the inherent conflict between Christianity and war. When Christians realized that either slavery must be stopped or Christianity be judged a failure, the outcome was assured: slavery was abolished. The Great War had drawn the ethical ultimatum once again. Christianity and war could no longer coexist. "Christianity will indeed have failed," Fosdick concluded, "if it does not stop war" (14–20).

Anyone who knew what was happening on the European battlefields and still called war glorious, Fosdick believed, must be morally unsound. War was no longer a gallant thing, with evenly matched knights fighting each other according to accepted rules of chivalry. War now meant dropping bombs from airplanes and killing women and children while they slept. It was shooting by telephone orders an unseen place miles away and slaughtering invisible men. War was murdering innocent travelers on merchant ships with torpedoes from invisible submarines. It was launching clouds of poisoned gas and killing men with their own breath. War meant men with jaws gone, eyes gone, limbs gone, minds gone. It meant countless bodies of boys tossed into the incinerators and prison camps vicious with the inevitable results of enforced idleness. It meant untended wounds and gangrene and a long time to die. War meant mothers looking for letters they would never see, wives waiting for voices they would never hear, and children listening for footsteps that would never come. After this war, Fosdick asserted, the possibility of a Christian war could never again be contemplated. He startled his Protestant audience with a vivid expletive of Walt Whitman: "Wars are hellish business—all wars. . . . And now I say God damn the wars—all wars!" (61–62).

Fosdick recognized that many would agree with his description of war's incredible horror but would respond by saying, in the name of realism, that war is inevitable. In view of the sadly inadequate solutions offered by Christian people to the problem of war, it was not surprising that many had concluded that war is a necessary evil. There was, Fosdick said, only one realistic way to rid the world of the scourge of war: the creation of a world federation of nations. This would require the development of "an international mind" and the sublimation of patriotism to a larger, worldwide unity. Only religion, Fosdick believed, was capable of bringing about such a moral revolution among the nations. Only religion could kill war.

A Bergsonian analysis of the predicament reinforced the need for a religious solution to the problem of war. Fosdick noted that humanity's spiritual development had failed to keep pace with scientific progress, the chief effect of which was to extend the power of the human body. Telescopes and microscopes had increased the power of the eyes, telephones the ears, telegraphs the voice, locomotives and steamship lines the feet. Guns had extended the blow of the fist from two feet to twenty-five miles. Never had the human body been so powerful. This was an age of giants. But these giants lacked the moral stature to control their superhuman strength (80–81).

In order for the world to escape the scourge of war, the church needed to lead in the shaping of a new moral vision. While the world wandered in an ethical wasteland, however, the moral power of the churches was being squandered in internecine squabbles over theology and church polity. Only organizations like the YMCA and the Federal Council of Churches seemed to offer a model of the kind Fosdick thought might lead the world toward the kind of federation that could bring an end to war.

Fosdick called for a more social concept of missions. "The missionary enterprise," he said, "is the Christian campaign for international goodwill." If there was danger of war with Mexico, then the United States should send "an invasion of school teachers and social workers and Christian preachers" to build a new quality of international relations between the two countries. If a clash with Japan was inevitable, then the United States should organize, through its mission agencies, expressions of goodwill that would help both countries to appreciate the best in the other. "The missionary enterprise at its very heart is the impulse to share our finest, and if the finest in America and the finest in Japan were thoroughly known to each other, the chances of collision would be minimized to vanishing," Fosdick concluded (94–96).

By the end of the war, Robert E. Speer could say that the slogan "This is a war to end war" had become a universal watchword. But, he said, the missionary enterprise had been doing "peacefully, constructively, unselfishly, quietly for a hundred years exactly the things that now, in a great outburst of titanic and necessarily destructive struggle, we were compelled to do through war." If the world was to be finally rid of this evil, Speer thought, it would be the missionary enterprise that would do it. For Speer as for Lyon, the missionary enterprise was the moral equivalent of war. After the Armistice, however, many students were more eager to wage a moral campaign against war than to enlist in the missionary crusade to make followers of Jesus. In the 1920s, when the Great War began to seem a less noble crusade, Speer's identification of the missionary enterprise with that conflict would seem a less fortunate alliance.

The war hastened the redefinition of evangelization. To respond to war, the gospel had to have a more social content. The European conflict demanded that footnotes be added to the Social Gospel—on war, on racism, and on democracy. But even with a new and larger definition of evangelism, the watchword was battered by the war. Even with a more social definition of the Good News, the credibility of the Western evangelists was impugned by a war that they endorsed, a war that did little more than set the stage for greater tragedy.

This redefined and larger gospel did not fit so easily with the neat dichotomies of the watchword's world, one world where missionaries were recruited and another world that was lost, that needed the Good News missionaries brought. The war evoked a new understanding of the spiritual geography of the world, a redefining of the topography of sin and of what was meant by being "lost."

The World: Who Are the Heathen?

Traditional Protestant missionary work, especially the crusade to evangelize the world quickly, had depended on a clear sense of who was right and who was wrong. The war relocated the mission field. Until 1914 it had always seemed clear to Western Christians where the balance of virtue lay. Although there was a growing awareness of the sins of the West, European and American civilization seemed comparatively virtuous. Asia and Africa—and probably Roman Catholic Latin America as well—needed the Good News that missionaries brought, whether shared in chapel, classroom, or clinic. The ready acceptance of Western education and medicines, if not always of the Christian gospel, seemed to confirm this missionary perception of need.

During the decades leading up to the war, there had been a growing tendency among student mission leaders to build their case for world evangelization both on the traditional claims of the Bible and also on the popular Darwinism of the period. Human societies as well as animals were engaged in a competitive struggle in which the fit would survive. Before the war, John Mott had argued that Christianity's ability to win out in the "struggle for mastery" among the nations was crucial, not only to the success of the missionary task but also for the credibility of the faith among young people in the West. "Only a Christianity powerful enough to conquer the minds and hearts of the followers of the non-Christian religions in Asia and Africa," Mott would say, "can show itself able to meet the deepest needs in the lives of the students of North America." On the other hand, in a situation in which many people in the West were drifting away from faith, the failure of the "foreign missionary propaganda" in this struggle for mastery could result in the mission and influence of Christianity being "shaken to the foundation."[20]

If the war could not give a final verdict in the case of Christianity versus the other religions of the world, it did hand down a sobering finding. Christianity as practiced in the West was found wanting. The heathen were not as far away as the missionary leaders had thought. As the United States was preparing to enter the conflict, John Mott wanted to distance Christianity from Western civilization. But there was also trouble at home. In spite of the efforts like that coordinated by Oldham of the British on behalf of German missions, missionary attitudes had not survived unscathed. "Bitterness has spread into these holy places," Mott wrote. Missionary unity that seemed to transcend national and cultural boundaries had been mutilated by the war. If Christians were confused, non-Christians were scandalized. Mott anticipated the actions that the British government would take against German missionaries in India, actions that would make it impossible for the latter to pick up their work after the war. The body of Christ was not, perhaps, broken by the war, Mott thought, but it was torn and maimed.[21]

In a 1916 pamphlet titled "Missionary Study in War Time," British SCM secretary Tissington Tatlow argued that a renewed emphasis on the missionary enterprise would be an antidote to "the poison of excessive nationalism" in Europe. The war demonstrated that material progress in the previous half century in Europe had outstripped spiritual progress. If Europeans were, in the face of the war, losing faith in "the power of spiritual ideals," then perhaps it was time to look to the non-Christian world to find dynamic Christianity. The world was now a unity, he asserted. If Christianizing the social order was a "home problem," it was also a problem for the world as a whole. The church in the West had missed the way. How better to find the way forward than "by studying Christianity at work in the face of heathendom?" Perhaps the gift of the Spirit could be recovered in Britain through seeing God's work in the growth of the non-Western church.[22]

It did not take long for Western fears about a loss of credibility for Christian missions to be realized. Soon after the war broke out, missionaries in Japan reported that the Japanese were becoming more resistant to the Christian message. For them, the civic and national influences of religion were of highest importance, and with the war, Christianity was seen as having compromised this public trust. The war was barely under way when missionary leaders in the West were hearing from Christians in the "mission lands." Six Japanese Christian leaders wrote a letter of concern to Christians in Europe and North America, asking why Christians in the West were powerless to stop the war. "We Christians cannot stand still and see such barbarous murder of other Christians in this Christian century," they asserted.[23]

From the Middle East came a different, more cynical response to the question of Christian culpability. In the Mosque of St. Sophia in Constantinople soon after the war began, a Muslim mullah was reported to have celebrated the fact that twenty million Christians in Europe were cutting each other's throats and prayed publicly that their number might increase. "That is Christian civilization," he said. "We spit in the face of such civilization."[24]

The Student Volunteer Movement in North America showed some awareness of the crisis of credibility that the war presented to the missionary message. There was a new deference toward other religions. In 1918, the SVM responded to a growing interest in non-Christian religions by giving special prominence in the official mission study course prospectus to Edmund D. Soper's new book, *The Faiths of Mankind*. It was described as "a sympathetic examination" of the world's great religions, comparing their teachings with those of the Christian faith. This humility seemed to deepen as the war continued.

In the call sent out to the colleges from the Northfield missionary conference in 1918, the war was said to be "a summons to penitent recognition that there has been something amiss with Christian civilization." This was Christendom's war. Christian nations were partners "in the sins that so sharply antagonized us one against the other and that at last ran their shears through the fabric of international society." Christians were at fault that war was even allowed to survive and were also culpable for the spirit of hatred in which the war was being carried out.[25]

When the SVM conference was convened, some of the old appeals for missionary action in response to the need "out there" were heard. But there was a new challenge as well. Social Gospel advocate Harry F. Ward declared that the first need confronting religion in the United States was for "applied Christianity" to be extended among intellectual and business leaders at home and among men and women working in American and European factories, mills, and mines. Few of these workers had heard the gospel, and even if they had, the conditions in which most of them worked denied its reality. They needed a new gospel, one that would bring real change to the injustices of their workplace.

Ward told the story of a striking worker in California who had recently been shot by a policeman. As he lay dying, he said, "Lift me up and sing with me our hymn." As he died, he and his comrades sang the socialist anthem, "The Red Flag." When would the red flag of socialism, Ward asked the volunteers, and the "blood-stained banner of the cross" come together? Ward was sure that neither would reach its goal until each absorbed the content of the other. That would only happen, however, if volunteers carried the Christian message "not simply to the ends of the earth, but into the very heart of our civilization."[26]

Shortly after the SVM Conference at Northfield, Channing H. Tobias, a black association worker from New York, challenged North American students to consider not only German atrocities in Belgium but white atrocities against blacks in America. A play on the popular wartime slogan,

Tobias's article "Shall America Be Made Safe for Black Men?" was a sobering account of "official" violence against blacks as well as the more traditional American lynching. He quoted congressional testimony on the recent East St. Louis massacre, which alleged that more than five hundred African Americans had been murdered by a rioting mob who had been watched—and perhaps aided—by city policemen and members of the Illinois militia.

Tobias described a shocking incident in which a ten-year-old boy, whose mother had already been killed by the mob, was running around sobbing, looking for his mother. Members of the mob shot the boy and, before he was dead, picked him up and threw him into the flames. A woman with a two-year-old baby in her arms was trying to protect the boy. She and the baby were also shot and thrown into the flames.[27]

Politicians might juggle the facts or dismiss the whole matter with a wave of the hand, Tobias said, but Christians, "on the peril of their own souls," needed to face squarely the reality of lynchings, economic exploitation, and public discrimination contrary to the Constitution of the United States. W. D. Weatherford, veteran YMCA worker with black associations, told students and volunteers at the January SVM conference that it would be "useless to look on the far fields unless we have in our hearts and in our own colleges the spirit of Jesus Christ, so we shall have the right attitude toward the man who stands by our side."[28]

In India, students returning from tours of study in the West described degraded city slums "under the very shadow of Christian institutions." International students noted class distinctions in Great Britain and racism in the United States. Indian students observed that missionary reports to supporters depicted only the darkest side of Indian life. Indians who served with the British forces in Europe came home reporting that Christian nations had been guilty of "the grossest excesses of selfishness and cruelty, frequently under the guise of religious conviction." In the light of wartime experience and revelations, Indian religious ideals of self-denial and sacrifice seemed superior to the self-assertion and dominance that caused Christians to engage each other and the world in a destructive conflict.[29]

In Great Britain, some Student Christian Movement members concluded that the churches prior to and during the war had shown themselves to be "nerveless and incompetent." The missionary impulse among students had shown some signs of weakening before the war, but by the time it was over, many students were clearly disenchanted with any missionary enterprise that seemed to be engaged in "the transplanting of the so-called Christian civilization of Europe to the East" or "the preaching of a purely individual salvation." General Secretary Tatlow reported in 1917 that any missionary apologetic of this kind "falls upon deaf ears."[30]

Even while admitting that the war had relocated the mission field for British students, in 1917 Tatlow did not see a waning of missionary interest among students. He recognized that the war had called attention to the "greater and more challenging task at home." But the war had also reminded Western Christians of "the solidarity of mankind, and of how hopeless it is to seek for our own national salvation if we forget the need for salvation for mankind as a whole" (83–85).

For many British students, the war had demonstrated that Europe needed Christian faith as badly as India or China. Although a similar argument was heard among some American students, the Europeans pushed the point to a place of devastating clarity. If human society is really one and not many, if all people are, at least in creation, God's children, then it follows that every society is equally in need of evangelization in every generation. A second point followed from this, one related to the evangelistic process itself: Christianity, the European students reasoned, is spread not by talking but by "contagion," by the influence of a living "Christian culture." If this is true, then "only a Christian society can conduct a Christian mission." It was only too clear to the European students who fought in the trenches of the war just how thin was the religious veneer on their society. And they now had profound doubts about the ability of this society to conduct a Christian mission.

The British students had a second, even more fundamental objection to the missionary enterprise. Many students began to doubt whether Christianity was "the one true religion." The war had brought increased contact between European youth and other cultures of Africa, Asia, and the Middle East. That exposure sometimes resulted in increased racial prejudice, but among many young people, it was the occasion for a thoughtful reflection on the relationship between culture and religion. Especially in the context of a war that was started and largely carried out by Christians, it was only natural that the other religions encountered by the young soldiers would seem more attractive than when previously described by missionaries. If the integrity of Christian civilization was in question and if other religions deserved a more sympathetic hearing, then it followed that a reappraisal of the missionary enterprise was in order. If Christianity was not the "one true religion," then certainly the missionary proclamation must be made—if it would continue to be made at all—with far greater humility and sensitivity.[31]

The war mocked the moral presumption implied in the watchword. Christianity, along with the civilization with which it was identified, was disgraced. There seemed to be as much or more need for evangelization at the home base as in the field. The world to be evangelized was not so much a place as a problem—war, race relations, political oppression, the industrial exploitation of workers. And these were moral challenges for the West as well as for the unevangelized nations far away. The war confirmed to students and to volunteers what Social Gospel advocates had been saying before the war, that in terms of social problems, Western countries were themselves very much in need of evangelization.

For students at least, the Great War led to a Copernican revolution in missionary thinking. World War I initiated a change that was completed in World War II in which the Christian center of gravity shifted away from Europe. Some saw the "center of financial gravity" moving from Europe to North America.[32] In a deeper sense, however, the war marked a shift of the moral center of gravity, certainly away from Europe and perhaps away from the West. No longer could the world be divided simply between "Christian" and "heathen" spheres.

The war gave the final blow to a wedge that the Enlightenment had driven between Christianity and Western civilization. Either the West was no longer Christian but pagan, or Christianity had lost its moral credibility. For many students, both had become true. Was the Constantinian "establishment" of Christianity in the West finally coming to an end? Was Christendom dead? Modern nationalism, it seemed, had created a force that neither king nor cleric could tame. With the weight of centuries behind it, the facile equation of Christianity and Western civilization might still be made after the Great War. But the moral force of the equation had been spent.

"In This Generation": A Comradeship Crushed

The war severely strained the international relations on which the crusade for world evangelization depended for both credibility and practical working partnerships. By the time of the Edinburgh Missionary Conference in 1910, there had been a growing recognition that the world could only be evangelized "in this generation" if the missionary forces of the West were united. Unity was needed not only to enable the work to be done but also to demonstrate the integrity of the gospel as it was being preached by Protestant missionaries. In a book published just before the Edinburgh meeting, Mott described how missionary work during the previous century had undermined vast Hindu and Muslim religious, social, and political systems. Now the constructive forces of Christendom were being visibly drawn together for the final "conquest of the world for Christ." This was the moment for "comprehensive Christian statesmanship and generalship."[33]

For many who attended the Edinburgh conference, John R. Mott himself seemed to have precisely that quality of leadership. Their confidence was symbolized by his being named moderator of the conference's business sessions and appointed chairman of the Continuation Committee that was created to carry forward the ecumenical missionary purposes of the conference. The war did not leave Mott's statesmanship unchallenged, nor did it deal kindly with the Christian forces united for world conquest.

The war threatened everything that the Edinburgh conference stood for, Oldham said in the letter he wrote to Mott on August 5, 1914, the day the United States declared its neutrality. There was still some hope, Oldham thought, of maintaining "the international fellowship and love which we began to learn at Edinburgh." American neutrality, it seemed, might serve the international interests of both the Continuation Committee and the international student enterprises with which Mott was associated. He went twice to Germany before the United States declared war.[34]

The German journal *Kirchenzeitung* commented during the war that although Mott's "fantastic optimism" had always been hard for the Germans to understand, they were dazzled by the enthusiasm his "magnificent goals" aroused at Edinburgh. The conference was such a triumph of missionary cooperation that Germans who distrusted Mott were forced to keep quiet. Then the war came. On Mott's second wartime visit to Germany during the Somme offensive of 1916, when American neutrality was beginning to waver, Mott was questioned warily by German missionary leaders. Was he coming to Germany on any sort of political mission? What was his attitude toward the American arms trade with the Allies? As a neutral, what did he have to say about the English missionary policy that threatened to permanently eliminate all German missionary activity and, consequently, to destroy the sympathetic working relations among evangelical missions?

Mott assured the Germans that he did not participate in political activities. When President Wilson had offered him the China ambassadorship just before the war, he had resolutely turned it down. He was planning to make a visit to Russia the next year on the personal invitation of the president but was merely going to see German prison camps to be able to give reliable information to the people at home. On the question of arms, Mott told the Germans that had Wilson anticipated how American arms would prolong the conflict, he would never have permitted American arms sales to the Allies. Of course, Mott did not approve of the British expulsion of German missionaries from their fields of work and from the English colonies, and he strongly condemned their disgraceful treatment. He had protested to the British, without effect. He promised to keep trying, whenever and wherever he could, to protect the "cooperating fellowship of missions." After a private conversation with Mott, German missionary leader D. Karl Axenfeld felt enough confidence in Mott's integrity to defend him publicly in one of the German missionary publications.

In 1916 Mott seemed to pass the test. If his credibility appeared diminished, it was not so much because he had changed as because the Germans had overestimated him. At least for the Germans, in the grim light of the war Mott's earlier successes lost some of their glory. The Germans began to recall their earlier questions about the watchword and their timid ponderings as to "whether the man really possessed a firm sense of Christian reality." The glowing pictures of the future that Mott had painted before the war, the organizational masterpieces that he created, had never failed to enhance the aura of glamor that surrounded him. "And yet," the Germans recalled after his visit in 1916, "which one of us would ever have seriously been willing to trust himself to his leadership?"[35]

A year later the quiet questions had turned into public accusations. The United States declared war on Germany in April 1917, the same month Mott left for Russia with the Root Commission. Any doubts the Germans may have had about the purpose of the commission's trip were dispelled by the American press. Its mission was to strengthen Russia's alliance with the Entente against the Central Powers, they read in *Zion's Herald* of Boston. German missionary leaders also had access to a May 17 report in the *Christian Advocate* that stated that President Wilson had called Mott to the commission precisely because of his international reputation in religious affairs.

To the Germans this was a serious breach of the neutrality expected from a leader of an international Christian movement. By accepting the Russian assignment, Mott seemed to have broken promises made the year before. In mid-1917 the German members of the Edinburgh Continuation Committee joined in signing a formal declaration stating that they no longer recognized Mott's position and leadership.[36]

In May 1920, Mott and German members of the the WSCF and the Continuation Committee took up these matters in a meeting in Berlin. Mott insisted that he had acted in good faith and that any failure on his part was unintentional. Professor Axenfeld was not convinced and explained his reservations in a long letter to Mott immediately after their meeting. He could not understand how Mott should have presumed to continue representing German interests on the Continuation Committee and the World's Student Christian Federation while clearly taking a partisan political role in the war.

If the Germans could have succeeded in making a separate peace with Russia, Axenfeld reasoned, Germany might not have lost the war. The Root Commission was clearly intended to prevent that from happening. How could this political agenda have escaped Mott when the American press—indeed the world press—had no doubt as to the purpose of the commission, Axenfeld asked. Axenfeld quoted Mott's words after his return from Russia, that Mott felt it to be "a religious duty" to win the war against Germany, since it would make the world "a safe place for democracy and especially for the democracy of Russia." In joining the Root Commission, Mott had used his unique international position of religious leadership to crush Germany. He had subordinated the kingdom of God to "the struggle of the nations." Anyone who preached a "democratic gospel" as an act of religious duty—and was ready to impose that gospel by force of arms—was preaching a false gospel, no matter how sincere his intentions.[37]

Even before America's entrance into the war, Axenfeld said, Mott had failed to speak out vigorously on behalf of German missions. The destruction of German missions was really a weakening of the entire missionary enterprise. As the British government's policy toward German missions in her colonies became clear, German Christians waited for a word from Mott. During the war Mott had spoken on many occasions about the "supranationality of missions." And yet, as chairman of the Continuation Committee, Mott took no firm action to prevent the "great disaster" that the war brought to German missions work. J. H. Oldham and J. N. Ogilvie, British members of the Continuation Committee, were perceived by Axenfeld and the other German members of the committee as having actively supported the British government action against German missionaries. Why had Mott remained silent about these destructive actions by members of a body committed to the success of the international missionary cause?

With regard to the Armistice, Axenfeld wondered why Mott, a personal friend of President Wilson, was able to do nothing about Article 438, the section that barred German missionaries indefinitely from returning to their fields of service and mission boards from recovering mission properties. How could Mott have left Paris at the time of the Armistice signing in 1919, and then Europe, without "sending any sign of sympathy to German Christians"? Mott had lost the respect that he had enjoyed among German Christians before the war, Axenfeld said. "If German Christians cannot participate in the international Christian enterprises except by recognizing you as the leader, many of them may hardly find a possibility of doing so," he added. If Mott wished to recover the confidence of German Christians, it would take more than money or the return of particular mission fields. In their hour of need, German missionary leaders had been deserted by the Anglo-Saxons who at Edinburgh had called them brothers. From Mott, German missionary leaders needed to hear a public defense of the "rights, the honor and the freedom of German missions," Axenfeld concluded.[38]

In spite of the German criticism during and after the war, Mott was able to sustain his leadership of the several international organizations with which he was affiliated. When he resigned from the position of general secretary of the WSCF after the war, he was elected its chairman. When the Continuation Committee became the International Missionary Council in 1921, he was appointed as the chair. And yet Mott must share responsibility, along with the other leaders of his generation, for the precarious peace that was made after the Great War, a peace that was but a prelude to a second and even more tragic war. William R. Hutchison writes that "American-European tensions, though they have been passed over very lightly in most histories of the missionary and ecumenical movements, had a bearing on the misunderstandings that led to the First World War, and then to the tragically incomplete reconciliation after November 1918."[39] Who can say whether the failure of German Christians to act more courageously in the face of a growing National Socialism in the 1920s and 1930s may not have been at least partly related to their bitter disappointment in the "comradeship of evangelical missions" during the Great War and after?

In any case the damage to the ecumenical missionary cause dashed the buoyant hopes of the SVM founders that the world could be evangelized in their generation. As Oldham had feared, the progress of the missionary effort received a serious setback. At least partly because of the conduct of SVM leaders in this war, the next generation would be far less willing even to carry on the crusade, to say nothing of finishing it speedily.

It was Christians from beyond the West who now stepped forward to take up the missionary task, and their presence and approach made it clear that the time for the watchword had passed.

Coming of Age

Churches in Africa and Asia had long been expected to become self-supporting, self-governing, and self-propagating—in a word, independent. With fund stoppages, the withdrawal of missionaries, and the inability to send replacements during the war, independence came somewhat abruptly to many younger churches. In many cases, work was carried on with improved effectiveness under local leadership, especially when contextual standards of effectiveness were used. In most instances where local leadership and control were advanced by the war, there was a reluctance after Versailles to return to business as usual. The Great War marked both a loss of innocence and a coming of age for many churches and Christian leaders in Asia and Africa.

If the war made the world safe for democracy, it made the missionary enterprise unsafe without it. Many Asian church leaders were unwilling to maintain the fiction of a self-governing church in which key decisions continued to be made in London or New York. They rejected the disingenuous distinction that missionaries were making between "church" and "mission" as a way of maintaining control of the budgets brought by the expatriate workers from the West. (By keeping the expatriate-staffed *mission* organizationally separate from the locally staffed *church,* foreign missionaries could maintain nearly complete control of mission budgets.) During and after the war, there was a growing demand for local participation in decision making and representation by national church leaders in the formerly all-expatriate mission councils.[40]

"When the Europeans came," the Africans say, "we had the land and they had the Bible. They taught us to close our eyes when we prayed, and when we opened them, they had the land and we had the Bible." The Great War created a climate sympathetic to such a cynical reading of recent history. There could be no denying that the great missionary movement of the nineteenth century coincided with the extension of European rule and European influence over the globe. But it was a cynicism bred by the war that could justify the grotesque misstatement that "the same Europeans assaulted the backward peoples of the earth materially with the gun and spiritually with the Bible."[41]

"The war has undoubtedly largely developed the spirit of nationality," the bishop of Madras wrote in April 1919, and his words were echoed by observers in many parts of Asia and Africa.[42] The war caused people to turn away from the exotic culture, often European, in favor of their own language, literature, art, dress, and proper names. There was growing resentment of colonial rule. Independence movements had gathered momentum rapidly during the war, and churches were often caught up in the drama. The gradual shift of authority from "mission" to "church" had been proceeding at a slow pace. During and after the war, national Christian leaders began to demand a more rapid devolution. Some were even beginning to say that the national church would never be strong until foreign missionaries left.

The problem was especially acute in India, where the missionary was "almost exclusively associated with the dominant and too often dominating race" (30). Among educated Indians, a growing nationalism made it more difficult to accept the faith of the ruling power. If Western civilization was representative of Christianity, then India did not need it. On the other hand, "the fact that Indians were taking their share in a world struggle quickened their sense of dignity and their idea of what India might be, if its powers were developed or were allowed free play."[43] Christians, however, typically coming from the depressed classes and castes and fearful of the implications of home rule, were slow to take part in political agitation against the British *raj*. This often resulted in their being branded as Westernized, oblivious to the aspirations of nationalism and no longer truly Indian. Because the labor movement in India was often championed by radical nationalists, Christians often found themselves distanced from the social justice issue that became increasingly important after the war.[44]

Despite a growing sympathy among missionaries toward Indian aspirations, there was a feeling among Indian Christians and missionaries that the church would not be able to continue growing in many parts of India unless there could be radical changes in the relationship of the churches and the foreign missionary societies.[45] In missionary work among students and youth, the war brought progress in the development of Indian leadership. The assignment of India's YMCA National Secretary Edward Clark Carter to the YMCA's war work in Europe provided the opportunity for K. T. Paul, a gifted association leader, to be named national secretary. Paul was the first Indian to hold that position. A strong advocate of indigenous Christian leadership in India, he believed that the Y was exemplary among missionary organizations in India in placing Indians in the highest and most responsible positions of leadership. His own position of leadership in the YMCA gave him a national platform from which to argue the case for Indianization. Paul believed that the reluctance of missionaries and mission agencies to give positions of leadership to Indian Christians was causing many of them to choose secular careers. Perhaps because of his work in an organization that stood outside or alongside the church, Paul pushed the question of Indian leadership to lengths that could make Western missionaries—and even leaders in the YMCA movement outside India—quite uncomfortable.

He pointed out at a conference in Calcutta early in 1918 that the Christian mission in India was an enterprise still largely financed and managed by Western missionaries. Paul insisted that there must be increased Indian representation in missions councils, the last retreat of foreigners who were committed to indigenous leadership in the Indian church, but were not ready to accept Indian leaders as equals in the inner sanctum of the mission. It was precisely in these missionary conclaves that Indian voices were needed to ensure the growth of the church and the corollary fading away of mission structures—the "euthanasia" of missions, as Paul called it.

But representation was not enough. Indian leaders should also be given executive responsibility in the mission itself, and on a completely equal footing with Europeans. Paul was willing to take the risk of weakening the Indian church—and here he acknowledged some disagreement with India missionary Daniel J. Fleming—in order to demonstrate in the mission and in the kingdom of Christ a transcending of racial bias. The ultimate goal, of course, was to transfer responsibility for all mission work to the Indian church, and Paul felt that this process was happening far too slowly.[46]

The wartime challenge to the watchword and the crusade for world evangelization could be summarized in two postwar reassessments of the missionary program. The first came from within the volunteer movement itself, and the second from the North American missionary establishment.

By the time the war was over, younger leaders were ready for a new watchword.[47] Tyler Dennett, an outspoken postwar critic of missions, suggested in 1919 that the slogan be changed from "The evangelization of the world in this generation" to "The democratization of the world in the next generation." That Dennett saw this as a change in vocabulary and not a change in content or purpose is a measure of just how much the war had changed student thinking about missions.[48]

The quest for a new watchword was really a reflection of the new missionary perspectives that the war had brought to the student missionary movement. One of the books being used in student mission study groups in North America immediately after the war was Kenneth Scott Latourette's *The Christian Basis of World Democracy*. In daily studies from the Gospels, Latourette led the student missionary and Bible study groups through a consideration of biblical principles that could provide a foundation for a new internationalism. Latourette believed that without these moral values and the new international relations that they could nurture, the entire fabric of civilization was threatened. Mounting social problems—labor unrest, the grievous disparity between rich and poor, injustices in the industrial sector, urban slums, a growing divorce rate, declining birth rates among the "abler classes," militarism, and war itself—could set back human progress a thousand years. "The last war shook human society to its foundations," Latourette wrote. "A second, necessarily more severe and exhausting than the first, might deal it an irreparable blow," he wrote in 1919 with startling prescience.[49]

Tempered by the war and perhaps as a professor more in touch with the student mood than the older generation of SVM leaders, Latourette outlined spiritual principles in the quest for a world democracy that revised the rhetoric of the missions crusade and challenged the key slogan of the Student Volunteer Movement. The extension of the ideal social order had been entrusted by God to a human agency, Latourette said, and to a peaceful propaganda of persuasion through the power of ideas rather than of the sword. So broad and comprehensive was Jesus' social program that it could not be accomplished in a generation, nor even in a century, especially with the use of force ruled out. Even after nineteen centuries, Latourette observed, no nation had yet learned to observe the "all things" which Jesus, in the Great Commission, had enjoined his disciples to teach. How long might the kingdom be postponed? It would take centuries, Latourette believed, for African peoples to catch up to the West, which itself had reached a point still quite far from the kingdom. Jesus' program for social transformation was so thorough that thousands of years might be required for its full implementation among the nations of the world.

This remarkable postponement of the evangelization of the world did not need to discourage the students, however. Himself a volunteer, a member of the executive committee, and an influential voice in the Student Volunteer Movement, Latourette told the students that the Christian ideal for society and for the life of the individual would scarcely be worth serious consideration if it could be attained in a generation. "All any one of us can hope to do is to make some contribution to the progress of the race, to aid his generation in seeing and observing a little more fully the program which Jesus revealed, and to insure to the generations after us the transmission of the vision and a somewhat richer heritage than was given to us." Here, from an SVM insider, was a radical restatement of the urgency in the missionary task that had always been kept, through the watchword, at the heart of the movement. The war, it seemed, had dealt a massive blow to the hopes for a speedy evangelization of the world.[50]

When North American missions leaders gathered in New Haven, Connecticut, in January 1919 for their first postwar conference, they paused to assess the effects of the Great War on the missionary enterprise. Senior missionary statesman Robert E. Speer was asked to address the question, "Is a restatement of the Christian message to the non-Christian peoples and a reinterpretation of the missionary objective for the church at home necessary?" In preparation for the New Haven assignment, Speer had put this question to twenty or thirty trusted and capable friends. Much of his address was a report of their replies.

Speer asserted that while there could be no tampering with the substance of the missionary message, the war called for a new statement of the Christian message. The war had taken the world from one era of human life and into another, one of Speer's respondents wrote. It was a new day that demanded a restatement of the Christian message both at home and abroad. Another said that the war had convinced him of the need for a more social, less individualistic message: "The war has emphasized the necessity of enthroning Christian principles in the life of society and in the life of the nation."[51]

For a prominent Japanese missionary, this restatement meant that the gospel must be stripped of its "Western philosophic mold, and offered in the simplicity with which Jesus himself taught it." The gospel as a metaphysical system or a plan of salvation for the individual had never been enthusiastically received by the Japanese. On the other hand, "the gospel considered as the power of God to create new personality, to reform bad social custom, and to produce ideal national institutions at once awakens sincere and hearty response." The gospel message in postwar Japan needed to be made "more practical and distinctly social in all its outlook and operation" (144).

From a missionary in China came the challenge to consider the messenger more than the message. "We do not need so much the 'restatement of the Christian message' as we do a reincarnation of Christ's spirit in the messengers." But the war was not so much a rebuke to the missionaries themselves as it was a denial of the reality of the Christian application in social and national life in the West. Another missionary leader had written to Speer that, in the aftermath of the war, "the most powerful restatement of the gospel message that could be made to the non-Christian people would be that the Christian nations practice it themselves" (150).

When Speer turned his attention to the second question set for the evening, whether there needed to be a reinterpretation of the missionary objective in the church at home, his time was nearly gone. In the final minutes of a long conference day, Speer quoted a respondent who captured something of the tragic meaning of the war for the missionary enterprise. Missionaries had been smug and provincial in assuming that the missionary movement with its individualistic message could achieve God's purposes. But Germany showed the poverty of such a program. Here was a nation that respected the Bible and supported the church. There were enough Christians to provide effective witness throughout the entire country. "In other words, Germany was a country that was evangelized as fully as our ambitions for the evangelization of lands now non-Christian would require. Nevertheless Germany was the cause of a great world tragedy" (149).

As the logic of these words settled into the consciousness of the missionaries and leaders after the war, appeals to the crusading rhetoric of the prewar era began to sound hollow, even shoddy. For the generation who had lived the tragedy of the war, there could be no easy appeal to the triumph of the watchword. For some after the war, there could be no gospel at all. For them, the war was the end of faith. For others, there would be new gospels, some competing, but none able to revive the soul of Christian civilization. And none would prevent the holocaust whose outlines were already sketched in the tragedy of Christendom's failure in the Great War and its peace.

But these meanings were not apparent to most American Protestants in 1918 as they turned from the military crusade back to the crusade to save the world. For many older leaders, the war seemed only to have heightened expectations of what could be achieved in peacetime.

Chapter Five

The Beginning of a New Era?

In the years of the Great War the world has crossed a new International Date Line. It is impossible for anyone to estimate accurately the full significance of the time in which he lives, but there is widespread unanimity of opinion that only one date has surpassed in importance to mankind these days in which we live. That date is the shining peak of time which separates A.D. from B.C.

—S. Earl Taylor and Halford E. Luccock, 1918

The Great War revealed as never before the limitless capacities of the students of our generation. There were disclosed within them latent powers of courageous and unselfish effort, of capacity for extreme sacrifice, of ability to lose themselves in great causes, of power of initiative, leadership and co-operation, which, if released and related to the great plans of Christ for all mankind, would make possible an absolutely unprecedented and hitherto unbelievable expansion of his Kingdom.

—John R. Mott, 1919

"Almost as suddenly as it began, the war has ended," the editor of the YMCA/YWCA campus magazine, *Intercollegian,* wrote in December 1918. The war had cleared the ground, he said, for the world democracy of which the Christian students had dreamed. But the nations would have to be reshaped, and reshaped in such a form that the glaring inequities of the old order would be checked or eliminated. This was a moment of danger, a moment of decision. The war might lead to "widespread and violent revolution and a welter of anarchy, followed by a restored despotism." On the other hand, democracy could triumph. What was needed, the American students were told, was "a greatly enlarged missionary program."

So far the church had been merely playing with missions, the editor thought. Comparatively few had taken the missionary task seriously. There were scarcely twenty-five thousand Protestant missionaries in non-Christian lands, a number that in contrast with the great armies of Europe was pitifully small. The war should mark a change. Missionary budgets must grow from thousands to millions of dollars, and recruits would have to be sent out by the hundreds and thousands instead of by the tens. "We must think imperially and with originality," the editor enthused, not for the expansion of a political empire but to spread the Christian gospel through the world so that the nations could be healed.[1]

The older leaders of the student missionary movement in America—along with Protestant leaders of most mainline churches—came to the end of the war believing its rhetoric, confident that the war's lofty moral aims had been largely achieved. If the war had not made the world completely safe for democracy, it had at least put the nations in a malleable state so that they would now receive the Christian message, the basis for democratic government. The missions crusade was needed more than ever, Protestant leaders thought. Now that the weapons of war had been laid aside, it was time to rearm students for the moral and spiritual battles that still remained to be fought. The postwar period was a time of unprecedented opportunity for the church, both at home and abroad. These magnificent opportunities demanded fresh leadership for the Student Volunteer Movement, and the organizing of a new and grand crusade for world evangelization.

The American SVM after Versailles was in many ways the same movement that had watched the world get swept into war four years earlier. Many of the same students were still in school, some seeking advanced degrees, others continuing their education where they had been forced to leave off during the war. There were more students than ever before. The years immediately after the war were marked by record enrollments in the United States, with more than three times as many students enrolled in colleges and universities in 1919 as five years earlier.[2] Much of the literature of the movement remained unchanged.[3] There had been little time to add to the student missionary library during the war, except on the subject of the Christian response to war.[4] The war had also postponed significant changes in the organization. At least on the surface, the Student Volunteer Movement at the end of 1918 seemed not to have changed at all—except for the more obvious seniority of its founder-leaders, who were now in their mid-fifties.

There seemed to be, after the war, a renewed mandate for the Student Volunteer Movement. Students began to take the volunteer pledge in greater numbers than at any earlier time. Mission agencies were recruiting with fresh vigor. An ambitious ecumenical venture—the Interchurch World Movement—was being launched to coordinate massive new programs of both home and overseas ministries in a final effort to evangelize the world. As the Interchurch Movement gathered strength, a great many new missionaries would be required. The volunteer movement would be facing a larger recruiting challenge than ever before.

The business of the movement continued as it had before the war with, of course, some energetic plans for growth, partly fueled by the Northfield Conference of 1918. By the 1919–20 school year, there were seventeen SVM secretaries at work, seven at the Madison Avenue headquarters in New York and ten traveling to all parts of the student field of about a thousand institutions of higher education in the United States and Canada. The headquarters staff and budget were at an all-time high.

The SVM had seen remarkable continuity in leadership in the first three decades of its existence. Several of the men in charge of the movement in 1918 had begun their service in the previous century.[5] But there were changes after the war. Long-time SVM general secretary Fennell P. Turner was called to a senior post with the Foreign Mission Boards of the United States and Canada. Instead of selecting a more youthful leader to replace Turner, chairman John R. Mott and the executive committee of the Student Volunteer Movement turned to the oldest and most experienced leader in the movement, Robert P. Wilder. He was also one of the most conservative in theological orientation.

After his key role in launching the Student Volunteer Movement at Mount Hermon in 1886, Wilder had helped to nurture the movement during its early years in North America and had served as a member of the first executive committee. On his way to India, where he served for several years as a missionary to students, Wilder spoke so powerfully at a Keswick Conference that he was invited by the leaders of that influential movement to make a tour of British universities. The British Student Volunteer Missionary Union was the result. Wilder had then gone on to the Scandinavian countries, founding volunteer movement chapters in Norway and Sweden. After leaving India, partly for health reasons, Wilder had returned to Europe, where he served as foreign students' secretary of the British Student Christian Movement and helped nurture the SVMU in Great Britain and its associated movements on the Continent. He had also served the World's Student Christian Federation as representative for Lands without National Organizations—countries in Europe that did not yet have full-fledged movements.

Midway through the war, when Mott accepted leadership of the North American YMCA, he had written to Wilder inviting him to return to the United States to head up a reorganized Religious Work Department. British student movement leaders were disgruntled that Mott did not consult with them before offering a position to one of their staff—and during wartime at that. Wilder nevertheless accepted Mott's offer to join his New York headquarters staff and had moved to a New Jersey suburb of New York. Now, shortly after the war, Mott wrote to Wilder with another invitation, this time to assume leadership of the Student Volunteer Movement.

Mott noted Wilder's unique qualifications and experience and praised him as a "missionary of missionaries," and "one whose life passion has been and is the evangelization of the world." Mott mentioned the launching of the Interchurch World Movement and the "unparalleled demand which it will soon make and continue to make for new missionaries." Wilder promptly accepted the position, noting that "the colleges are able to furnish the workers needed, and the country has funds sufficient for the speedy evangelization of the world."[6] When Wilder explained to friends his decision to move from the the Religious Work Department to the SVM, he said that the new position would allow him to "do more for the Watchword."[7] With a new and seasoned leader in charge, the SVM was ready for the larger challenges of the postwar world.

Turning Point

After the war, the older SVM leaders were more optimistic than ever about the future of the missions program. So profound was the optimism of this generation, who in the 1890s had plotted the campaign for world evangelization, that even the shock of the Great War did not shake them from their bold plans for world conquest in the name of Christ and democracy. This optimism was the product of a century of growing Protestant confidence, and, at least for many middle-aged leaders, it remained undiminished by a war fought half a world away, one that resulted in an industrial and financial boom that was the basis of American economic predominance through most of the century to follow. To these men, the outcome of the war seemed to demonstrate the righteousness of their cause. Although the war had been forced onto the world by the decadence of European culture and the failure of its Christianity, the United States had been willing and able to put the world right.

The war was a tragedy, to be sure. But to men like John R. Mott, the serendipities of the war seemed to completely transcend its tragedies. The world's extremity was the Christian movement's moment of greatest advantage, Mott reasoned. The war had smashed many of the pillars of modern civilization. Governments had fallen. Military power had been proved inadequate. Education and diplomacy had been insufficient; international relations were shattered. The war had discredited every major human institution except one. The church was missing from Mott's list. Apparently unable or unwilling to say that the war had not discredited Christianity, Mott shifted the logic of his argument to say that no claim of Christ had been invalidated in the tragic war years. "Against the black background of disorder, destruction and chaos so widely prevalent in parts of the East and of the West," this was the time, Mott thought, to put the Christian movement "in its central place in the thinking, planning and relationships" of human society.[8]

Now in his mid-fifties, Mott's already brilliant career had been taken to new heights of popularity and political influence by the war, through his leadership in the American YMCA's war work and related involvement in the United War Work Campaign and also in his participation in American diplomatic missions to Mexico (1916) and Russia (1917). During the war, Mott had resigned his position of leadership in the intercollegiate YMCA to assume responsibility for the parent American YMCA body. In his continuing leadership roles in the Student Volunteer Movement in North America and the Continuation Committee of the Edinburgh Missionary Conference (after 1921, the International Missionary Council), Mott was convinced that the postwar world presented an even greater opportunity for world evangelization than had the turn-of-the-century world to which he addressed his book *The Evangelization of the World in This Generation*. "The Christian movement holds a position of advantage today because of the unprecedented openness of the world," Mott told a group of Christian leaders in England in 1922. "In all the Christian centuries there has been nothing like it."[9]

Mott was not alone among national Protestant leaders in holding such views of the decisiveness of the postwar period. Brown University president W. H. P. Faunce put it even more dramatically. In May 1919, he declared to a national gathering of Protestants, "This one year will shape the thousand years that follow after. The world is a molten mass, and before it cools, Christianity may stamp upon it the image and superscription of God."[10] This reaction to the war was a logical extension of the optimistic and progressive ideas that had shaped the careers of the student generation that founded the SVM and the WSCF: "For at least thirty years prior to the world war," historian Eldon G. Ernst wrote, "American intellectuals and social leaders had sensed the dawning of a new era defined not only by revolutions in industry, science, and urbanization, but also by the social and intellectual awakening of non-Christian and comparatively non-industrial peoples hitherto subjected to Western colonial powers. The war and its aftermath intensified the conditions of social and intellectual change."[11]

The war was the apocalyptic threshold of the new age, the inevitable labor pains in the birth of a new age in which Christ's kingdom would finally be established among the nations. So dramatic was its impact worldwide, the war was widely viewed in America as a turning point in history. One popular book, written as a part of a Methodist centenary missions program, noted a widespread unanimity of opinion that only one date had surpassed in importance these postwar days—that of the birth of Jesus. The current era would likely be viewed by future generations not only as a turning point in history but as having determined the destiny of mankind for ages to come.[12]

Along with other mission leaders, the SVM founders were more convinced than ever of America's providential role among the nations. The Great War had given birth to a new era in world civilization. The Armistice seemed to pave the way for the worldwide extension of Christian democracy, the one means by which world peace and brotherhood might be preserved. There was widespread agreement that military force had only removed the hindrances to democracy. "No military victory can foster the intelligence and moral character which are the foundations of democracy," Earl Taylor and Halford Luccock wrote. Only Christianity could "make democracy safe for the world"; only Christianity could set in motion those moral, educational, and religious forces that would provide a context in which democracy could flourish in the developing nations. "To complete the task of the soldier demands an adequate and aggressive program for the worldwide extension of the kingdom of God," the Methodist leaders wrote. A democratic world order could be realized only if it rested on "the foundation of the world's first and greatest democrat—Jesus Christ."[13]

Because America had suffered comparatively little during the war, the older volunteer movement leaders reasoned, she must shoulder a larger share of the responsibilities for reconstruction after the war. American colleges would need to carry a larger burden in finding leaders for the missionary enterprise that would give integrity to this reconstruction. This meant that the volunteer bands would need to describe more forcefully and accurately the task remaining to be done, so that students could really understand the missionary task. It also meant that postwar college students would need to be challenged to find and live a genuine Christian faith. Without a corroborative faith, the Christian mission would be merely "propaganda" and would spread only the "externals of American culture" to the other nations.

This was not to say that cultural imperialism was in decline. The war had, on the contrary, served to strengthen some of the relations between the missionary enterprise and American political, economic, and military agendas. The Americans had been fighting to make the world safe for democracy. With the fighting done and the world becoming safe once again, SVM leaders were ready to get on with the business of spreading democracy, and with an evangelistic fervor. The springs of democracy, Tyler Dennett argued soon after the war, lay in the open Bible, the free school, and the free church. The "backward" or subject races could come to the "council tables of civilization" and become part of the emerging international democratic partnership only if they received the Christian values on which these institutions were based. The end of the war, the student readers were told, signaled the beginning of a new age in which the foreign missionary would find himself or herself standing forth as "the master-builder of world democracy." There was a need, the Methodist leaders wrote, "to think imperially in the cause of the kingdom of God."[14]

A Magnificent Expression of the Missionary Spirit

The SVM founders were aware, of course, that the war was viewed by some young people as representing the failure of Christian civilization and as a fundamental challenge to the Christian message they wished to propagate. Movement leaders could agree with much of the growing critique of Christianity without applying it to the missions movement. Instead, they saw the missions movement as a way of correcting what was wrong with Christianity. While applauding the ideals of the Allies, they were willing to admit that the war showed a tragic, evil side of Western civilization. As such, it was an expression of that which the Christian mission would have to put right. It was the duty of an expanding Protestantism to "Christianize the impact of Western civilization."[15] As we have noted in the last chapter, the SVM founders believed the missionary movement to be "the moral equivalent of war"—equivalent to the ideals of war but without its wastage and destruction.

Along with other Protestant American mission leaders, volunteer movement leaders saw themselves as "chaplains and tamers" of Western expansion and imperialism. "The mission establishment could feel that a torn and confused political order needed its ministrations now at least as much as a ruthless imperialism had needed them before," William R. Hutchison wrote in his history of Protestant missionary thought.[16] Because the conflagration had been kindled by European hands, and all its battles fought on other continents, American Protestant leaders looked on the war with a kind of moral condescension. American soldiers had never fought more honorably and valiantly; civilians at home had never been more generous. Wiliston Walker, the Yale church historian, wrote that "no action in which the nation has ever been engaged has been so unselfish." "We had no vision of territorial enlargement, of financial gain or of political aggrandizement, "the editor of the *Watchman-Examiner* wrote. "We coveted no foot of land and no dollar of wealth belonging to another nation. We were moved by no passion save the passion for righteousness and liberty. For humanity's sake we bowed our shoulders to the burden, we bared our breast to the storm, we stretched out our hand to the sword."

There was no pause for a humble reappraisal of the missionary enterprise. Among Protestant leaders like the SVM founders who had come of age in the nineteenth century, this was no time for pessimism or morbid introspection. Winning the war had extended democracy at home and abroad. The enforced common life of military service had helped to do away with remaining class distinctions in America. Overseas thrones were now tottering, and dynasties dissolving—"the spirit of freedom stalks abroad." Russia was struggling through the darkness toward the light, while Germany, "crushed, punished, shamed, will come forth purified and sweetened to take her place among the free nations." The United States was now called to take her place as a world power as she gave leadership in world reconstruction. The missionary services of previous generations, along with the successes of war, had given America a new mission. "The welfare of the whole world has now become our concern," concluded the editorial, written immediately after the war.[17]

These men were not unaware of other voices. In an address to the Foreign Missions Conference of North America in 1920, John Mott admitted that some people were "specializing in darkness" and that the "zone of pessimism" was constantly widening in many parts of the world. He tried to explain this pessimism, curiously avoiding any direct reference to the war. Some people were physically and emotionally exhausted.

Others were isolated from "the great movements of Providence" or were unable to see the full sweep of the battlefield. "I defy anyone to take the long view backward and not become a genuine optimist," Mott said. There were some, Mott concluded, who were pessimists because of a wrong philosophy of life. Pessimism was, after all, a "spiritual disease" and "not to be tolerated in the life of any Christian."

Mott was willing to admit that there were difficulties. But appealing to a military metaphor once again, he declared that these were "the drill ground of the strong faith and the triumphant character." Mott was convinced that "a greater day than Christianity has ever known" was at hand. Finally, referring euphemistically to the war as the "recent great struggle," Mott acknowledged that victory had brought with it very serious handicaps. The nation was facing grave dangers, and Mott outlined some of these. And the war was perhaps not quite finished. "We are now fighting twenty-three wars as a direct result of the Great War, and the tides of bitterness are surging on every hand," Mott said. At such a dark moment, Mott believed, the Lord Jesus Christ had never appeared so unique, so necessary, and so sufficient. This was "a great day for Christian missions." At a time when some were beginning to talk of Versailles being a Pyrrhic victory, Mott argued that only the missionary program could ensure the realization of the aims for which the war had been fought.[18]

Daniel Johnson Fleming, professor of missions at Union Theological Seminary, thought that the war was "one of the finest examples on a national scale of the embodiment of the Christian motive." The United States had gone to war to make democracy available to every people, to ensure that even the smallest nation would be given the opportunity for self-realization and free development, Fleming wrote in a study text for colleges. He quoted approvingly from the words written by President Wilson when the United States declared war on Germany: "We have no selfish ends to serve. We desire no conquest, no dominion. We seek no indemnities for ourselves, no material compensation for the sacrifices we shall freely make. We are but one of the champions of the rights of mankind." America's participation in the war, said Fleming, was "in reality a magnificent expression of the missionary spirit."[19]

War as a Model for Missions

It did not seem possible that men who had shared in the drama of the Great War could "ever be content again to wear out their voices 'barking' second-rate side shows." The tragedy would end in a farce "if a

whole nation of young men who have followed a great cause with devotion to the death should settle down to the busy rebuilding of a whole series of petty loyalties," the editor of the *Intercollegian* wrote in December 1918. "We have seen what a body of men can do when they settle
down unitedly to a big job."[20] The war and the YMCA's war work campaign had, at least for the leaders, placed missionary hopes and plans in
an altogether new frame of reference. Mott believed that the new concepts, plans, and activities that had emerged out of the student Christian
movement's encounter with war had "schooled the present generation
for dealing with world responsibilities in larger terms." The cause of
world evangelization was the appropriate channel for the newly aroused
energies of those who had served as war workers, for the fighting men
themselves, for women who had found liberating opportunities for leadership during the war, and for thousands of young patriots at home who
had thrown themselves unstintingly into the war effort. "Shall there be a
great outpouring of life, not on the shell-scarred fields of Europe, but on
the far-flung battle line of the church in Africa, India, Turkey—yes, in
Russia and the Central Empires?"[21]

The war raised the expectations of SVM founders by demonstrating
A comparison of the missions cause with the war effort was a common theme among the older Student Volunteer Movement leaders after
the war. They had always used military metaphors to describe the missions enterprise—phrases like "evangelization crusade," "planning and
waging a world-wide campaign," "the mobilization and advance of
Christian forces," "strategic points in the world's conquest," and "Christian statesmanship and generalship." Now there was an example of a war
with global aims and impact against which to measure the effectiveness
of the worldwide missionary campaign. Not only were the two campaigns seen to be similar in scope and nobility of purpose, they were also
thought to demand a parallel public commitment and personal engagement. SVM leaders adduced evidence for the similarity of the two campaigns from the fact that student volunteers in Canada, Britain, and the
United States had been "the readiest to volunteer for military service."
Similarly, the sons of missionaries were noted as having enlisted in especially large numbers.[22]

The war raised the expectations of SVM founders by demonstrating
just what could be done with a full mobilization of a nation's resources.
Germany's "total mobilization" was unprecedented in the annals of war
and was judged by contemporary observers to have been unsurpassed in
effectiveness among the belligerent nations. But the United States had
learned quickly enough and had been willing to bend the principles of

democracy in order to fully exploit the potential of a "scientific" mobilization. "With her passion for democracy fanned into flame, the United States has been willing to take measures seemingly inconsistent and undemocratic and subject herself to more paternalism in government than she had ever known before," J. Lovell Murray wrote. "She found, as other nations found, that all the elements in her national life must be laid under tribute to the common end."[23] Perhaps the missionary movement could learn from such total dedication to a cause.

The war demonstrated just how much money could be raised when churches, synagogues, and religious organizations were united by a common cause. "Great pyramids of gold had been laid upon the altar of humanity's need," one church publication proclaimed after the war.[24] The vast sums of money raised for relief purposes during the war proved that mission organizations had been too modest in their expectations of support for the gospel crusade. The average church member in the United States was said to be contributing only $1.22 per year to foreign missions, with many Christians giving nothing at all. By contrast, the YMCA in the United States had easily raised $50 million for war relief—a sum much larger than the combined annual budgets of the home and foreign mission boards of all the churches in America.[25] In November 1918, just as the Armistice was signed, the United War Work Campaign—in which the YMCA was one of seven cooperating agencies—brought in more than $200 million. Mott described it as "the largest voluntary offering in history" and said that it had demonstrated the value of cooperative, interdenominational efforts.[26]

The student movement had always been known for its educational efforts, its missionary propaganda. On both sides of the Atlantic the student Christian presses had continued to roll, in spite of the restrictions of paper supplies during the war. In comparison to military intelligence, however, the missionary movement was found wanting. Efforts to inform Christians about missions were thought to be far less effective than the government's propaganda campaign during the war. Schools, pulpits, and press had been drawn into the battle for democracy. "How meager in comparison are the church's efforts to inform her membership regarding the world enterprise of missions," the SVM educational secretary wrote. Here was an incentive to more thorough research, more effective propaganda, a higher degree of "missionary intelligence."[27]

The war became the context in which the missionary challenge was set. The need in the mission field was dramatic enough to put American churches and Christians on a "war basis." At home the ratio of Protestant pastors to citizens was one to five hundred; on the mission field, one to fifty thousand. There was one doctor for six hundred fifty people in the United States, one to two million people in unevangelized countries. The Christian response to these facts gave little evidence of "a flaming Crusader spirit in the church," and the military crusade was held up as a challenge for the churches to put new forces in the field. If a political and military crisis could cause the nation to send millions of young people onto the battlefield, certainly the human needs of the non-Western world should cause a similar mobilization of missionary recruits for a cause just as worthy and no less urgent (126).

In spite of the poor showing of Christian missions in this comparison of the mobilization of missionary forces with those of a nation at war, SVM leaders were still hopeful. They believed that the fine qualities of loyalty, courage, and patriotism that had been recently mobilized for the war were now awake and ready to be engaged in the "enterprise of spreading Christ's kingdom throughout the earth." Mission leaders had been too modest in their expectations. If the true nature of the mission cause were "brought before the Christian college men and women of today, and a ringing call made for volunteers to go out to the frontiers of the Kingdom, there should be such a response on the part of able and devoted students as will crowd the ranks of the Foreign Missionary Legion of the Christian Church and keep it up to full strength" (145). What was needed was the same kind of mobilization that had just been witnessed during the war—the gathering and dissemination of missionary intelligence, leadership, material and human resources, and prayer.

For the SVM founders, the war was a renewed call to the battle for world evangelization. Expectations seemed higher than ever before. If war in a mundane sense could bring into existence in a few weeks such massive programs as the YMCA's work with soldiers and prisoners of war, free the vast sums of money that had been tapped by the United War Work Campaign, and unleash social forces that could change, at least for several years, the entire face of American higher education, how much more could now be accomplished by the war of international spiritual conquest to which they were committed? Wartime had always been "the birthday of missionary advance." American foreign missions had begun during the War of 1812, and all the women's missionary organizations were said to have been founded either during or after the Civil War.[28] There seemed to be little pause, among Protestant missionary leaders, to ponder the war's revelations about the soul of Western civilization, about its gods and its goals.

The Interchurch World Movement

But for activist American Protestants, there was time to launch a new organization. As the decade dominated by World War I came to an end, a new movement took shape that expressed nearly all the dreams of Protestant leaders for the postwar world. The Interchurch World Movement was a cooperative Protestant venture whose purpose was to solve the most urgent social problems at home while finishing the job of world evangelization abroad. It combined fervent evangelical piety and a rigorous Social Gospel. It was the largest, boldest, and most ecumenical crusade for national and international salvation ever launched by American Protestants.

For the mature Protestant leaders of the Great War generation, developing massive programs in a brief time for specific goals had become a way of life. Involved first with the tide of progressivism and then swept into the wartime crusade, church leaders had learned to confront the unusual conditions of modern urbanized and industrialized society aggressively and optimistically.[29] The success of the United War Work Campaign in raising $200 million had underscored the practical benefits of ecumenical cooperation and had set a new standard for the resources that might be released by an interdenominational fund-raising effort. This generation of men, most of whom had not themselves fought in the trenches, saw no reason to doubt that the greatest of all wars could usher in the greatest era of worldwide Christian missionary expansion.

If the Interchurch World Movement extended the metaphors and organizing methods of the war that had just ended, at a deeper level it represented an adult version of the Student Volunteer Movement. Some of its key leaders were SVM founders still active at the highest levels of the student missionary movement. A uniting of the major Protestant churches to apply a social Christianity to the problems of America and the world, the Interchurch Movement had more experienced leadership, better financing, more sophisticated networks among the participating denominations (and at higher levels), and a better grasp of secular reins of power than any previous expression of the Protestant crusade in America.

William Adams Brown, a friend of the SVM who was present for the December 1918 launching of the Interchurch World Movement, recalled "the thrill of expectation which stirred those who had gathered there"—experienced church leaders, professors in theological seminaries, veteran workers in the cause of home and foreign missions. These were people who should have been familiar with the weaknesses and limitations of the organizations they served. "But they had seen a vision—the vision of a united church uniting a divided world; and under the spell of what they saw all things seemed possible. Difficulties were waved aside, doubters were silenced. In the face of an opportunity so unparalleled there seemed but one thing to do, and that was to go forward."[30]

And go forward it did. The Interchurch World Movement was a bold plan that became extravagant as it gathered momentum in 1919. Involving more than thirty denominations and enlisting such notables as Secretary of State Robert Lansing as chairman of the general committee and John D. Rockefeller Jr. as a major financial backer, the movement sought the active support of half of the American population. Its projected budget matched the extravagance of its goals—$300 million in the first year and $1.3 billion within the next five years. With characteristic hyperbole, John R. Mott called it "the greatest program undertaken by Christians since the days of the apostles."[31]

As the new decade dawned, the tragedies of the war seemed almost forgotten by the Protestant leaders who met in Atlantic City to finalize the details of their new and greatest crusade. But the spirit and the rhetoric of combat were never more vivid. "This is war!" declared the editor of a leading denominational paper. "The supreme issues of the military war were not settled; the way was merely cleared for their settlement. It is the Christian war that must permanently save the world from greed and lust and tyranny."[32]

Chapter Six

Rallying the Troops

They went out, boys; they will come back like the Judgment Day.
— Harry Emerson Fosdick, 1919

It is doubtful if any student enterprise in the history of education so seized upon the attention and imagination simultaneously of an entire student generation.
— David R. Porter, of the Des Moines convention

There are men here in this Conference, and women too, who are saying that Christianity here in America, and as expressed in this Student Volunteer Convention, is a failure because it is not fearlessly and openly facing and grappling with certain great present and living issues of social injustice and economic wrong and the unequal distribution of wealth, and the growth of tendencies of tyranny and of oppression that bid fair to rob us of some of the very liberties for which our fathers died.
— Robert E. Speer, at the Des Moines convention

The one fact which stands out is the tremendous responsibility that was placed not only on the delegates but upon the whole student generation. Immediately following upon this thought came a feeling of real apprehension for fear that *my* generation of college men and women would be found wanting in the great task imposed upon them.
— A student delegate to the Des Moines convention

"We stand on the threshold of the greatest opportunity which North American students have ever confronted," declared John R. Mott on December 31, 1919, in his opening address to the first Student Volunteer Movement quadrennial convention after the war.[1] It was a vintage Mott address, ebullient and optimistic, with a ringing challenge to the greater tasks ahead. Mott's addresses had never failed to galvanize student audiences into action—to take the student volunteer pledge. But the audience had changed. The world had changed. In their response to the first SVM convention after Versailles, students demonstrated just how profound these changes had been.

Young people are disillusioned, even brutalized, John F. Carter Jr. wrote, by the cataclysm caused by the complacent folly of their parents. "We have seen man at his lowest, woman at her lightest, in the terrible moral chaos of Europe. We have been forced to question, and in many cases to discard, the religion of our fathers." Though no doubt more cynical and eloquent than most of his peers, Carter expressed some of the raw emotion that the war left in its wake, the disillusionment and cynicism the Student Volunteer Movement faced as it picked up the missionary crusade after the war. "We have seen entire social systems overthrown, and our own called in question. In short, we have seen the inherent beastliness of the human race revealed in an infernal apocalypse." And of course, it was the older generation who had engineered the apocalypse. There was little doubt that they had "pretty well ruined this world before passing it on to us," Carter said. "How intensely *human* these oldsters are, after all, and how fallible!"[2]

In his opening address to the Des Moines convention, Mott seemed to be aware that students were restless, even bitter, and that many were becoming critical of the leaders and institutions that had taken them to war. Mott tried hard to convince his listeners that he understood the postwar challenges to optimism and faith. He outlined some of the drastic changes brought about by the war. It was a new world, torn and embittered, confused and bewildered. While nations were still divided "vertically" one against another, the Bolshevik movement was throwing "a horizontal cleavage across the entire human race, arraying class against class." The war had sent millions to their graves, but some were estimating that more would die from starvation and exposure during the current winter than during any one year of the war. How could students face such a world? God spoke to each generation of students, Mott said reassuringly, and never had the divine word come with greater clarity and power than to this generation. The call was for leadership in building a new world order after the war. Hundreds of thousands of students had "laid down their lives with smiling faces," Mott said, so that their lives could become foundation stones of this new order.[3]

Mott and the older volunteers came to Des Moines to celebrate the achievements of the first generation (thirty-three years) of the Student Volunteer Movement. And they were now ready to renew the crusade for world evangelization. But the generation of students whose representatives gathered in Des Moines in December 1919 had just finished a crusade. Its outcome was revealing deep and bitter divisions in the nation. The month before the opening of the quadrennial convention, the U.S. Senate had refused to approve the peace treaty that President Woodrow Wilson had signed in Paris. This was a new and bewildering world. What was there to celebrate? Was this the time to relaunch the crusade?

No Pause for Repentance

The first major task confronting Robert P. Wilder, newly appointed SVM general secretary, was the planning of the quadrennial convention that had been postponed because of America's entry into the war. The rationale for this convention was, in a subtle way, different from that which had dominated the conventions in the two decades before the war. In the early days of the movement, quadrennials were held primarily for the benefit of students who had already become volunteers, with a secondary emphasis on the recruitment of new volunteers. They were attended by volunteers, mission organization recruiters, missionaries on furlough, and students who had serious interest in missionary work. The convention to be held in Des Moines would have a remarkably different composition. It was intended, said Chairman Mott, to assemble "a representative body of the best qualified students, together with professors and instructors and leaders of the Christian forces of North America, to face the oneness of the task and the wholeness of the task of Christian America and Christian Canada, as they look out upon the world field."

A YMCA secretary from Columbia University in New York wrote to John R. Mott just before the Des Moines convention, describing the makeup of the Columbia delegation. Forty-two delegates had been selected from among more than one hundred candidates. There were two class presidents, the chairman of the student government organization, captain of the track team, editor of the university newspaper, and representatives of athletics and other extracurricular activities. There were two Jewish and two Roman Catholic students. "I am hoping that the speakers will command the respect and interest of these students who have no Protestant tradition," the YMCA leader wrote to Mott at the suggestion of Mott's son, who had done much on the Columbia campus to create enthusiasm for the Des Moines convention.[4]

Still plainly guided by prewar assumptions about North American students, the SVM had given a broad invitation to the convention. As the Columbia delegation illustrated, it was often general leadership qualifications rather than commitment to the missions cause that determined who would attend. The convention attracted the brightest and the best from the campuses, only some of whom were inclined toward foreign missionary work when they arrived in Des Moines. Although the purpose of the convention was repeatedly pointed out in the printed materials and in the personal interviews, many students seemed only to hear "something about making the world over." David R. Porter, the national college YMCA secretary, reported that "even some of the most experienced volunteer secretaries stirred up delegations not all of which were ready for a missionary gathering." The students insisted on coming. The world did need to be made over.[5]

The SVM executive committee had been requested to make room at Des Moines for up to one thousand students who had already graduated from college, in addition to currently enrolled students, in order to accommodate students who had graduated during the war who would not otherwise have had the opportunity to attend a quadrennial convention. The net was being thrown wider than ever before. Those with less commitment, it was expected, would be swept along by the enthusiasm of the convention. By the end, even some who had come as spectators might find themselves at the altar, signing the volunteer pledge.[6] The SVM founders seemed confident of their ability to rally the troops once again as they summoned to Des Moines the largest and most diverse group of students ever assembled in North America. The world needing America's aid as never before, Wilder expected an unprecedented harvest of volunteers from North America, its manhood "practically unscathed by the war."[7] The world was ready to be saved, and American students would rise to the challenge. "We have not been putting hard enough things on the students," Mott had said during the war. "It is time to appeal to the heroic. Students will respond and we will save our nation, and we will take our part in the world's work."[8]

As the convention began, all the signs were positive. In the months since the Armistice, the number of volunteers had nearly tripled, and the meeting convened in Des Moines, Iowa, from December 31, 1919, to January 4, 1920, was the largest student gathering to date. The students came in force, more than five thousand from nine hundred colleges and universities across the United States and Canada. Every state and province was represented, and nearly every institution of higher education.

Thousands of students were turned away because of space limitations. Porter said that "it would not have been difficult to secure an attendance twice as large."[9] The first eight rows of seats in the coliseum were reserved for the more than three hundred foreign students and overseas delegates who came to Des Moines from forty countries. In addition to the students, there were one thousand honorary delegates—missionaries, mission board secretaries, local and traveling secretaries of the YMCA and YWCA, and editors of church papers.

A New Agenda

The program had been carefully designed, as in past conventions, to move the students to give their lives (or renew their commitment, in the case of volunteers) to the task of world evangelization. On the first day the students were confronted with the world's crying need and reminded of God's power to meet these needs. The following day John Mott reviewed the accomplishments of the first generation of the SVM (1886–1919), concluding that, after thirty-three years, the movement had never been more "strong and vital." Then the students were given a survey of the potential of the present student generation, in Europe as well as in North America, and reminded of the tasks at home and of their responsibilities to the churches at home. By the end of the third day, the convention turned its attention to "the worth and failure of the religions of the world"—first Hinduism, then Islam, and finally Christianity. One address focused especially on "the failure of the non-Christian religions in relation to women."[10] The convention was planned to end with a ringing affirmation of the indispensability of Christianity as the answer to the needs of the world. Students would be called to "self-denial and the spirit of conquest," to the "hard tasks" and difficulties of world evangelization, and to a considered signing of a declaration card to become a foreign missionary.

The program went as planned, but the students did not fall into step. When Robert Speer took up the final address—the personal worth or failure of Christianity—on Friday evening he acknowledged that questions not on the program of the convention had dominated much of the informal discussion among many delegates. Was there enough worth in Christianity to justify missionary activity? Were there not quite enough challenges for the faith at home, without attempting to confront the great faiths of the non-Christian world? Some delegates were saying that Christianity in America and as expressed at the convention was a failure because it was not grappling with the great issues of social and economic injustice and the growing tendencies toward tyranny and oppression that threatened "to rob us of some of the very liberties for which our fathers died." Speer said that he could sympathize with his critics on this point. He recalled his wartime address at Columbia University, when he challenged Christian students to see that wrong is wrong, wherever it is found. "We were fighting them not because they were German," Speer said, "but because they were wrong." If we find these same wrongs in America, calling them American does not make them right. Speer noted that he had received a whole drawerful of newspaper clippings and letters from across the nation bitterly attacking his remarks. These were people, Speer said, who were determined to deny "the rights of free speech, and honest loyalty to the moral law, for which our fathers died."[11]

Some were criticizing the convention and the SVM, Speer admitted to the packed convention hall, because the quadrennial lacked the courage to pass a resolution in support of the League of Nations. Others seemed to be leveling their charges against Christianity itself. On this point Speer became defensive. "Christianity just as it is in Canada and in the United States today, imperfect, incomplete, discredited by the weakness of men, is the richest and purest and greatest power that there is in the world." It was worth carrying to the rest of the world, he asserted. "You young men and women who never have been outside these Christian lands may not feel that," he said patronizingly, "but all of us here who have come back to America out of the great non-Christian areas of the world, we have felt it and we know that even what we have got is worth carrying to all the world of men." In any case, Speer argued, it was not the integrity of Christianity that was at stake but the trustworthiness of Jesus Christ. Christianity had failed a great many times in the past and had still lived on. There was no danger that Jesus would fail, said Speer. "But there is a danger here tonight that we ourselves may fail."[12]

Speer was not the only one of the old guard who spoke from the platform to a gallery of growing criticism. The following morning, Sherwood Eddy acknowledged that he had been confronted by critical delegates. "Why do you bring us this piffle, these old shibboleths, these old worn-out phrases," they asked. "Why are you talking to us about the living God and the divine Christ?" Eddy discarded his prepared text— "Have We a Gospel Indispensable and Adequate to All Mankind?" — and instead focused on students in North America. "I am not going to speak about the heathenism in Africa," he said, "but I am going to speak about the heathenism in our hearts right here." He began with a sharp rebuke to the spirit of isolationism that was then spreading across the United States.[13]

The most popular nation in the world was on the way to becoming the most hated nation in the world, Eddy said. He quoted European leaders who were questioning the integrity of America's wartime aims. "You said you entered the war, not like other nations. You wanted no land nor indemnity, you were fighting for ideals, you were going to make the world safe for liberty and democracy and righteousness. Those ideals of yours were proclaimed *ad nauseam* through the daily press of Europe and of Asia." America had come out of the war the richest nation in the world with most of the world in its debt; but Americans were now threatening to repudiate the ideals they had so loudly and boastfully proclaimed. America, alone capable of coming to the aid of its recent military partners, seemed willing to let Europe sink in starvation, famine, and revolution, "apparently aiming to get the world's trade rather than to give the world peace." Would Americans stand for world selfishness or world service?[14]

Although Eddy urged the students to join him in breaking the conspiracy of silence on the League of Nations that he said existed in many parts of the United States and to write to Washington in its support, it was clear that he, like Speer, was on the defensive. He spent more than half of his address confronting the students to deal with the "great personal problem of sin." He and the other SVM leaders seemed unable to respond to the questions that the students were raising about the integrity of the Christian mission and message. Instead of grappling with the social perversion of war, a live issue for many students, Eddy asked them whether they were pure, free from personal sexual sin. Rather than facing the viability of the world evangelization crusade in the light of the recent global failure of Christian civilization, Eddy wanted to know whether his critics were honest or whether they might be cheating on exams. Perhaps they were hypocritical, standing on the "sidelines of criticism," unwilling to get into the game, to do something positive to solve the world's problems. Eddy might have warmed his critics by tackling the relationship of Christian missions to the aggressive chauvinism and power politics that had been major underlying causes of the war just ended. Instead, he talked to the students about individual selfishness and the need for self-sacrifice. "In thirty-three years," he boasted, "we have placed 8,100 men in the ends of the earth. What are you going to do with your life for the world of your generation?" (192–96).

The SVM conference at Northfield in 1918 had recognized the need for penitence in the face of the war and the failure of Christian civilization. There was little pause for repentance at Des Moines as the SVM stalwarts dished out the warmed-over rhetoric of missionary militancy and Christian conquest. In Mott's exhaustive review of the history of the SVM at Des Moines (the report of the executive committee), he made only passing reference to the war. When in the report he spoke of the movement's contribution to the "Christianizing of international relationships," Mott mentioned the war only to laud "the courageous Christian influence which has been exerted by officers and enlisted men of the Army and Navy who received their original Christian impulse through the volunteer movement and the closely related student association movement." Mott did not allow a war already won to distract him from calling the students to "the world's greatest cause." He believed the Student Volunteer Movement had maintained its vitality by keeping "a continuous human stream flowing out from the American and Canadian universities to the nations of the earth." This had preserved "its reality, its contagious enthusiasm and its world-conquering power." While other organizations had stagnated and died, the crusading character of the SVM had maintained its vitality.[15]

A Weariness of Crusades

But the students were weary of crusades. They were apparently expecting less celebration of a movement, more realistic grappling with the issues of the day. They had looked forward to a discussion of "broad religious problems with their economic and political bearings," reported one campus publication after the 1920 convention. "What they got for the most part from the speeches in the big coliseum was narrow sectarian religion." Although that may have been an extreme point of view, it represented a growing body of opinion among students active in the campus YMCA and YWCA programs after the war.[16]

For the young, the war seemed to have severely strained the bond between words and reality. "The long bombardment with war propaganda," Sydney Ahlstrom noted, "had probably served to cheapen and degrade popular idealism."[17] As the real facts of the war came home to America, often along with the soldiers, a growing number of student volunteers were disillusioned by the gap between the ideals for which they had fought and the reality that had often been masked by their government's propaganda. The church's countenancing of the war brought

Christianity, and, by association, the missions movement, under attack by disillusioned and increasingly cynical students.

"I went off like a little tin hero and joined the Navy in 1918," wrote one volunteer who served on the SVM headquarters staff during the postwar period. "And for what? Who can answer? We went to 'make the world safe for democracy,' to fight the 'war to end wars,' [for] Wilson's Fourteen Points, etc. What colossal jokes! Not a mother's son of us knew what we were fighting for and most of us have forgotten the dead slogans and are again ready to goose step off again to another slaughter of the innocents when capitalism commands. We were fed up on [sic] vicious lies and propaganda to make us hate so we would fight our duped brothers in Germany who were fed on just the same kind of damnable lies about us so they could hate and fight us. And the pity of it all is today that nearly all of that stuff has been proven to be lies which our 'Intelligence Department' dished out, and most people don't know it."[18]

Although this degree of alienation may have been rare, most postwar undergraduates were not ready to take on another crusade. As the student department of the YMCA reported, many were "afflicted with the traditional spirit of national isolation." This isolationism, which increased in the years after the war, dampened enthusiasm for missions among students. It was combined with a conviction that there were problems enough at home—problems of poverty, race relations, and industrial strife—without looking to the "heathen" world. An increasing number of students felt that these problems must, in fact, be addressed before American missionaries took the gospel to needy lands beyond. There was a renewed interest in home missions, and the SVM was asked to begin recruiting students for home missions assignments. The question was even raised as to whether the volunteer pledge should not be changed to include home as well as foreign missions.[19]

In 1919, Kenneth Scott Latourette, a volunteer who had served in China and joined the SVM executive committee after the war, described the postwar student mind as restless and uncertain. There was a kind of ethical lethargy, he thought, and "a lowering of the moral tone." He noted that American campuses had been stripped of their upperclassmen, "with the result that in some institutions the underclassmen have run riot." Latourette, at this time a professor at Yale, noted a declining interest in current events among college students in the United States, with only "a languid curiosity about Europe and with but scant appreciation of the gravity of the problems which still face us."[20]

It was not only students who were restless and uncertain. The nation as a whole seemed to have lost the sense of purpose that had character-ized the war years. Going against the churches and an apparent majority of Americans who favored America's entry into the League of Nations, a partisan Senate refused to ratify the Versailles treaty and blocked U.S. participation in the League. "It seems that God won the war and the devil won the peace," said former Secretary of the Treasury William G. McAdoo to an Interchurch Movement gathering in response to the vote. S. Earl Taylor, general secretary of the Interchurch World Movement, expressed the anger of many Protestant leaders when he stated, "I am hu-miliated and sore at heart. If there ever was a time when men needed to be big and broad-minded, and generous and sympathetic, as well as statesmanlike, that time is now. It is unthinkable that America will throw away her unique opportunity for moral and spiritual world leadership."[21] To the church leaders it was obvious that the time had finally come for America to save herself and the world. But the politicians and the Amer-ican people at large, it seemed, were "tired of going forward with lifted eyes."[22] The senators who voted against the League of Nations were no doubt piqued because Wilson had excluded their leaders from the Paris delegation, but they were also in touch with the mood of a country weary of war and of propaganda. Now, after the crusade to make the world safe for it, democracy had her say.

The Fate of the Interchurch World Movement

If the politicians were unable to keep the nation's wartime promises, per-haps the Interchurch World Movement could be, as one of its spokesmen said, "America's chance to make good before a disappointed world." The war was not over! During the first five months after the Des Moines convention, the Interchurch Movement was spending $1 million a month to raise the massive budgets pledged for "the Christian war that must per-manently save the world from greed and lust and tyranny." The Protes-tant churches "bombarded the nation with propaganda to raise their spir-itual weapons, their men, and their money."[23]

But there was already trouble in the movement. In spite of their out-cry against the politicians, the churches themselves found it difficult to rise above partisanship. Conservative Northern Baptists and Northern Presbyterians had voted to withdraw their support because of the promi-nence of liberal Social Gospel thinkers in the movement. In addition to Fundamentalist-Modernist quarrels, denominationalism was on the rise after the war, making cooperative ventures increasingly difficult.

But it was money that finally brought the moment of truth for the Interchurch Movement. In spite of the most advanced fund-raising techniques and endorsements by the most powerful men of America, money from the so-called friendly citizens did not come in fast enough to sustain the central organization of the movement. When the results of the big campaign were tabulated in May 1920, it was clear that income would fall short of the ambitious goals set. With pledges nearly reaching the $200 million mark, the denominations would be able to finance most of their own programs in the Interchurch Movement's master plan. But the participating denominations seemed unable to find funds to sustain the Interchurch Movement bureaucracy itself. Even a secret Rockefeller loan of $1 million was not enough to keep the failing movement on its feet. In the end, Protestants were unwilling to pay the ecumenical costs of their last great campaign.[24]

Less than two years after its birth, the Interchurch World Movement was dead. There was new hyperbole in describing the abrupt demise of the movement. "The most colossal collapse in the church since the days of Pentecost," read one epitaph, "the greatest blow to Protestantism since the Reformation." One supporter of the movement called it "the greatest tragedy that has occurred in the history of the Christian church." The collapse of this grandest of all Protestant enterprises in America struck an ominous note at the beginning of the new decade. The dreams had been so magnificent, the risks so compelling. Protestant leaders across the nation were stunned.[25]

The lament turned bitter when the Interchurch World Movement's extravagant expenses turned into denominational debts. The churches that had underwritten the large headquarters budgets of the Interchurch Movement took several years to repair the damage done by the postmortem debts left when the movement collapsed. Although the Student Volunteer Movement had no financial stake in the Interchurch Movement, as an interdenominational program it was rocked by the tremors caused by the failure of this grand ecumenical venture. The SVM was soon having trouble finding money to keep its own modest but expanding bureaucracy going.

Eldon G. Ernst, whose excellent study of the Interchurch Movement remains a solid interpretation of American Protestantism after the war, asserted that "the single most important impact of the Interchurch World Movement on religion in America was its demonstration that crusading Protestantism—indeed Protestantism in general—was losing its traditional hold on the American people as a whole and on the social and cultural tone of the nation." Crusading idealism had not made the world safe for democracy. It could not even bring a common vision of what the world should become. "The Protestant community, it seemed, would have to forge its way in the post-war world with uncertainty, disunity, and diminished vigor," Ernst concluded. Believing that the drama of war could be sustained in a peacetime equivalent, Protestant leaders had marched boldly forward only to discover that few were following. The prevailing spirit after the war was not idealism but apathy. The greatest Protestant crusade was over, and the missionary movement would not survive the crash unscathed (170, 166).

Giving Students Voice

Criticism of the Student Volunteer Movement at the Des Moines convention added urgency to already planned changes in the structure of the SVM. A student volunteer council was formed in 1920 to provide a student voice in the affairs of the SVM. A democratically elected representative body, the council was made up of two student volunteer representatives—one man and one woman—from each volunteer movement in the United States and Canada. The council appointed student representatives to the executive committee, which was enlarged to thirty members, half of whom would be volunteers appointed by the council.

Twenty-nine student volunteer unions elected representatives to the first council, which met in April 1920. Its fifty-five members came from fifty-four different educational institutions, 85 percent of which were privately funded. Nearly 90 percent of the council members came from east of the Mississippi, with only four persons attending from the West Coast. At Des Moines, by contrast, the largest single delegation came from the University of California, and all but three of the thirty colleges on the Pacific coast sent full quotas to the convention. By 1920, 30 percent of American college students attended colleges west of the Mississippi, and nearly 40 percent were now enrolled in public colleges and universities. If council membership was even roughly representative of the volunteer movement's presence on American campuses, the movement was not keeping up with the changing student population, either in terms of the geography of the student population or in its burgeoning growth on public and nonsectarian campuses.[26]

High on the council's agenda was the matter of finances. How could the volunteer unions help to raise the fourteen thousand dollars that was the projected deficit for 1920? When the council was told the story of how Mott and Wilder had almost single-handedly "valiantly and victoriously [borne] the burden of raising the fourteen hundred dollar deficit on the first budget of three thousand dollars at a time when foreign missions were exceedingly unpopular," the delegates realized that their task was but a "small thing." They felt that "each volunteer would want to help make up this fourteen thousand dollar deficit as a thank offering for what the movement has meant." The council addressed the question of possible changes in the watchword—"The evangelization of the world in this generation." Some students felt it should be changed, perhaps even set aside altogether. With the benefit of Wilder's explanation and vigorous defense, the group agreed that the watchword "has a greater challenge as it stands" and that what was needed was "more frequent definition and explanation of it." On the question of the SVM and home missions, the council endorsed the executive committee's recommendation that the SVM lend assistance to the home missions boards in their task of recruitment. But the SVM stopped short of offering to recruit for the home mission boards or to expand the volunteer pledge to include home as well as overseas missions service.[27]

Wilder was euphoric. "Nothing since I have returned to this country four years ago has filled me with greater hope than the meeting of the council," Wilder wrote to Mott the month after the Yonkers meeting. One of the New York City Union delegates, Warren S. Dudley, had been among the outspoken critics of the volunteer movement at Des Moines. After the council, Dudley reported to his friends at Columbia University's Teachers' College and Union Seminary that "the gathering was thoroughly representative of the student volunteers of North America, but that they must remember that neither Union Seminary nor Teachers' College was representative of the country." Wilder was delighted with the "hearty reaffirmation" of the watchword and impressed by the delegates' readiness to pray. "It seemed as if it was Mount Hermon over again," Wilder wrote.[28]

It seemed that the council had silenced the voices of dissent that had emerged at Des Moines. But as the 1924 convention approached, there were signs of division more troubling than anything the SVM had experienced before. Sherwood Eddy did not remain silent after the Des Moines convention, either about the League of Nations or about the future of the SVM. He continued his usual itineration among college students as a kind of YMCA missionary-at-large, listening to students and occasionally offering advice to SVM officials. In a July 1922 letter to the executive committee, he reported that "a very real change has come over the students of the country." The "insurgent revolution" of Des Moines was just the beginning of a growing demand "for a more socialized and broader presentation and conduct of our whole missionary movement."[29]

The demand for foreign missionaries was declining, Eddy said. There were several thousand volunteers who could not be sent abroad, either because of the lack of openings overseas or because of the inability of foreign boards in North America to finance new missionary assignments. In the foreign field, there was "a widespread and insistent demand for the transfer of authority to the native church," while at home, financial support was "no longer keeping pace with our former ideas of expansion either in America, England or on the continent of Europe." The growing demand for a broader concept of Christianizing the impact of the West on the Orient, Eddy said, called for a new deployment of Christian businessmen, educators, and civil servants, as well as "a few foreign missionaries." Furthermore, foreign work could no longer be carried out without reference to problems at home. Lynchings in America were now being reported in the Christian press in India.

Before Eddy left for Asia, he proposed a new approach for the 1924 convention: the students should be encouraged to deal directly with "pagan" industrial and race problems at home and abroad. They should be challenged to use Christ's power to combat "pagan" nationalism in the United States as well as in other lands. This would make it possible "to hold every man and woman in the convention responsible for making America Christian in all the departments of its life," even if foreign assignments were not possible.

The Student Volunteer Movement was standing at the parting of the ways, Eddy declared. It could remain conservatively true to the ideals and methods of the last generation and become "a reactionary body unresponsive to the demands of the present student generation." Or it could become truly representative and "follow through the reorganization begun after Des Moines, broaden its scope in the next convention and respond to the demand of the majority of students and the best practice of the more advanced student movements of other lands."[30]

The criticisms of the 1920 convention and Eddy's suggestions for radical change led in September 1922 to a vigorous executive committee debate about the shape of the next SVM convention. The Volunteer Council, meeting earlier in the year and aware of the controversy, had called for a continued "foreign missions" emphasis. Some executive committee members agreed with Speer's call for a clearer declaration of "missionary responsibility of nations as well as of individuals." Speer believed the United States ought to "purge its own life of all untruth and wrong and to make its influence and contact of every kind with other nations, and especially with the non-Christian nations, a Christian influence and contact." He saw a need to "mak[e] it plain that we can only give what we have, and that if Christianity dies out or dies down or goes wrong in America, the missionary enterprise is attacked at its very roots."

Student volunteer and Presbyterian missions executive Speer challenged the executive committee with the need for thousands of new missionaries in vast areas still unevangelized. "I have spent the past year in the heart of the great missionary problems of Hinduism and Islam," Speer asserted, "and I speak of conditions which I know. Let us hold fast to the work given us to do and not allow the movement to be dissipated or dissolved as will be the sure result if there is any unfaithfulness to its still unfinished task."[31]

From the college associations came a strikingly different note. Association leaders had been discussing the student mood and the future of the SVM in the aftermath of Des Moines. The relationship of the college associations to the next convention would need "most careful thought," declared Leslie Blanchard of the YWCA. The next convention should encourage a much larger expression of the missionary motive, she said, and this could not happen if there were a replay of former SVM programs or a simple shift to the general convention model then being used by the Student Christian Movement in Great Britain and its student missionary department, the Student Volunteer Missionary Union. Blanchard believed that American students were currently getting a fragmented picture of the gospel and that the factors that produced missionary motivation among students had "totally changed since Des Moines." She proposed a conference of representatives from the various student movements during the next several months, to consider "the whole scope and message of the next convention" (9).

A November consultation, attended by ninety-five representatives of the SVM, the college associations, and the foreign mission boards, came to the conclusion that the next convention should remain under the direction of the SVM. But there would need to be changes. "The next convention should consider the needs of the whole world with due reference to the total impact of North America upon the world in all its aspects of life." It would aim to recruit volunteers for work in domestic as well as overseas missionary service. It would "secure decisions for life service in all vocations, especially international commerce and diplomacy." The next convention would place equal responsibility upon those who remain at home "both to repent of the injustices and wrongs in our own national life and to give their whole lives to Christ in such a way that all the relations with and impacts upon other lands may become Christlike." The next convention needed the full cooperation of the officers and members of the associations, and the program should be planned by an enlarged committee that would include representatives from the college Ys of the United States and Canada as well as foreign student representatives.[32]

The controversy over the content of the Indianapolis convention highlighted weaknesses in the new SVM structure. The council had called for a foreign missions convention. The executive committee, with strong counsel from college association leaders, overruled. Because volunteers were members of the council for a one-year term and therefore attended only one meeting, a lack of continuity hindered the effectiveness of the council's work. Significant issues were considered, often with vigorous discussion. But action was usually limited to recommendations to the executive committee, where the real decision-making power still lay. Although volunteers now made up half of the executive committee's membership, the problem of continuity again muted the student voice. Students were, in the nature of the case, transient. When they were volunteers, they were even more so. They were working toward a missions assignment that would take them out of the country and off the SVM executive committee.

Student voices in the SVM executive committee were often drowned out by stronger, more authoritative voices. There were the foreign mission board representatives, mature men of national reputation and international experience. And there were the association leaders, professional full-time workers who knew the college scene regionally or nationally and who could seem to speak more authoritatively on student issues than a student who spoke from the context of only one campus. The Y leaders and the mission board representatives—professionals in a volunteer organization—both had vested interests in the SVM, but these interests did not always coincide.

The mission boards valued the SVM because of its recruiting strength, which of course depended on the movement continuing to keep in touch with the goals and strategies of the mainline agencies and at the same time understanding the students and how to motivate them for missionary service. The mainline mission boards, with their need for a continuing flow of competent missionary recruits, had come to depend on the SVM's recruiting muscle among America's students. The association representatives, on the other hand, needed the SVM only as long as it continued to enhance their influence and strengthen their work with the students. As we see in more detail later, the associations tended to view the SVM as an adjunct to the campus Y rather than as a separate organization. If the missionary cause lost its appeal to their members, then the campus associations would have little motivation to continue their patronage of the volunteer movement.

The SVM was caught between a rock and a hard place. If it lost favor with the Y, the SVM would lose the privileged access that the associations provided to the students through its national campus programs and publications. The favor of the associations seemed increasingly to depend on the SVM's ability to adjust to the new campus mood. But students after the war were more interested in a domestic social agenda than in foreign missions. Following the popular student mood could threaten the distinctive purpose of the volunteer movement. If the SVM stopped recruiting missionaries, the support of the mission boards would not last and its very raison d'être would be in doubt. The Indianapolis convention of 1924 posed the challenges of this dilemma more starkly than ever.

If youth are often victims in tragedies that they have had no hand in creating, they are sometimes also outriders, the first to see and describe the world that is coming to be. With the war over, the SVM founders were ready to return to the missionary crusade as they had known it, as they themselves had shaped it. Student volunteers, on the other hand, saw the hypocrisy of an evangelistic crusade that seemed to presume the moral superiority of Christian civilization. They saw an enormous need for salvation at home. They were ready for a rethinking of missionary premises and practices.

The older generation still looked at the world through the lens of a nineteenth-century optimism and Protestant consensus. The young, with a conscience shaped by a Christian world at war, sensed that the West needed to stop and take stock before renewing the missionary crusade. Why had Christians gone to war? If militarism and racism lay at the roots of war, then Christians should address these wrongs before rushing off to put the world right. Many students began to see that vast numbers of Americans had been excluded from the "kingdom of God in America." Perhaps the first and most compelling mission was a home mission.

Chapter Seven

A Youthful Revolt

The first angry notes of youthful revolt against the management of
the Student Volunteer Movement's quadrennial convention were
heard at Des Moines in 1920. Four years later that revolt had organized itself into the quasi-independent gathering of Indianapolis,
when the spirit of lawlessness seemed to express its challenge:
"Now we will show you venerables how a student convention
should be managed." . . . The students were trying to carry out the
latest ideas of Teachers College, but were foiled by tumultuous ri-
valries, as all insisted on being heard, whether or not their ideas
were relevant to the subject.
   — Harlan P. Beach, 1928, about the Indianapolis convention

The conservative and restraining hand of the Old Guard was there.
It was a great convention, but they were out of touch with its greatness, and consequently its greatness didn't go far enough. Leaders
in a day that is past, they now can't think things through. It's too
bad the convention wasn't left in the hands of the young.
   — An international speaker at the Indianapolis convention, 1924

The Indianapolis convention was opened on December 28, 1923, not by
John R. Mott, as was the tradition, but by a recent medical school grad-
uate and SVM volunteer, Walter H. Judd. The chairman of the fourth
SVM council that had met in New York earlier that year, Judd took pains
to describe how democratic this convention program was, that much student input had been garnered and that eighteen of the twenty-four members of the business committee coordinating the convention were students. "This *is* a student convention," he asserted. But Judd became
cautious, even defensive, when he began talking about the missionary
purpose of the convention. The needs in America might be no less urgent, no less acute, no less desperate than those over there, he admitted.

Yet the specialized nature of foreign missionary work justified this quadrennial challenge to foreign missionary service.[1]

Sherwood Eddy, back from tours in Russia and the Orient, was on the
platform to describe the social and intellectual unrest in the world with
which the missionary message would need to wrestle. It was a dreary
world, torn by strife—national, racial, and industrial. Everywhere Eddy
had found conflict and revolution. "In Orient and Occident alike," he
said, "I found a semi-pagan social order of selfish materialism, autocratic
exploitation and strife. Everywhere men are in revolt, especially in the
ranks of youth, against these three great evils of the present social order."

After a survey of conditions in the East, he turned his attention to
the United States. America had emerged from the war, Eddy said, with
one-third of the world's wealth and about half of its gold supply. Two
percent of the American people owned 60 percent of this national
wealth, while two-thirds of the people owned no property at all. One
hundred families owned or controlled most of the railroads and a large
proportion of the basic industries. Eddy reported to the convention that
there were nearly two million American children at work who ought to
be in school. Since 1885, there had been four thousand lynchings of
black Americans by white—an average of two per week. In some
cases, he reported, a majority of the lynching mobs were professing
Christian church members. These lynchings, Eddy said, were being
regularly reported in the newspapers of Japan, China, and India. On the
side of government policy, Eddy was alarmed by a federal budget in
which 85 percent of expenditures were going "for wars past and future." The secretary of war was asking for a larger army. "Is the course
of America to be one of competitive militarism and economic imperialism," asked Eddy, "or that of high moral leadership for the world
back to the paths of peace?"

Why was there "no real youth movement in America?" Eddy wondered. "Why is there no widespread passionate demand for a new social
order?" He called the students to consider the "constructive spiritual revolution" of Jesus. This revolution involved a radical transformation of
human nature and society in the building a new social order called the
kingdom of God.

Jesus was the greatest revolutionary in history, Eddy said, offering a
constructive revolution to a new way of life. Jesus offered an abundant
spiritual life in place of selfish materialism. He offered the infinite worth
of the individual and the commonwealth of democracy in place of autocracy's inhuman methods of exploitation. Jesus launched the great

offensive of love and the full sharing of life against the strife of hatred and war. Judged by actual results, Eddy declared, the spiritual revolution of Jesus was the greatest revolution in all of history.[2]

Making the Case for Missions

It fell to Robert E. Speer to make the case for foreign missions to a generation that was changing its mind about the evangelization of the world. In an address that followed Eddy's, Speer acknowledged that the world was changing, that "the old conceptions of struggle and conflict" were challenging the nineteenth-century view of an emerging world in which a common set of "liberating and transforming ideas" would bring nations and races into a growing community of experience and faith. Young people were now being urged not to lose the old ideals of warfare and conflict and to keep at hand the sharp sword. Professors were expounding new, more sophisticated theories of race with an old claim—the right of the white race to dominate peoples of color and to exploit them for the comfort and advantage of the Caucasians. "There can be but one result of such a doctrine," Speer observed, "the same result that came in 1914 only on a wider and more deadly scale."[3]

Speer went on to give an eloquent but familiar defense of foreign missions, "the errand of men and women who have gone out to love and serve the world in the name and the spirit of Christ, to bring his redeeming life to bear upon all the needs of the world" (139). He defended the missions enterprise against charges that it had preached a narrow and individualistic gospel. With James Dennis's *Christian Missions and Social Progress* as reference, he asserted that everywhere missionaries had gone, they had promoted temperance, opposed trade in drugs and alcohol, reduced gambling, raised the personal ethical standards, cultivated the virtues of industry and frugality, enhanced the status of women, suppressed antisocial customs such as polygamy, concubinage, adultery, child marriage, and infanticide, helped to stamp out slavery and the slave trade, abolished cannibalism and human sacrifice, organized famine relief, improved animal husbandry and agriculture, introduced Western medicines and science, founded leper asylums and colonies, promoted sanitation, and prevented war. To validate such a catalog of achievements, Speer evoked more recent testimony from national, colonial, and diplomatic leaders in mission countries. They confirmed the missionary achievements, and one, a Japanese educator, said that even more missionaries would be needed in the years to come (141–44).

A Radical Departure

Speer's words carried echoes of what some students had come expecting to hear. "When I was asked to attend the conference at Indianapolis," one delegate wrote, "I thought I was going to hear the usual speeches about those supposedly backward peoples of Asia and Africa, who needed to be converted to Christianity. I thought I was going to hear the usual superlatives about the splendor of Western civilization without mention of all its adorning economic, social, and political complexities, which have been the causes of all the exploitation, prejudices, and destruction in the world today."[4]

This delegate, an African American student from New York City, was pleasantly surprised by what he described as "the greatest outburst of frank, honest, sincere expression ever made by the young people of America." This convention should have convinced the guardians of human society, he thought, that the old order of things was unsatisfactory and that there was among young people "a burning thirst for light." He heard Americans denouncing their own imperialism, racism, and militarism. He heard a Chinese speaker deploring America's lack of knowledge of things Oriental and an African "telling of the new Africa and of the spirit of unrest throughout the continent." A Hindu asked for America's help without Americanization. An African American denounced segregation, Jim Crowism, lynching, and other forms of social and economic oppression.

No previous SVM convention had witnessed such a range of opinions expressed, from the platform or in the hallways. A major reason for this diversity was the use—the first time in a major student convention—of student-led discussion groups. The discussion group approach was vaunted as producing a convention conducted according to the principles of democracy, and the successful use of this approach in Indianapolis led some educators to see the 1924 SVM convention as a model for future religious and educational conventions.

Students participated in small, two-hour group discussions of subjects such as war and military training, race relations, industrial problems at home and abroad, and the imposition of Western civilization and Western Christianity on other nations. Led by students trained in group facilitation, the groups were free to set their own agenda and determine the subjects on which they would offer findings or recommendations. In each of the forty-nine groups, the issue of race relations was discussed, and in forty-one groups it was a major question. A second issue considered by a majority of the groups was "the attitude which students should take toward war and the means for securing world peace." Eleven groups spent time considering a third question: to what extent could Americans rightfully adopt methods of missions, or of colonization, that would tend to impose Western civilization or Western Christianity on other peoples of the world.[5]

Discussion was reported to be vigorous, with widely differing opinions being expressed on emotionally sensitive subjects. In one group where race relations were being discussed, a Christian student admitted, in the presence of African American students, having been part of a mob that had hanged an African American. White and black students together were forced to confront the fear and prejudice of the statement made by a white student: "We must protect our women." African American students told whites that racial purity meant as much to them as it did to the whites. In view of the obvious racial mixtures present in American society—resulting from the white man's double standard—"the question was one which the whites ought not to stress." One discussion group participant was quoted as saying that "segregation and ill-treatment are the only means of keeping the Negro in his place." The indignation of black members in that discussion group was taken by the reporter as appropriate, as was the question from a Chinese student who asked why America was sending missionaries to her people when Americans themselves needed Christianizing so badly.[6]

It was an important question, but one that was pushed aside by the democratic will. Most students at the Indianapolis meeting appeared not to be interested in missions issues. By the time the discussion groups reported back to the assembly, racism and war had clearly emerged as the two critical issues of the convention. The groups came up with a wide variety of practical responses to these problems. On racism one group proposed to initiate interracial prayer meetings on campus. Another pledged its members to work to break down discrimination in dormitories, fraternities, college athletics, churches, and college life in general. One group decided to do what they could to change the history curriculum so as to give a more balanced and Christian interpretation of racial issues.

On the question of war, there was general agreement that war was beastly and horrible and that no effort should be spared to deal with its causes. The students favored educational polices that would promote peacemaking. "We should cease to glorify war in our history books" and "positively exert ourselves by all the ingenuity of love to eliminate attitudes which blossom forth into war." The students wished to "establish and strengthen agencies of justice" and to use all legal means to outlaw war. They wanted to "do all in our power to Christianize the social order and the industrial system, realizing that predatory economic motives lie at the root of many military operations."[7]

Because of the strong, but not unanimous, feeling on the issue of war and the League of Nations, the convention leaders agreed to an unusual experiment in democracy. Student representatives would give brief statements of four different positions in response to war, after which there would be an informal vote on the convention floor to allow the delegates to express themselves on these four divergent positions:

1. *Military preparedness:* We believe that preparation for the emergency of war is the best way to avoid war; therefore we urge our nation so to prepare that any future war shall be brought to a speedy and righteous termination
2. *War as Last Resort:* We believe that war is unchristian and should be abolished through a process of education, but that nonresistance is now impracticable, and that occasion may arise wherein it is our duty to engage in war, after all means of prevention have failed
3. *League of Nations:* We believe that war is unchristian and that the League of Nations is the best means of preventing it, but we should resort to war in case an unavoidable dispute had been referred to the League or World Court without successful settlement
4. *Pacifism:* We believe that henceforth war is an utter denial of Jesus' way of life, ineffective as a means of settling differences between nations. Therefore, we declare our resolve not to sanction or participate directly in any future war.

An overwhelming majority (about 85 percent) of the students voted for the League of Nations, with about equal numbers (6 percent) showing support for war as as last resort and for absolute pacifism. Only about 3 percent favored military preparedness.[8]

Student Power

Some volunteers saw the use of discussion groups at the Indianapolis convention as a superficial and inadequate change in a student movement that had already lost touch with the students. T. T. Brumbaugh, a student who had become a volunteer at Des Moines, reported that the Indianapolis convention made him feel "too insignificant to be of any use on the field." That was proof, he said, of the greatness of the convention. "As the mighty conclave reached its inspirational heights, I confess the effect upon me was far from inspirational; on the contrary, it was one of depressed anxiety lest the mighty challenge of the world's great needs, as presented by the masters of appeal whose names have graced so many foreign missions programs, should find me lacking in those qualifications necessary for effective Christian work."

This feeling of depression—of being a "mere student faced by such mighty problems"—grew stronger after the convention as the volunteer realized that this so-called student conference had provided comparatively little opportunity for student participation in attempting to find a solution to "some of these perplexing social and religious problems." An officer of the third (1922) SVM council, Brumbaugh was tempted at first to withdraw from the movement for awhile. After further thought, however, and with the realization that he would be a student only a few months longer before sailing to the field, he decided to "strike out to help correct from the 'inside' some of the faults of our much criticized organization."[9]

Brumbaugh's comments, billed as those of an inside student observer, were published in the February issue of the *Student Volunteer Movement Bulletin* under the title "Convention Mistakes." It was presented as the first instance of a new *SVM Bulletin* feature called the Open Forum, the purpose of which was "to encourage thinking on the part of volunteers on all questions related to the activities of the movement and the relation of these to the world-wide missionary enterprise." Neither the SVM nor the editors of the *SVM Bulletin* would be responsible for the views expressed, and freedom of expression in the Open Forum—clearly a response to growing student criticism—would be limited only by the policies and principles of the movement as set down by the executive committee.

The planning and execution of the convention, wrote Brumbaugh, like other recent activities of the student Ys and the SVM, was too much controlled by the "higher ups," a group of nonstudent "dictators" in American student affairs. They had themselves constructed the program with only token input from the students, and they had largely excluded students from a significant speaking role in the convention. Student attempts to change the direction of the program were usually frustrated. "These plans have been in the process of making for many weeks," the students were told, "and we should be reluctant to change them at this late date." The result was a program that was "altogether too inflexible for a democratic gathering in which the hope was to challenge, call out and reflect student opinion on the vital issues of the day" and to relate those opinions to the foreign missions enterprise (122–24).

Brumbaugh's harshest remarks, excluded from publication, were reserved for the "big four"—Speer, Mott, Eddy, and Wilder—and for the future of the SVM. Speer, he said, had failed to give "any outstanding new idea," and Mott demonstrated an "ingrown mind," the natural result of age and reason enough for him to pass his leadership on to others. "As for Sherwood Eddy," Brumbaugh wrote, "how can I criticize this powerful, modern social leader?" But even Eddy failed to understand the current situation, Brumbaugh thought, "in his presumption that the worldwide dissatisfaction and urge of youth to change things could find its American counterpart in the activities of the student Christian movement." Even though there had been no unfavorable reaction to Wilder's public part in the program, this volunteer, who had "seen something of the inside workings of the movement," felt that Wilder was "hardly in a position to reflect student sentiment." His reluctance to yield to student desires for change in the program was a major cause for its inflexibility, Brumbaugh said.[10]

For volunteers like Brumbaugh, the discussion group approach seemed to be little more than window dressing for a program whose content was really no different from those of past conventions. They realized that convention discussion groups had limited influence on the ongoing life and decision-making process of the SVM, and asked for more substantial changes in the structure of the movement itself. In a concluding comment on the future of the SVM, also not included in the excerpts published in the *Bulletin,* Brumbaugh quoted a missions professor as saying that the SVM faced one of two possible reactions from students. Either the present generation of students would assume responsibility for the movement and initiate a genuine *student* program of world service, or else the students would desert the present SVM organization and give their support to another movement, more sensitive to student sentiment and with a broader agenda. If students were to assume responsibility for the movement, it would be through the SVM council. But Brumbaugh, a former council member, was not optimistic about this student forum. Council recommendations were accepted by the SVM executive committee—where students "silently outnumbered" the "higher ups"—only if the student voice agreed with the will of the older generation. Here was the crucial point, Brumbaugh said: either the Student Volunteer Movement would become a student movement once again, or it would cease to be a movement of significance.

A New Look at the Watchword

Persons who had attended both the Des Moines and the Indianapolis conventions noted many differences between the two. The control of the convention was visibly passing from the hands of the founders and into the hands of younger persons. At the same time, there were fewer foreign mission board and church representatives on the platform in Indianapolis, suggesting a change in the emphasis of the convention and its relation to the church mission agencies. One mission board representative thought the convention to be less of a foreign missionary convention than its predecessors, and he believed that the convention failed "to bring the average delegate sufficiently up against his specific responsibility for foreign missions." A Canadian student observed that "the present generation of students does not regard the challenge of foreign missions as of paramount importance in the Christian program." If this represented a greater commitment to the "unoccupied mission field" at home, it was a good thing. If, on the other hand, the challenges of war and industry were usurping the priority of missions, then "it is unfair to the actual conditions as they exist in the world today."[11]

One student felt that the Student Volunteer Movement was on the defensive. As for the watchword, "The evangelization of the world in this generation," only one speaker appealed to the words on a banner above the convention hall. "Don't throw it away too lightheartedly," Speer had admonished the students. The new generation required it just as much as the old. Even though the world had become more accessible, even though there was a new and larger concept of evangelization, still the central task remained: making Christ known, that is evangelization.[12]

But the watchword appeared to lack voltage for most students, and many were outspoken in their readiness to have it changed. According to one volunteer, the new student generation was thinking not so much of evangelization of individuals as of the reconstruction of society. The world of the watchword was exclusively the non-Christian world. Students were now aware of the shortcomings of Christianity as witnessed by non-Christian nations. With the task conceived somewhat differently, the new student generation could not imagine its being completed in a single generation.[13]

One of the reasons that students in Indianapolis were less sure about missions is that they had become, during the war years, less sure about their faith. A Canadian delegate observed that "there was not any expression of conviction on the part of the students that the way of Jesus is the way." A majority of the delegates seemed to him to lack a "vital expression of belief" as far as the Christian way of life was concerned. Another delegate thought the students at the 1924 convention had very high "spiritual ideals" but a certain lack of "Christian devotion."

At the close of the student session, Princeton student Henry P. Van Dusen suggested that the convention had focused on themes of self-expression, self-development, and self-realization, giving too little attention to the needs of the world and the task of bringing God's kingdom to earth. The principle of self-expression and self-realization, he said, stood in antithesis to the principle of the cross and the absolute surrender of the self to God that the cross represented. There had been a pretense, Van Dusen wrote after the conference, that the spiritual life of American students was continuing strong. All the while the foundations of that deeper Christian spirituality were "rotting away." Had the delegates not been "so happily busy in discussion and thinking and planning at Indianapolis," the Princeton student wrote, "we might almost have heard the slow, quiet settling of the platform." Van Dusen, who later became dean and then president of Union Theological Seminary in New York, recognized as a student that there had been in the war years a loss of faith among students, not merely a loss of enthusiasm for foreign missions.[14]

According to historian Paul A. Varg, the Indianapolis convention was nearly transformed into "a Christian revolutionary meeting aiming at reform at home rather than the Christianization of China."[15] The movement that had once been galvanized into action by the plight of the heathen abroad was now incensed by "paganism" in America. University of Chicago Divinity School professor Shailer Mathews had, in the last quadrennial before the war, reminded the students that Christianity could not hope to conquer the world if it were not first able to conquer the social problems of America. After the war, student activists were gripped by a new realization of the unfinished task at home. For the students, the proverbial "Physician, heal thyself" seemed a more appropriate script than the watchword. If America (and by extension, the West) could not solve her own social problems, could not "set her own house in order," what message of civilizing salvation could she take to other lands and cultures?

Eddy's appeal for more attention to the home front was underscored by a request that had come to Wilder before the Des Moines convention.

On behalf of the Home Missions council, the general secretary had formally asked the SVM, in its work on college campuses, to recruit for home as well as foreign missions. If this was not possible, the home missions leaders were ready to see launched a new Student Volunteer Movement for Home Missions. This seems to have been a vexing question for the leaders of the SVM, and they spent a large amount of time in the decade after the war trying to find a solution to a request that, logical though it was, threatened to dilute the essential purpose of the movement. The SVM never yielded ground on the home missions question. They were supported in this debate by the Foreign Missions Conference of North America and the Federation of Woman's Boards. In their annual conference early in 1924, the boards voted a resolution urging the SVM to maintain its original policy of recruiting for foreign missions, "not diverting its energies to other forms of service."[16]

Through the democratic discussion group process, Indianapolis had further polarized the question of home versus overseas missions. This clarifying of the student point of view could, on one level, simply push the discussion back to the basic history and definition of the movement. The Student Volunteer Movement had been founded to recruit students for foreign missions. It would take more than a change in student mood to erase the distinctions between home and overseas missions that had long since been institutionalized in American Protestant life. On another level, however, the debate exacerbated a growing tension between the SVM and the Y.

The missionary cause was losing its appeal to many of the brightest and the best on campus. The volunteer movement had enjoyed a privileged position with the Associations as long as it continued to be on the cutting edge of student life and opinion. For three decades the SVM quadrennial had been the only national student conference in America. (It was, in fact, a continental conference for the whole of the United States and Canada.) The war had shifted the attention of the students to new issues: the problems of war, racism, and economic injustice. For the SVM these were not unimportant, but they were only a part of the international missions program. When these social problems were considered purely in an American context—as was often the case in student discussions after the war—they seemed to have no point of connection with the volunteer movement program. The foreign missions cause had always appealed to a minority of students. But that minority had been the opinion shapers, the campus leaders. Now, foreign missions was becoming the cause of a less popular and less powerful minority. The college Y became increasingly reluctant to have its national program tied to a specialized campus ministry that was losing its luster, its student drawing power. After Indianapolis, the differences between the two organizations finally led to an amicable compromise. The SVM would continue to hold its national foreign missions conventions. And the Associations would have, starting in 1927, their own national convention, where the focus would be on other issues, issues closer to the postwar student's heart.

A Movement in Decline

In 1920, the Student Volunteer Movement recorded the largest number of volunteers enrolled in its history, and in 1921 a record number of volunteers sailed to foreign mission assignments. For a moment it seemed that the extravagant optimism of the older volunteers was being confirmed, that the American missionary force was ready to seize this moment of "plasticity," as Mott often described it, and finish once and for all the task of conquering the world for Christ. But suddenly the tide turned. In the years between the Des Moines and the Indianapolis conventions, the enrollments of new volunteers, which had grown more or less steadily since the beginning of the movement to the 1921 peak, plummeted by nearly 50 percent in only three years. By the end of 1924, the number of new volunteers enrolled had fallen to a level not seen since the turn of the century. The number of volunteers taking assignments abroad, after peaking in 1921, dropped by nearly one-third in the three years following. The war was finally taking its toll. Students were voting with their feet, with their careers. While some were still willing to do missionary service overseas, many were not. The war and its aftershocks seemed to have changed their minds about foreign missions. The number of volunteers continued its relentless downward plunge. A volunteer movement without volunteers was clearly in trouble.

The decline in volunteer sailings roughly paralleled that of the deployment of missionaries from the mainline denominations during this period. But the decline in volunteer enrollments, which might have been expected to follow a decline in the number of missionaries being sent abroad, actually seemed to anticipate that decline. By 1925, the number of new volunteers recruited fell below the number of missionaries being sent out by the mainline mission boards to which the SVM was closely related, the first time this had happened since the early years of the movement (see fig. 7.1). There was also a decline, during the war and after, in the percentage of the total number of sailed missionaries who were

Figure 7.1

The Volunteer Movement in Decline, 1920-1930

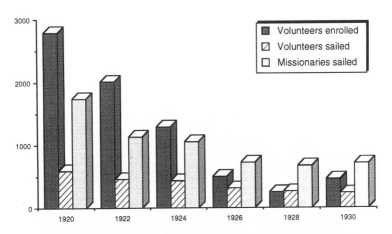

Based on statistics from William H. Beahm, "Factors in the Development of the Student Volunteer Movement for Foreign Missions," p. 234.

volunteers. Soon after the candidate department was begun in 1908 (to track the volunteers more carefully, from pledge to the field), out of a total of 530 new missionaries who sailed, 385, or more than two-thirds, were volunteers. By 1920 only about one-third (595) of the North American missionaries sailing (1,731) were volunteers. Although the percentage climbed again somewhat in the mid-1920s before the long slide toward the movement's eventual dissolution, it never reached prewar levels. The SVM was losing its recruiting ability, its reason for being.[17]

The volunteer movement also began to lose its national clout in terms of the national student population represented at the quadrennials (see fig. 7.2). The high point had been at the 1906 convention, when more than 1.33 percent of all American students were present at the quadrennial in Nashville, Tennessee. From 1914 to 1920 college enrollments climbed by an astonishing 55 percent. Quadrennial attendance kept pace, with Des Moines attendance surpassing Kansas City by 54 percent. During the period 1910–20, the percentage of students attending the SVM convention held at about 1 percent. After the Des Moines convention, the SVM's numerical impact on the American student population declined as precipitously as new volunteer enrollments. By 1932, quadrennial at-

Figure 7.2
Quadrennial Convention Attendance as a
Percentage of Total U.S. Student Population

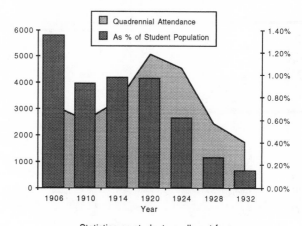

Statistics on student enrollment from
Reports of the Commissioner of Education (Washington 1906-14) and
Biennial Surveys of Education (Washington 1920-32).

tendance as a percentage of student population had dropped to less than
one-fifth of its prewar level and was less than a tenth of what it had been
in 1906. Only about three students in a thousand attended the 1928 convention in Detroit. As a popular movement, the SVM had lost its earlier
clout.

Finance

Late in 1923, Robert Wilder wrote to John Mott, asking him to contact
an SVM supporter in Boston who had for many years contributed five
hundred dollars annually to the movement. In the past year he had given
nothing. This was because he had read a *Christian Century* article in
which Arthur Jorgensen, a YMCA secretary in Japan, lashed out against
"the old 'imperialistic' plan" of evangelizing the world. Jorgensen had
asked why the church was failing to evangelize the world in this generation and answered that it was because mission organizations were not
turning over the evangelistic enterprise to national Christians. Aggressive Western schemes of Christian conquest, if they had ever been ap-

propriate, could no longer be justified. Christianity's superiority was not something to be "shouted from the housetops," particularly "in the dark shadow of the past ten years of Western history." There needed to be a frank recognition that the genuine Christianization of the West was a far more urgent and difficult task than the evangelization of the East, Jorgensen wrote. The Student Volunteer Movement, the only mission organization mentioned by name in the article, shared the failure of the church in acting as if the Great War had only rejuvenated the old slogans and strategies.[18] If Mott would assure the Boston supporter who had read Jorgensen's article, Wilder concluded in his letter to Mott, "that the stream of foreign missionaries from the West should continue to flow into the East, at least for several years to come, I think it would change his mind."[19]

But many supporters did not change their minds. Within two years after the war, the SVM was for the first time in many years experiencing serious financial difficulties. General Secretary Wilder reported in 1924 that the movement had weathered the most difficult year in its history, at a time when spending was at an all-time high (see fig. 7.3). A major part

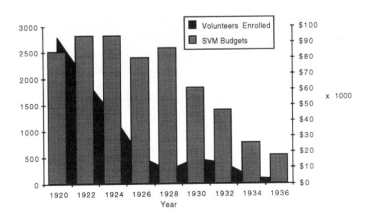

Figure 7.3
SVM Budgets, 1920-1936

Based on statistics from William H. Beahm, "Factors in the Development of the Student Volunteer Movement for Foreign Missions," p. 234.

of the problem was declining student revenues, which had always provided the largest share of the SVM's income. After Des Moines, students "subscribed" some $25,000 annually for the work of the movement. The amount subscribed at Indianapolis was less than $15,000, and the students in fact failed to deliver even that amount. Another problem that the SVM faced on the financial side was the graying of its support base. The friends of Mott and Wilder who helped to bankroll the movement were aging along with the founders. As some supporters died, there were significant one-time gifts to the SVM, but these were also last-time gifts. Gifts from the Rockefeller Foundation continued during the 1920s but decreased during the Depression and finally stopped altogether after 1935. This was less a measure of Mott's decreased involvement in the movement than an indication of how John D. Rockefeller Jr.'s ideas about missions were changing, along with those of his American contemporaries in the Protestant mainstream.

By the time the Indianapolis convention was over, Robert Wilder, now in his sixties, seemed to realize that the American postwar generation would not evangelize the world. Although the opportunities abroad were more inviting than they had ever been and prospects of success more assured, Wilder believed, the war seemed to have changed permanently the generation of youth who had fought it. In a report to the SVM executive committee at the end of the academic year in which the Indianapolis convention was held, Wilder reviewed the five years since he had assumed leadership of the movement.

"The war was followed by a period of marked unrest among students all over the world," Wilder wrote. "This was evidenced by the youth movements in many lands, movements showing dissatisfaction with things as they are and a clamoring for change in social conditions, in international relationships, and in organized Christianity. The elders have failed, otherwise the world war would not have come. Turn out the old, bring in the new. It was the youth who won the war, the youth alone can bring in the new age which must come or humanity will perish."[20]

But the irony in Wilder's words could not forestall the changes. As Wilder wrote this report, his own leadership of the movement he had founded was being challenged. After the recent quadrennial convention, some of the volunteers were making it plain that Mott, Wilder and Speer were no longer in touch with the students and their world and should make way for younger leaders.

By the mid-1920s, Wilder was acknowledging that student attitudes were having a profound impact on the SVM in North America and abroad. Enrollments of new volunteers after Indianapolis were less than half what they had been after the Des Moines convention. Some were calling for major changes in the SVM and the missionary program that it supported. More radical voices suggested that, since the day of missions was coming to an end, the SVM was no longer needed. The volunteer movement had already been abandoned in some countries, and it was almost everywhere far weaker now than it had been before the war. Wilder reported to the SVM executive committee on the new evangelical student movement that had started in England and spread to most of the university centers of Great Britain and Ireland. Meanwhile a new Calvinist movement had emerged among students in Hungary and a liberal Christian movement in the Netherlands, neither holding membership in the WSCF. It was a time of turbulence and change in the student world.

In Canada, a new unified Student Christian Movement had been formed, marking the end of the dominance of the YMCA and YWCA on campus. In 1922 the Canadian SVM had taken action to give the Canadian volunteers a measure of independence from the New York-based organization that had previously assumed responsibility for the movement in all of North America. The student Associations in the United States were beginning to face the reality that they could no longer represent all American students or institutions and that some new kind of united student Christian movement must eventually emerge, of which the college YMCA would be but a part. Although the college Associations had demanded a larger role in planning the last quadrennial convention, the Indianapolis experience with a broader-than-missions agenda had convinced Wilder that the next convention should be planned and carried out solely by the SVM. The college Associations, he reported, would for the first time have their own national convention, freeing the SVM from the pressure to adapt to their divergent agenda.[21]

In the 1920s the SVM experienced a loss of power internally as fewer students chose to take the volunteer pledge. It experienced similar loss of power externally as a growing number of American Protestants began to have doubts about the continuing need for foreign missions. It was the crisis of an organization whose program had been built around cultural and religious assumptions that had now changed—or were at least being strongly challenged. The association of the SVM with the old world— the world that had made the war—brought the movement under increasing suspicion, even attack. For those who had moved to a more radical critique of Western culture and institutions, the SVM and missionary programs were viewed with indifference. The SVM's endorsement of the recent military crusade now made it difficult for the movement to be seen as representative of the internationalism that the new student generation demanded. After Versailles, many students wished to ensure that war could never come again. The wartime intimacy of the missionary and the military crusades gave little assurance that the SVM's ideals could guarantee peace in the troubled world of the 1920s.

The problems of the volunteer movement in North America were proportional to its earlier successes. Other volunteer movements associated with the WSCF also declined after the war, but with less visible impact. The volunteer movement, as an expression of student missionary outreach to students, had actually given rise to the student Christian movements in Australia, Great Britain, and other European countries. The child had now outgrown the parent. In most countries outside North America, the volunteer movement had become little more than a department of the student movement. After the war, the influence of these missionary departments diminished rapidly, at least partly because the WSCF was itself developing a new mission, one that had less to do with missions.

Chapter Eight

That All May Be One: Missions Displaced

The last federation conference at Lake Mohonk, in 1913, had broken up in a spirit of great optimism and international goodwill, and set out as they thought to build a new world at once. Actually they set out to kill each other, singing the same hymns as they did so, and praying for victory to the same God. The ghastliness of that tragedy haunted us at Peking, for we knew it would happen again unless desperate things were done to make it impossible.

—A British delegate to the WSCF Conference in Peking, 1922

When I was traveling for the movement, I felt sure God was calling many more students into missionary work than were responding to his call. Perhaps I was right, but now that I have become a missionary and have seen many more, I wonder if they are as indispensable to God and his plans for bringing in his kingdom as I had thought. Perhaps he wants other people out here who are not regular missionaries. I do know that the time is almost upon us in Japan when the native Church will not welcome many more regular missionaries.

—Jesse R. Wilson, 1922

In Europe, students and young people who had borne the brunt of the ugliest conflict the Continent had ever seen became victims of the turmoil and suffering that followed. There were widespread political disturbances as national boundaries were redrawn and new nation-states created. Nationalism ran rampant, often becoming the pretext for an increasingly vicious racism. The Continent staggered under the cumulative blows of famine and starvation, unemployment, homelessness, and epidemics—plague, malaria, typhus, and the Spanish influenza. The flu took more lives in a few months than the war had taken in four years. Millions of refugees, many of them students, wandered across Europe, trying to return home or looking for a home that no longer existed.

World's Student Christian Federation student leader Ruth Rouse, who spent the years after the war visiting European campuses, described the spiritual chaos that reigned in the universities. War had blown to pieces the world of the students. Bitterness, a sense of injustice, skepticism, and cynicism were common among the Christian students of the defeated nations. "Successive waves of anti-militarism, fierce nationalism, communism, license, idealism or despair swept through the universities," Rouse wrote.[1]

If, after the war, the Student Volunteer Movement was in trouble in the United States—a country physically untouched by the war—how would it fare in the chaos of Europe? If the movement faced a serious crisis in the land of its birth and its greatest strength, what would it find in Europe, where, except for Great Britain, its hold on the student movements had never been strong? And how could the missionary cause gain a hold among students in the Orient, where Christianity faced its largest missionary challenge?

The fate of the student missionary program in Europe and the Orient after the war to a large degree shaped the missionary policy in the World's Student Christian Federation. Would its younger members be ready to carry on the battle for world evangelization? The WSCF was, like the SVM that had given it birth, a nineteenth-century student organization now ready for a changing of the guard. How would the torch be passed?

Decline and Revival

"One of the most striking differences between American and European Protestantism," a European student leader told the American students at the Indianapolis convention, "is that American Protestantism is dynamic, optimistic, forward-looking, and aggressive, while European Protestantism, at least on the Continent, seems to be defensive, pessimistic, and passive."[2] But European student leaders seemed less reserved than their American colleagues in registering their disillusionment with crusades in general and with this war in particular. Less diplomatic than the Americans in describing the generation gap, European students were sometimes cynical. There seemed to be a pronounced alienation between the generation that had decided for war and the generation that had fought it. The disillusionment of the battlefield was charged to the account of those who might have prevented the war. The editor of the *Student Movement,* the official publication of Great

Britain's Student Christian Movement, described the generation gap thus: "The old men and their ways are known. None of them will turn prophets in their old age; that does not happen. The prophets of the better world must come from among the young men and women. The reformers in industry, in church, and in state must arise from the younger generation, or they will not arise to aid our need at all."[3]

The war seemed to many British students to make a mockery of "schemes for world evangelization." Nevertheless, 560 students had signed the volunteer pledge during the war, and 4,500 had participated in mission study activities. Among the mainstream of British students after the war, however, there were new concerns competing with the missions agenda. Many British students supported the emerging League of Nations. Study circles on internationalism were as popular after the war as missions study circles had been before. There was widespread interest in the new study of comparative religions. The growing popularity of Eastern religions and internationalism was often accompanied by a decline in missionary interest.

For many, the reasons were not only, or even primarily, intellectual. "Men and women have not that grip of Christianity which can convince them of its missionary urgency," the British Student Volunteer Missionary Union reported in 1922. Students who had had no faith encounter with Jesus Christ could "have no good news to pass on to others." This was understood by some of the leaders as being the result not only of the war but also of the waning influence of the nineteenth-century evangelical revival. The number of students who came to college sincerely believing and practicing the Christian faith had been decreasing for some years, SVMU leaders reported. Those who did come to the colleges as Christians, or who found Christ while in college, often did not have enough faith in "institutional Christianity" to make a career of foreign missionary service. Students were willing to serve abroad but reluctant to do so under a traditional missionary society. "Those who know the student generation today will know that there is no lack of consecration, no shirking of self-sacrifice, no fear of ridicule behind this general refusal," one movement leader wrote, "but rather a profound distrust of organizations."[4]

When the SVMU wanted to gear up for a renewed emphasis on missions recruitment among university students after the war, they were aware that conditions were not propitious, that the end of the war had brought what one SCM leader described as "a revolt against orthodoxy in general and the churches in particular." The SVMU asked for a commission to be appointed to study the missionary work of the movement and to learn as much as possible about student attitudes toward missions. The report of the Commission on Missionary Work was hardly encouraging.[5]

Many British students had returned to their studies after the war highly critical of the church at home and the church's mission abroad. They did not want to perpetuate British denominational differences in other countries, the commission found. The war seemed to have made students sensitive to divisions in British society that produced conflict. They did not want to be guilty of exporting these divisions and conflicts to Africa and the Orient. They were generally critical of missionary societies and their policies, although they admitted to being largely ignorant of their work and the needs of the younger churches abroad. Because of the presence of a growing number of foreign students in Great Britain and the popularity of comparative religious studies, there was a growing belief among British students that other religions contained much that is true and were better adapted to the needs of their adherents than an imported religion like Christianity. At a deeper level, the commission reported, some British students expressed grave doubts as to whether there was any longer a word of good news that Christian missionaries could carry to other peoples. Many students were, after the war, no longer sure that there was any distinctive Christian message at all.

Some of the most pungent criticism of the SVMU and the missions movement came from women, and the commission addressed specifically the relationship of the British movement to women. Women were serving in higher positions and holding greater responsibility in British society after the war than was the case in the missions movement or the SVMU. University women in particular were not visible in leadership positions in the foreign missions movement in Great Britain. Some women students were critical of the fact that female missionaries often did not receive allowances and furlough pay on a par with their male counterparts. These inequities needed urgent attention, the commission felt.

The commission's recommendations led to sweeping changes in the SVMU. The watchword was abandoned, as it was judged to be already "virtually obsolete" for the current generation of students and was believed incapable of being revived.[6] The SVMU committee was dissolved, and its work transferred to the general committee of the Student Christian Movement, of which the SVMU had long been a department. The volunteer declaration was revised to read: "It is my purpose, if God permit, to devote my life to missionary service abroad." This broadening of the pledge was an attempt to move away from a narrow definition of missionary to include persons who served abroad with a missionary purpose without actually becoming foreign missionaries.[7]

A New Movement

In listening to the mainstream of British students, the SCM seemed to have missed or ignored the voice of a growing minority of students who held to traditional theological beliefs and who had not lost interest in foreign missions after the war. Leadership for this more evangelical minority emerged from one of Britain's oldest universities. Already before the war there had been a serious rift in the SCM when the influential Cambridge Inter-Collegiate Christian Union (CICCU, usually pronounced "kick-you") was disaffiliated by the SCM because of theological differences. Even though the great facts of the Christian faith do not change, SCM leader Tissington Tatlow had argued in 1910, human insight into these eternal truths does change. "Theology is dynamic and not static," he insisted. For the CICCU leaders, on the other hand, the differences had been too great, and "compromise could not have papered over the gap for long." According to Douglas Johnson, leader and historian of the evangelical student movement in Great Britain, it was a case of two essentially different Christianities confronting each other. "One was endeavoring to preserve the historic Christian faith under the control of the plain statements of Holy Scripture. The other aimed to embrace all possible views and to adapt the faith into terms which the modern mind could accept."[8]

After the war, a meeting was arranged between SCM and CICCU leaders in an attempt to heal the rift. After an hour of discussion, the CICCU representatives felt the meeting was at a stalemate. CICCU member Norman Grubb—who would leave for missionary service in central Africa immediately after college and later return to lead the influential evangelical mission, Worldwide Evangelization Crusade—finally turned to the SCM chapter president and asked point blank, "Does the SCM put the atoning blood of Jesus Christ *central* in its beliefs?" "Well," the president responded, "we acknowledge it, but not necessarily as central." That seemed to settle the question for the CICCU members. They were not interested in reunification with such a student movement.

With SCM ties broken, the Cambridge students began to look elsewhere for support. They turned naturally to Oxford, where their aggressive efforts to recruit participants for an intervarsity conference aroused stiff opposition from chaplains and students alike.[9] Among medical students and hospital Christian unions in London they found a more sympathetic reception, and the first intervarsity conference was convened at the head-quarters of the Egypt General Mission at Drayton Park, London, in December 1919. In addition to the usual Bible studies and addresses, the program included a missionary meeting that featured speakers from Asia, Africa, the Islamic countries, and South America.

The intervarsity conferences fostered a renewed missionary interest among evangelical students in Great Britain and Ireland during the postwar years, when missionary enthusiasm was waning in the SCM. Returned missionaries or missionaries on furlough were often invited to speak at these conferences, and they found students with a strong, if not enthusiastic, interest in foreign missions. The new movement drafted an evangelical theological statement in 1924 and four years later organized itself formally as the Inter-Varsity Fellowship of Evangelical Student Unions. The new movement was soon commissioning its members for overseas mission assignments.[10]

But the war had taken a toll even among evangelical students in Great Britain. In spite of reminders by the older pioneer missionaries of the thousands of volunteers who had, at the turn of the century, responded to the call for the evangelization of the world in this generation, the postwar generation seemed unable to rekindle the old enthusiasm. Their ranks had been thinned by the terrible wartime losses, and those who were left were not always qualified or free to go. Nor could the more evangelical students in Britain ignore the changes taking place in the mission field, changes that are outlined in chapter 4. Younger churches were now looking for "experienced advisors and colleagues" rather than an army of new missionary recruits.

Postwar student volunteer interest in Great Britain and Ireland, as measured by new volunteer enrollments, showed an early and sharp decline (see fig. 8.1). But there was an immediate recovery to prewar levels. Clearly, many students were still interested in missionary service. The SCM, however, was attempting to reach out to the majority of students, many of whom were sharply critical of the church and its mission. Some no longer chose to call themselves Christian at all. In its effort to make its message and program attractive to these students, the SVM alienated evangelical students who were still interested in foreign missions. By giving priority to its outreach to students in Britain, the SVM gradually lost its effectiveness in recruiting students for the foreign field.

Figure 8.1
Student Volunteers after the War,
Great Britain and Ireland

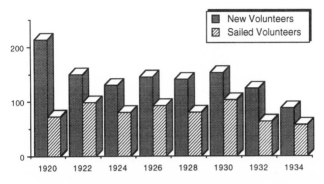

Data compiled from SCM, *Student Christian Movement of
Great Britain and Ireland*, 1920-34.

France

While the volunteer movement in Britain predated the SCM, in France
it was just getting started. The environment was hardly favorable. In
a 1920 federation survey of student attitudes toward Christianity, male
students in France were reported to be no longer hostile toward Christianity but indifferent. The war seemed to have turned them away from
intellectual issues and toward the practical tasks of reconstruction.
Some women students, on the other hand, were turning with renewed
interest to the church, while others, repelled by the formalism and
mysticism of the Roman church, were abandoning Christian belief altogether.

In Switzerland and France, missions interest among students did
not grow much after the war, in spite of efforts to promote the new
volunteer organization, *Les Volontaires du Christ*. In 1923 the fledgling volunteer movement was reorganized in France to include not
only ministers, evangelists, and missionaries "but all who declare that
the spread of the gospel is the chief aim of their lives, whatever pro-
fession they may adopt." This broadening of the missionary career,
however, did not result in the recruitment of more volunteers. Rather,
it seemed to have the effect of diluting the call until it lost its distinctive appeal.[11]

Germany

In Germany, impoverished by the war and by the stringent terms of the Armistice, students who often lacked the simple necessities of life seemed nonetheless eager to find intellectual and spiritual moorings. Various philosophical approaches were popular among students, from Nietzsche to Feuerbach and the historical pessimism of Spengler. In the vacuum left by Germany's political and military collapse, many students were finding escape in primitive German religion or in anti-Semitism. Others turned to radical pacifism.[12] Among Christian students there was hostility toward the WSCF because of the federation's perceived failure to ameliorate the conditions of the Versailles treaty, which had virtually eliminated German missions. "The fact that the World's Federation has been able to do no more for our missions than it has done is the strongest argument that can be urged against the World's Federation and its general right to existence," a German student leader wrote in 1920.[13]

With German missions effectively stifled by the treaty, there was little possibility of turning the new prestige gained by the student alliance during the war into gains for the student missions movement. Missionary study circles were reported to have almost disappeared in German universities, and no new volunteers were reported to have joined the German Student Missionary Union after the war. The volunteer movement in Germany, which had never recruited a large number of students for missionary service, was for all practical purposes dead by the end of the war.[14]

Australia

Many students in postwar Australia were reported by student movement leaders to be plagued by an uncertainty aggravated by the rapid pace of change. There was a reluctance to join great causes, and many students appeared to be less interested in religion. A practical materialism, more than intellectual barriers, was thought to be responsible for the growing secularism. When students observed that effective, respected leaders in Australia were apparently able to serve both God and mammon, some wondered if Jesus had not perhaps been wrong in his attitude toward money.[15]

In this context the Student Volunteer Movement was abandoned by the Australians in 1921, in the conviction that "the Student Volunteer Movement which had brought the student movement into being had attained its purpose by permeating it with a world outlook." Since the student

Christian movement as a whole "stood for the devotion of the life to the service of the kingdom of God, and sought to inculcate the ideas that all callings—whether at home or abroad—demand this kind of devotion," the existence of a separate organization like the SVM to recruit foreign missionaries was deemed unnecessary, even inappropriate. There was but one "standard of dedication" for the followers of Christ, and "the distinction between 'home' and 'foreign' must be utterly abolished." At the same time, the attitude of students toward foreign missions was described by student worker Margaret Holmes as "one of dense ignorance and complete indifference."[16]

American leaders were aware of and concerned about these developments in Europe and Australia. When Robert Wilder, veteran European student worker whose wife was from Norway, was asked by John Mott in 1921 to interpret the needs of the student movements in Europe, Wilder began by noting that the strength of the student Christian movement in North America was due largely to the Christian home and church. When a group of student volunteers were asked when their thoughts were first turned toward Christian service and the foreign field, nearly all said that it was between the ages of six and fifteen. Wilder reported that many recruits were signing the student volunteer declaration in their freshman year. They had come to college already primed for the student volunteer challenge.

This stood in sharp contrast to the situation in Europe, Wilder said, where homes and churches usually showed little evangelical life. Christian leaders frequently did not believe in the supernatural or in the resurrection of Christ. Many European churches, Wilder thought, could be characterized as Unitarian in theology. Seminary professors were not much help in the development of students' faith. Wilder recalled a recent statement made by a student worker at a federation meeting in Europe: "If we in Germany asked our theological professors to address us, one of two results would inevitably follow: either the address would be so *wissenschaftlich* [scientific] and dry that students would not come to the next meeting, or else it would be so destructive critically that our members would lose their faith."[17]

It was an exaggeration, Wilder admitted, but not without truth. What was needed in Europe, he thought, was an approach based on evangelistic and Bible study work—less glamorous, he conceded, but probably more effective in the long run. There needed to be in every location where student work was attempted a core of converted students, trained in the model of Jesus' relationship with the twelve disciples. Social service was essential, Wilder said, and currently attractive to European students. But unless it was accompanied by authentic spiritual development, it would lead to student programs that would eventually collapse for lack of foundation.

One Family under Heaven

When Mott and Wilder went to Europe in the 1890s, they went as advocates of the watchword, of the student missionary cause. Wilder was the catalyst for the founding of volunteer movements in several European countries, and Mott for the organizing of the World's Student Christian Federation. Out of the volunteer movement in Great Britain grew the Student Christian Movement, a uniting of campus Christian ministries throughout England, Scotland, and Ireland. The WSCF sought to unite campus ministries throughout the world, including the non-Western countries. But for Mott and Wilder, the chief cause was world evangelization. The ecumenical apparatus was a means to that end. Until the Great War, the missionary ideal had continued to take center stage in the federation. The war marked a seismic shift of attention among the students and leaders of the WSCF.

In China, one of the federation member countries, students have periodically given expression to the duty—a legacy of Confucian scholarship—of putting the world in order. In imperial days, students coming to the examination centers would often stage a demonstration to show their concern for China's future. After the Great War, Chinese students in the new institutions of higher learning began to give modern expression to the ancient tradition. On May 4, 1919, after hearing the bitter news from Versailles that Japan would be allowed to stay in Shandong, some three thousand students gathered in Tiananmen Square at the entrance to the imperial palace. "China's territory may be conquered," they declared, "but it cannot be given away! The Chinese people may be massacred, but they will not surrender."[18]

In the 1920s, China was caught up in the tumultuous events associated with the May Fourth and New Culture (Renaissance) movements and the political changes that would later be called the Nationalist Revolution. While the New Culture movement, with its roots in both indigenous and missionary influences, was shaping a new leadership elite in China, James Yang-ch'u Yen, a YMCA secretary, was launching a mass education movement for villagers. Yen's "foundation character system" grew out of his work with the Chinese labor corps in France during the war. After the war, Yen refined this simplified approach to learning the Chinese language and with his Y colleagues began to use it for advancing literacy among peasants in the villages. It was the beginning of a mass education movement that had a wide influence in China, later becoming a model for Marxist education. The early 1920s was the heyday of YMCA influence in China and the period of greatest success for the student Christian movement. But life for missionaries in China was becoming more complicated.[19]

In a 1921 *Atlantic Monthly* article, veteran China missionary Paul Hutchinson discussed the future of religion in China. He analyzed the status of the major religions in China—Confucianism, Taoism, Buddhism, and Islam—turning finally to Christianity. After several centuries of Roman Catholic work and a century of Protestant effort, China's Christian community numbered about 2.4 million, with six thousand foreign missionaries at work throughout the country. "Christians, as a whole, are winning a position of respect and influence out of proportion to their numbers," Hutchinson wrote. As for the future, Confucianism, "a wonderful philosophy," would live on as the distinctive philosophy of the Chinese. As such it was "much better adapted to the practical working out of a Kingdom of Heaven on earth than most of the philosophy that has come from the so-called Christian lands." It provided an enlightened materialism that could easily be "fulfilled" by elements of Christianity.

In the end, the contest among religions would be decided by a pragmatic test, characteristic of Confucianism. Which civilization could provide the best models for life in the modern world? The Chinese nation would choose the religion that had formed that civilization. Given such a test, Hutchinson thought it clear that Western civilization would win the day, with Christianity emerging as the dominant religion in China. It followed that the purpose of the foreign missionary was to "vindicate the civilization from which he has come." When that was done, the work of the foreign missionary in China would be finished. Christianity had already demonstrated the superiority of its civilization in medicine, education, agriculture, and spirituality. Only in international politics had Christianity so far failed the test. But even there, vindication would come soon enough, Hutchinson thought, especially if a labor government were elected in Great Britain. A broad acceptance of Christianity by the Chinese, however, would only come after the missionaries had left and Christianity was fully under the direction of Chinese leaders. That development would be well under way, Hutchinson thought, by the end of the century.[20]

It was an unusual argument for the postwar period, and it brought a cogent reply several months later from Chinese leader Chang Hsin-hai. Chang argued from history, Hutchinson's history. After the Reformation, he said, Christianity lost control of the state and was gradually deprived of its decisive influence over Western civilization. The scientific, intellectual, and political advances of the West during subsequent centuries were possible precisely because civilization had been freed from the church's autocratic control, Chang contended. It followed that the intellectual and political developments in eighteenth- and nineteenth-century Europe were essentially unchristian in their origin and in their consequences. Christianity's record so far in the twentieth century might well vindicate Nietzsche's conclusion that the gospel died on the cross. But at the very least there needed to be a recognition that the spirit of Christianity was none too powerful.[21]

Although there had always been individuals who lived up to the principles of Jesus, Chang wrote, "I find nothing in the history of Chinese relations with the so-called Christian powers that would recommend the Christian religion to our attention and appreciation." In a concession to Hutchinson's cultural logic, Chang agreed that it would be the actions done in the name of the nation, not those of an individualistic morality, that would "produce the greatest effect upon destiny of our people." China had been wronged at the peace table in Versailles, Chang said, and that public wrong could not be undone by the altruistic actions of missionaries. But that was only one example. "We have always observed a strange gap," Chang wrote, "between the teachings of Christ and the spirit in which the Christian nations do their work in China."

It was an unusual dialogue, one that could hardly have taken place before the war. When discussing their work, missionaries had usually talked to themselves or to their own supporters in the West. When they had addressed a larger Western public, they could assume a sympathetic audience. Because missionary addresses were on the order of preaching to the converted, there had been little concern as to the accuracy of observations made about another culture. Before the war it was assumed that no one else was listening. Whether or not that assumption had been correct at the time, it clearly no longer held after 1920, as this exchange illustrates. The world was now listening to—and disagreeing with—missionary claims. After the Great War, these claims were increasingly scrutinized in the light of Western national and international behavior. The world beyond the West became more vocal in registering its judgments on the moral and missionary implications of Western foreign policy.

Young volunteers sometimes participated in the new international and cross-cultural dialogue about missions. A Princeton Seminary volunteer, preparing for missionary service in the Middle East, responded to Chang's letter. The young volunteer considered Chang's response inadequate but admitted that he had brought "a serious charge against the Christian nations of the world." "Is not this challenge of an unbeliever one which should ring throughout the Christian church," the volunteer asked, "and awaken us to a relentless and dynamic endeavor to Christianize national motives and international relationships?" Only then, he thought, would the gospel of Christ find an unhindered response in the Orient.[22]

Some of the hindrances to the gospel in China in the 1920s had more to do with a loss of faith among intellectuals in the West than with China's loss of face at Versailles. About the time Chang's article appeared, T. Z. Koo, the assistant general secretary of the YMCA's China national committee, went to the Netherlands to press the invitation for the WSCF to hold its next general conference in Peking. "China is at a crossroads," he told the federation leaders. She could take the line of least resistance and be swept along in the rush of a nationalistic materialism; or she could embrace the new humanism from the West.[23] John Dewey had been touring China for the past two years (1919–21), riding the crest of a wave of enthusiasm for the humanistic educational philosophy taught at New York's Columbia University Teachers College, where many of China's educated elite had studied. Bertrand Russell followed Dewey on the China lecture circuit during the 1920–21 academic year. Russell's opposition to the recent war had earned him time in prison and an eager following in China, as had his views on socialism, sex, and Christianity. Dewey's religious agnosticism and Russell's "roaring atheism"[24] had not gone unnoticed by Chinese students, Koo reported to the federation executive committee. If the WSCF would hold its 1922 conference in China, it could make "a profound impression on the minds of the entire nation which will bear its fruit for the kingdom of God for many years to come."[25]

The Peking meeting, like that held in Tokyo in 1907, was planned as a general student conference with "evangelistic deputations" to "the leading student centers of the Far East." The WSCF meeting took as its motto an ancient Chinese aphorism, "One Family under Heaven." By the time it was convened in April 1922, the conference had received so much attention that it sparked in China the formation of a short-lived but highly visible Anti-Christian Student Federation. Staging demonstrations and printing literature in protest of the WSCF meeting, the anti-Christian movement attempted—sometimes successfully—to break up the associated evangelistic deputations by federation members to China's major urban centers. Within a few days of its opening, the conference "was suddenly and unexpectedly thrust upon the front page of every Chinese and foreign newspaper." Historian Ruth Rouse wrote that the movement "proved at the time a help rather than a hindrance. It gave wide publicity to the federation and secured a larger hearing for the deputations than might otherwise have been the case."[26]

Oriental scholar Jonathan T'ien-en Chao has identified two streams of influence behind the Anti-Christian Student Federation. One was the broad religious critique of the New Culture movement. In 1920 and 1921 the Young China Society had sponsored public debates on the role of religion in society: "Is there still a place for religion in the modern world?" "Does modern China need religion?" Christianity found itself on the defensive in these debates, which concluded that, in the history of human progress, religion belonged to the past. Religion had been displaced by science.

Also behind the Anti-Christian Student Federation was the Shanghai-based Socialist Youth Corps, recently reorganized along Marxist-Leninist lines according to international Communist Party directives. Its official publication, *Hsien-ch'ü,* published a special anti-Christian issue on March 15, about a week after the launching of the Anti-Christian Student Federation, containing its constitution, declaration of purpose, and information on how to organize anti-Christian activities. "The first step is to contact anti-Christian students and bring them together in a grand organization," one writer explained. "The next step is to guide them in fighting a decisive battle against the Christians."

The anti-Christian movement had been bolstered by the report of Chinese delegates who had just returned from the January 1922 Congress of Far Eastern Toilers in Moscow. Lenin's explanation of the need for collaboration between oppressed peoples in colonized lands and the proletarian revolutionaries in capitalist countries, Chao wrote, had convinced the Chinese delegates that all reactionary forces in China were instruments of foreign imperialism. "It is no wonder that when these delegates returned to China, they began to interpret the World's Student Christian Federation conference as an example of the imperialist expansion of capitalism," Chao concluded.[27]

Missions Issues

While the Peking meeting attracted opposition to Christian missions from without, it stirred controversy on missionary questions within the federation as well. The issue of racism in the missionary program was put on the agenda by an unusual letter addressed to the federation by the African Student Union of America. African American students were concerned about the issue of justice for Africans under the rule of European colonial powers. They alleged that African American missionaries were often prevented by colonial government policy from serving in Africa. They asked federation students from Europe to take up this cause with their respective governments, asking that African peoples be treated justly and that African Americans be free to carry on missionary work and Christian education in the European colonies. "At present it is difficult for American Negroes to enter certain parts of Africa to carry on Christian education," they wrote. "We feel that such action is contrary to the teachings of Jesus Christ and will delay the coming of Christian internationalism and brotherhood to all men."[28]

African American students were asking why they should have enthusiasm for student volunteer conventions and their recruiting drives for new missionaries when most avenues for the expression of service were securely closed to them. They also questioned the integrity of the missionary message to a world that was largely made up of people of color when foreign mission boards seemed to be drawing a color line in recruiting and sending out missionaries. They looked to the WSCF as the international student organization that might be able to pry open doors of missionary opportunity closed by racist policies on the part of both governments and mission boards.

From its beginning in 1895, the federation had declared its intention "to influence students to devote themselves to the extension of the kingdom of God in their own nation and throughout the world." At the same time, it had carefully avoided involvement in political issues. Here was a question that clearly related to the federation's missionary mandate, but one that called the WSCF to make a statement in the political arena. In a carefully nuanced statement, the Peking conference responded to the request from the black Americans as part of its discussion of the missionary purpose of the federation and its student volunteer policy. "Our attention has been called to the fact that it is at present very difficult for Negro student volunteers to enter many parts of Africa, their fatherland, to carry on missionary work," the Peking statement read. "This is obviously unfair, and more, contrary to the accepted conceptions of missionary policy, which long ago recognized that no group can be wholly won to Christianity by members of another entirely different group."

The statement was as significant for what it did not say as for what it said. There was no direct challenge to the European colonial governments such as Great Britain, France, and Belgium to deal with the question of racial discrimination in their colonial policies. Nor was there explicit encouragement to the students or their leaders to raise the issue with their governments, as the African American students had requested. Instead the federation called on the recently formed International Missionary Council to use its influence to ensure that qualified black candidates would be "accepted for service in every part of Africa." Student movements in countries with colonial control in Africa were urged in the most general terms "to use their influence to break down any barriers which may work to prevent the acceptance of Negro student volunteers in Africa."[29]

The Problem of War

It was war, not missions, that dominated the Peking discussions. The conference had delegates from thirty-two countries and included more than five hundred from the various provinces and territories of China.[30] With a program entirely in the hands of a committee appointed by the Chinese Associations, the meeting had been planned to find ways to challenge the New Culture movement in China. Many in the New Culture movement saw pacifism as the only original and useful religious idea in the New Testament, and they were watching to see whether the federation would be willing to follow the radical example of Jesus. A world conference with a local agenda, the Peking meeting was structured so that participants would work in six forums, each discussing a different part of the larger theme, "Jesus Christ and World Reconstruction." Because of the large number of Chinese delegates and their interests, the forum dealing with war and race relations upstaged all other discussion groups, with many participants from the other five forums leaving their groups to join the war and race forum.

While these topics—war and race relations—would also preoccupy American students in Indianapolis the following year, the weight of opinion and the way opinions were expressed were quite different. The Chinese delegates were joined by other Orientals and the delegates from Australia and New Zealand in a passionate desire for the conference to make a unequivocal statement in support of Christian pacifism—to pledge themselves never under any circumstances to engage in war. The Europeans were unwilling to take that position. "We longed, many of us, desperately, to see eye to eye with those who had pledged themselves never to engage in war," a British delegate wrote after the meeting. "But we could not and would not surrender our right and privilege to lose our own souls, if need be, in defending the weak from the evil we have made in the world."

The Americans, ambivalent, were caught in a clash of convictions that made many fear the federation had been wrecked, or would at least be split. "We doubted each other's sincerity, even Christianity," one American delegate wrote. "Many of us even doubted our own. Prayer appeared to fail. We were too honest to be hypnotized into seeing a solution which did not exist. . . . The agony of disagreement, when we had come with such high hopes from all corners of the world, was nothing to the dreadful fear that we were failing, failing those who had sent us, failing him who had brought us together."[31]

The Peking resolutions anticipated the ambivalence of Indianapolis:

> We, representing Christian students from all parts of the world, believe in the fundamental equality of all the races and nations of mankind and consider it as part of our Christian vocation to express this reality in all our relationships.
>
> We consider it our absolute duty to do all in our power to fight against the causes leading to war, and war itself as a means of settling international disputes.
>
> As a result of our discussion at the Peking conference, we declare frankly that we have not succeeded in reaching an agreement as to what our individual attitude ought to be in the event of war. Some are convinced that under no circumstances can they as Christians engage in war; others that under certain circumstances they ought to take their share in the struggle.[32]

In the international movement as well as in the United States, the student missionary movement was dealing with a new generation that looked at the missionary program with consciences chastened by war. If there was a difference in the international arena, it was demonstrated in a greater impatience with the traditional patterns of missionary work and a stronger reluctance to postpone action on the questions of war and racism. The European student movements had never been as gripped by the missionary cause as the American movements. For them, the volunteer movement could more quickly be set aside.

Student Volunteer Method

The Peking conference did pause in its discussion of war long enough to affirm the student volunteer method, noting that it was "still the responsibility of student movements to enlist their members for life service in specifically religious work." With Australia and New Zealand having just abandoned their volunteer movement chapters, and with declining enrollments being reported in Great Britain and the United States, the WSCF acknowledged that its experience in student volunteer work had been uneven. But there were still "large circles within the federation which are convinced that the student volunteer method is of very great value and who believe that they have learned in their work of recruiting that no other method has been so effective in obtaining workers for life service in home and foreign mission fields." Perhaps because the method was unfamiliar to many students and leaders outside Great Britain and the United States, the federation minutes required a paragraph to define the student volunteer method. The non-Western setting may have influenced the description—a method of recruiting candidates not for "foreign missions service" but for "neglected forms or undermanned fields of Christian service."[33]

In recognition of the changed postwar situation with regard to missionary service, the WSCF had some words of caution. The need in mission lands was not for greater numbers of missionaries but rather for persons "of the right type." The postwar missionary needed to have "a growing mind," and the workers were to be ready not only to share what they knew of Christ but "to learn still more of him from the people they go to serve." While there was a need for more missionaries to be sent from the "older churches" to the "younger churches," these missionaries needed to come "as servants of the church universal," not as leaders but as fellow workers (28).

Linguistic Imperialism

There was another struggle in the postwar federation, internal, perhaps, but one that would bedevil many an international organization in the twentieth century. "Twenty years ago," a German delegate wrote, "the critics of the federation used to say: the federation is merely an American organization; the conferences have the American stamp; the American influence is always prevailing."[34] A Dutch delegate used a broader term: "During the first period of its existence the federation was in name and organization a world organization, but in reality it was directed by

Anglo-Saxons."[35] While the Peking meeting demonstrated progress toward a more representative federation, the "process" was controlled by what would later be described as "linguistic imperialism." The use of English limited the selection and quality of non-Anglo-Saxon delegates to WSCF meetings, H. C. Rutgers believed. When Anglo-Saxons then complained about the absence of students from the Continent, it brought Rutgers "as near swearing as a Christian is allowed to go." The use of English also inhibited participation in the federation sessions. The use of a language foreign to them prevented many delegates from "being truly themselves." While he recognized the need for a common language, the Dutch delegate confessed that he was "getting tired of being constantly obliged to protest against being driven too hard in a foreign language" (129–31).

The federation meeting in Peking did not reach the highest expectations of its Chinese planners. Christians from every part of the world had been unable to speak clearly to the problem of war. Many felt that the federation, and perhaps Christianity itself, had failed. Others saw another possible significance in this failure. Was this failure the betrayal of a trust, or could it be the "pale shadow of the cross of Christ?" "We must indeed pay for federation, but truth is not the price," wrote one delegate. "It is something much more costly than truth. It is the admission that *we* are not the elect; that the truth we have is not the whole truth, or even a higher truth than anybody who differs from us, but rather as it were one color in the spectrum, one letter in an endless word, an essential part, but not by any means the whole." To follow Christ was to follow him in death as well as life. "Jesus Christ began the reconstruction of the world by sacrifice, and where progress has been made in history it has been always by further sacrifice." Only sacrifice could make the world safe for humanity. The call to federation was a call to self-sacrifice and international service. Only sacrifice could unite the "one family under heaven." The alternative was war and more war.[36]

By the summer of 1922, the Anti-Christian Student Federation had mostly disappeared, only to be reborn in August 1924 as the better-organized Anti-Christian Grand Federation. "This resuscitated anti-Christian movement maintained a sustained and increasingly fierce attack against Christianity and all its institutions throughout the years of the Kuomintang-Chinese Communist Party collaboration (1924–27)," Chao writes. This attack led to a separation of the Chinese church from foreign missions and helped Chinese Protestant leaders to see the need for Chinese indigenous churches that would be independent and nondenominational, "suited to the ethnic characteristics of the Chinese people, and integrated with Chinese culture and ways of life."[37] Although the Chinese indigenous church movement of the 1920s that emerged in response to the anti-Christian movement did not achieve those aims on any broad front, it represented a time of unsurpassed creativity in the twentieth–century encounter between Christianity and culture in China.

After the Peking meeting, Mott asked member countries for counsel as to the future direction of the federation. Five British representatives responded with an affirmation of the concept of "a federation of self-governing national movements, each with its own genius, gifts and experience to contribute, standing shoulder to shoulder as brothers in Christ to serve their generation by the will of God." But the postwar student world had changed. Christian students were now "more analytical and less creative" than they had been. They were unwilling to accept without discussion the assumptions on which, before the war, federation work had been based. The federation needed to chart new directions for the future. British leaders believed that the task of the WSCF lay in three main areas: efforts to eliminate war, linking constituent movements for the good of all, and pioneer work with new national movements. Traditional methods of evangelism would need to change in the postwar world. It was inappropriate, the British thought, for "evangelists from abroad" to create expectations that could not be met by local churches. In some European countries, on the other hand, the fields were ripe, and securing speakers and audiences was "largely a matter of organization." In these places, evangelistic work should be pursued without delay.[38]

A Growing Diversity

After the war, federation discussions tended to be more concerned with international issues than with evangelization. The shift away from traditional missionary work coincided with a growing diversity of opinion in the federation. At the federation meeting in England in 1924, participants found it more difficult than ever to agree on how Christian students should respond to vexing international questions. The commission on international study and action gave a report that had to have qualifying statements attached. Even these could not capture the full range of opinion expressed in the conference debate, and the chairman was asked to appoint an editorial committee to receive and edit statements submitted by delegates after the conference and to append these statements to the minutes. The commission that discussed matters of basic Christian belief ran into such sharp disagreements that they were unable to report anything at all to the plenary gathering.

The debate on pacifism and social justice was painful, leaving many delegates weary and a few disillusioned. The social Christianity to which the federation had committed itself in Peking was undoubtedly distracting the student movements from the priority of the missionary task as traditionally understood. For some, this was a necessary distraction. But the federation seemed unable to unite around the social agenda that many believed to be the appropriate new expression of the missionary task for the WSCF after the war. Social activists in the federation saw clear-cut principles that could be applied in the fight to abolish war. Others feared legalism—bringing Christians under the law again rather than being dependent on the "inward guidance of the Spirit of Christ." The social activists believed war was diametrically opposed to the principles of Christianity. If Christian civilization was to prevail, war had to be eradicated. It was useless to wait for some "spectacular intervention of God in human affairs" to eliminate war. The growth of God's kingdom had always been aided by human efforts. Although it was not a new debate, it was part of a continuing federation attempt to refine its mission in the light of the war.[39]

The war had altered the message of the federation. Before the war, the federation had been dominated by an aggressive commitment to evangelism—to present the living Christ to students, both in the West and in the emerging colleges and universities of Africa and the Orient. After 1920, the federation gave much of its attention to a Christian response to war and its causes—racism, economic injustice, and international disputes. The message of the prewar federation was both personal and positive. It called students to a radical reorientation of their personal lives (conversion, or becoming a Christian) and to an identification with a religious movement committed to conquering the world with love, goodwill, and the fruits of Christian civilization (the kingdom of God). The postwar federation was grappling with the apparent failure of Christian civilization and, by implication, of the crusade for world evangelization. The debate on war very nearly split the federation. Unable to agree on a Christian response to war, the federation compromised in urging a vigorous attack on its root causes.

The euphoric ideals of the prewar federation had been shattered. The missionary and ecumenical programs of the church had been powerless to stop the war. Now paralyzed in its efforts to shape a Christian response to a future conflict, the federation seemed a victim of the very foibles that made for war. There was an unmistakable aura of pessimism on campuses everywhere. A new program of action was desperately needed. Any attempt to pick up the old crusade—even to build an alternative platform for action—was sure to spark vigorous debate. And missionary claims were now widely disputed, in the West and beyond. International relations were now taken to be more important than ever, but they had become, by the same token, far more difficult than they had been in that nineteenth-century atmosphere when the world had seemed so close to being saved. The federation, having become a victim of the extravagance of its own claims, now struggled to survive in an international arena where common ground was hard to find.

An Ecumenical Agenda

When the WSCF met in Denmark in 1926, some leaders were hoping to revive its missionary purpose. French representative Suzanne de Dietrich presented a report on the evangelization of the universities. While affirming that this activity "went to the very core of the vocation of the federation," the leaders—and the reports of the meeting—were blunt in describing universities "plunged into a turmoil of conflicting philosophies and religions." The comparative study of religion was demonstrating the spiritual vitality of other religions and challenging the exclusive claims of Christianity. Many students were gravitating toward the position that one religion is as good as another. Among Christians there were deep differences of opinion as to whether Christianity was essentially a moral code or a personal experience of God with little or no relation to the life of society. Students were asking how the findings of science could be reconciled with the claims of Christianity. For many students, psychological analysis had shaken the belief in the validity of religious experience. Throughout the world students were being drawn to secular and even atheistic philosophies as Christianity was judged to have failed in establishing justice and preventing war.[40]

"The federation on the eve of war had appeared more as an organ of conquest," committed to the slogan "the evangelization of the world in this generation." The term evangelization, rather than calling students to action, now stirred up defiance among them. Students in the whole of Europe were said to be in a state of psychological fatigue. This was thought to be partly responsible for an indifference to and distrust of absolute ideals. Students expressed wariness about religious conversion because it seemed to be based merely on an appeal to the emotions. In a tendency that had been observed first in Europe and later in most other parts of the federation world, postwar students were said to be at once idealistic and skeptical in their religious views. They could grant Christ an important place but were inclined to reject organized Christianity and to mistrust dogmatism and ready-made beliefs. Students after the war were more "pragmatic, experimental and subjective" and would no longer listen to "the dogmas and ways of expression of the older generation" with regard to Christian faith. Students wanted facts, not emotionalism. They wanted an interpretation of the gospel with intellectual credibility as well as spiritual reality. The spirit and message symbolized by the watchword simply did not appeal to the new generation of students.[41]

On the other hand, when students did turn definitely toward Christianity, they often chose, in these postwar years, "the most traditional forms of faith." According to de Dietrich, it was precisely because they lived in an atmosphere of religious, moral and intellectual relativism that students in the 1920s were struggling to find "positive certainty," an anchor to an unchangeable order (182). Though they were a distinct minority, some outstanding French students were reported to be turning to the neo-Thomist movement in Catholicism. Fundamentalism was popular among some students in America, and neo-Calvinism in Europe. All of these movements had in common a new emphasis on external authority and "the absolute." The fundamental articles of faith were removed from "individual caprice, from fluctuations of feeling," and from the vagaries of religious experience.[42]

A remarkable change in the attitude toward missions had taken place worldwide since the war, student leaders noted in the Denmark gathering. Everyone agreed that interest in missions among students had dropped sharply. The old spirit of missionary conquest was fast disappearing from the federation. Was there a loss of conviction for this founding principle of the WSCF or merely a change in how it was being expressed? Members of the commission on international and missionary questions could not agree. Some felt that the declining missionary interest was caused by indifference and doubt among students, a loss of faith, a spiritual bankruptcy. Others noted that students had a new kind of world interest and that this had led them, along with many missionary leaders, to question traditional missionary methods. A changed world situation called for new missionary approaches. Student interest in international and interracial questions could be seen as an expression of

Christian internationalism, if not of the traditional missionary spirit. Many members were not sorry to see students more interested in questions of international relations than in the traditional missionary work of the churches. The problems revealed by the war had to be addressed if the Christian message was to be proclaimed with integrity. Grave international and interracial problems demanded prompt and effective action if the Christian enterprise was to be justified at all. Could the work of missions demonstrate a Christianity robust enough to deal with the relations of nations and races—in short, a Christianity vigorous enough to address the problems that had led the world to war?

No longer limited to an individualistic mission of "snatching burning brands from the fire," the missionary witness of the church was now needed more than ever in the international arena to ensure that discussions did not stop with economics or politics. The missionary voice would push international bodies to a consideration of "fundamental questions of national and racial tradition and culture, the corporate mind and spirit of peoples" that lay behind economic and political issues. Federation members believed that the missionary movement could serve as a reminder that moral and spiritual issues were at the root of international conflicts and that Christianity held a uniquely adequate solution to such problems. Christian missions were believed to be making a particularly significant contribution, both intellectually and practically, toward the solution of the race problem.[43]

While the federation still recognized the obligation to evangelize, at a practical level there was a greater concern for unity. Conflict and divisions among Christians bred disloyalty to the missionary cause among students in the West and a barrier to the achievement of authentic indigenous expressions of Christianity in the mission lands. The federation seemed to be aware that its words about war could be consistent only if Christians were willing to deal with conflicts in their own ranks. At both the High Leigh (England) and Nyborg Strand (Denmark) meetings, the federation spoke of a Christian role in an emerging world society. "We believe it to be God's will that all those, in every race and nation, who know him through Jesus Christ, should be drawn together into a common fellowship of faith and service," they declared. They believed that after centuries of disruption and disunion there was "an ever growing desire to re-experience the life of the church universal as the soul and conscience of the world society."[44]

The war and its aftermath turned Christian students away from the prewar emphasis on evangelization and conquest and toward a concern for "true nationalism and internationalism." Misguided nationalism had led the world into war, J. H. Oldham, the editor of the *International Review of Missions,* wrote in an evaluation of the WSCF after the 1924 conference. The federation could provide a model community in which the world would see that differences between races and nations need not divide but could, like the differences between the sexes, "be complementary and a source of mutual enrichment."[45]

The federation's new ecumenical spirit had immediate echoes in its view of missionary methods. The desire to find common ground in situations of religious conflict applied not only to the relations among Christians in the West but also in the way Western churches related to the younger churches in mission lands. Already at the meeting in Denmark, the commission on international and missionary questions called for changes in missionary strategy that could soften the negative effects of Christian "denominationalism" in the mission field. In the missionary approach to other cultures, religious belief and practice should not be imposed from the outside but should be allowed to express the religious experience and "peculiar genius" of the given society. The missionary should come as a "co-seeker" for truth, expecting to find a new revelation of God from the encounter of that culture with Christ. The church could be at home in a new culture when it came in a spirit of friendship rather than condescension or control.[46]

Even though the federation was, during the years after the war, talking more about its relations with the churches, it still had no official connection with nor official representation from the churches. For the first two decades it had been a predominantly Protestant evangelical movement. As the federation grew, it came into contact with a variety of non-Protestant church bodies. Some leaders began to feel that the evangelical test was too restrictive. Some movements were already accepting students from any Christian church, including the Roman Catholic and Orthodox churches. Should not the federation acknowledge the new reality? North Americans like John Mott, conscious of the feelings of their more conservative Protestant supporters, were willing to liberalize the membership informally but did not want this reflected in written statements.[47]

Since its founding in 1895, the federation had struggled to find an acceptable basis of membership. Should it be a personal basis—what the individual student believed? Or should it be an evangelical basis—the student's membership in a Protestant church? The federation was never able to agree and maintained a fairly loose standard of membership that allowed for either personal or evangelical criteria, depending on the national situation. In the meantime, while the general committee continued its ongoing discussion of the criteria for membership, the constituent student movements placed less and less emphasis on membership or a membership test. After the war, the student movements came to include an increasing number of students who were seeking for faith but were not ready to declare themselves Christians. Many movement leaders feared that any kind of confession of faith would become a barrier to students who were "becoming Christians." By the time the WSCF was in a position to articulate a new definition of membership more mindful of the variety of churches from which its members came, campus practices rendered the two-decade-long discussion irrelevant. Virtually anyone could belong to the federation.[48]

Not everyone was happy with the changes in the federation and its affiliated movements. After the 1920 meeting of the federation in Switzerland, the Norwegian delegate—not a person of conservative views—expressed concern that some of the movements were "giving nearly their entire emphasis to the moral side and were ignoring the religious side of Christianity." A North American YMCA missionary observed in 1924 that student movements in both Europe and North America had "gone over to the extreme liberal wing, lock, stock, and barrel." The idea of definite decisions, of recruiting, of an enthusiastic pressing of the missionary enterprise as the most important thing in the world—all of this the liberals found "distasteful," he believed.[49]

Not all the criticism came from within the family. In 1922, Gerard Brom, a Dutch Catholic student worker, wrote a critique of the Protestant student movements associated with the WSCF. He observed that the existence of the federation was an indication of weakness in Protestantism. The federation "completed" the Protestant churches, Brom said. It was a movement that "must save itself by doing, with desperate heroism, what the Protestant churches either cannot or do not wish to do themselves," Brom wrote. Its lack of an "ecclesiastical foundation" was corrected in the short term by the warmth of its "personal piety." It would continue to be a strong movement as long as it could sustain its missionary enthusiasm. When its missionary force was spent, Brom predicted, the lack of ecclesiastical roots and the federation's vague religious basis would eventually undermine its apparent strength and unity.[50]

By the time the movement was thirty years old, an ecumenical agenda was taking the place of the earlier missionary enthusiasm. Avoiding the echoes of an imprialist era, the WSCF took as its watchword the pacific words of Jesus, *Ut omnes unum sint*—"That all may be one."[51] To a generation who had come of age in the brutal clash of empires, it was a watchword that reflected new priorities at home even as it intoned a gentler expression of Christian outreach to the non-Western world.

The federation was, of course, no more than the sum of its national member movements, and the bitter lessons of a world war had inclined this generation toward a message of reconciliation and ecumenism rather than one of spiritual conquest and evangelization. And the new humility that the war had brought to any discussion of the "heathen" was clearly in evidence. As WSCF members looked forward to a 1928 meeting in Mysore, India, they recognized the opportunity for "education throughout the federation concerning the spiritual heritage of India and its contemporaneous currents of life and thought." Such preparation for the Mysore conference would enable the federation to both contribute to the Christian cause in India and also "receive the great spiritual contribution India has to give."[52]

The changed watchword symbolized the new spirit of mission in the federation. It was a spirit congruent with the diversity of the postwar federation. The WSCF at age thirty was far less homogeneous than it had been in the years when Western students rallied around the old watchword. This diversity made it awkward to even talk about a one-sided crusade for world evangelization. There were new voices speaking new languages. It was time now for the West to listen rather than call the shots. In any case, the indigenous principle meant that wherever foreign missions succeeded, the local church must increase while the mission decreased. A lack of respect for the indigenous principle was beginning to have public consequences. Widespread sympathy for the anti-Christian movement in China illustrated just how vulnerable the church—and Christian organizations like the WSCF—were to the charge of imperialist aggression.

It was war, however, more than diversity or the church's association with capitalism, that had shattered the crusade to save the world. Crusades are called by old men sure of their cause and fought by the young with innocent ideals. The Great War had impugned the leadership of the elders and left the ideals of the young lying shattered on the battlefields of Europe. Had there been no war, the cry of the watchword would certainly have had to compete with the rising clamor of secularism. Its claims would have been no less sharply challenged by a rising nationalism in Asia and the new orthodoxies of science. Without war, the missionary appeal would have struggled to compete with the distractions of affluence. As it was, the shame of the war gave the watchword a certain air of hypocrisy that made it unpalatable, especially on the world stage of the federation. To the generation that fought the war, the watchword seemed to evoke images of an era whose crusades had brought the world not to salvation but to the brink of disaster. After the Great War, it was the ecumenical rather than the missionary vocation that occupied the attention of the World's Student Christian Federation.

Chapter Nine

Search for a New Crusade

Woe is me if I preach not this Social Gospel.
—Sherwood Eddy, 1927

The slogan of the last generation of students was "The evangelization of the world in this generation." I do not say that this new slogan is not also theirs, but in a particular sense our slogan must be,
"If any man would come after me, let him deny himself, take up his
cross and follow me."
—Reinhold Niebuhr, 1927

"The Student Volunteer Movement started with a group of five in my student days at Princeton," Robert Wilder recalled in a 1926 letter to a Swiss
missions leader. "We used to meet Sunday afternoons in the home of my
father who had been a missionary in India thirty years and then retired to
Princeton where he founded and was editing the *Missionary Review*. The
college men would discuss missions in one room, while Wilder's sister,
Grace, prayed in the next. Robert recalled that "for two and a half years
she and I prayed together night after night that the little beginning at
Princeton might become intercollegiate."

When Robert left for Dwight L. Moody's conference in the summer
of 1886, Grace said to him, "I believe that our prayers will be answered
at Mt. Hermon, and that the beginnings at Princeton will become intercollegiate at Mt. Hermon." Four weeks later, one hundred of the two
hundred and fifty delegates had signed the Princeton declaration card.
"This was the beginning of the Student Volunteer Movement," Wilder
wrote. "Since that beginning 11,218 student volunteers have gone from
Canada and the States to foreign lands as heralds of Christ. Three thousand four hundred and seventy-six have gone to China, among them one
of my daughters; two thousand one hundred and forty-nine have gone to

India and another daughter of mine is planning to go there as a missionary."[1]

Could the fervor of that crusade be rekindled? By the mid-1920s there were still some who believed it possible, in spite of many signs to the contrary. Forty years had passed since the founding of the SVM, and the world and the church had changed dramatically. The college associations, in a reflection of broader mainline Protestant trends, became more liberal, gradually losing interest in foreign missions. It became increasingly difficult to find student volunteers on the campuses. Missionaries were not so welcome in some countries as they had been before the war, and many Protestant churches were increasingly ambivalent about sending them, an ambivalence aggravated by mission revenues that declined sharply after an initial postwar peak. Churches, denominations, and mission organizations were being rocked by theological controversy, the aftershocks of which were often felt in campus organizations. But there was still hope in the student movement that the crusading spirit of the 1890s could be rekindled among postwar youth, and there were new campaigns calling students to a radical new gospel. Could the volunteer movement be reborn?

A Troubled Marriage

By the mid-1920s, there were growing tensions between the SVM and its traditional campus partner, the student associations—the YMCA and the YWCA. In 1921, the general secretary of the college associations had stated in his annual report to the WSCF that the Student Volunteer Movement did not exist on campus, at least not in theory. Within the local institution the individual volunteer, rather than any group or band, was the functional unit of the SVM.

This arrangement had been worked out between the associations and the SVM over the years as a way of defining their organizational symbiosis in the college or university setting. From 1889 it had been agreed that the SVM would be the missionary department of the college associations. The SVM would not become a separate organization competing with the campus associations. In exchange, the association would actively promote SVM literature and programs, including such off-campus events as regional SVM conferences and the quadrennial conventions, the only national Protestant student conference during that period. Because the SVM was a national movement without a local organizational expression on the campus, the arrangement benefited both parties. The associations depended on the SVM for their missionary education and recruiting policies, and the SVM had the advantage of association staff, buildings, campus programs, and administrative infrastructure, along with the visibility of being closely associated with the best-known Christian ministry program on American college campuses.

For three decades it had seemed an inspired partnership. Organizationally, however, it had always been a tense relationship that had worked because of one man, John R. Mott. Since its beginning, Mott had been the principal leader of the SVM, while also serving in key leadership roles in the YMCA's college work. He ensured that each organization continued to respect the other, both on the campus and in the respective national programs. He could make sure that conflicts between the organizations were talked out in such a way that philosophies and policies remained compatible. Mott had been the guarantor of the three-decade marriage between the SVM and the student associations.[2] But three changes took place during and after the war to challenge the harmony of the Y-SVM relationship.

Mott's Leadership

First, Mott's leadership roles changed, and he was no longer able to provide the personal leadership link between the two student movements. Mott had already, during the war, handed over the student association work to another when he assumed leadership for the national YMCA administration. Soon after the war, he also stepped down as chairman of the SVM and after that only rarely attended SVM executive committee meetings. It was no longer possible, because of the growth and evolution of the two organizations, for a single person to head both as Mott had done.

In the absence of unified leadership, conflicting understandings of the respective on-campus roles of the SVM and the YMCA soon became visible, and the YMCA also challenged the SVM's ownership of the quadrennial conventions (see chapter 7). In 1923 the college YMCA reported that "the student associations are now entirely responsible for the missionary program, since the present policy of the volunteer movement and the local practice in most institutions is that local members of the volunteer movement shall express their missionary interest through the regular campus organizations rather than as a separate movement." The SVM report the same year acknowledged the traditional principle that the unit of membership on the campus was the individual volunteer.

Wilder then went on to report, however, that "in institutions where there are sufficient numbers of volunteers to group together, a band is usually formed." Wilder reported that there were bands functioning in 342 institutions, nearly half the number of campuses covered by the college YMCA program, with bands in the process of formation on another 250 campuses. Even before the Indianapolis convention, the SVM was working aggressively to make itself less dependent on the associations, even as the YMCA was asserting its control of the missionary program on campus.[3]

New Campus Ministries

The SVM's effort to establish a more autonomous campus presence in the years after the war was related to a second major change in the relationship between the volunteer movement and the student associations. The YMCA began to lose its position as the sole, or even dominant, Christian organization on the American college campus. After the war, the number of Americans in colleges and universities increased dramatically, doubling in the decade after Versailles. During the same period of time, membership in the college associations peaked in 1921 (at ninety-four thousand members) and then began a long and steady decline. In 1920 there were college associations actively promoting SVM activities on more than 70 percent of the American college and university campuses. By 1930, associations were present on less than half of the campuses (see fig. 9.1). But these numbers do not tell the full story of the decline of the YMCA on the American college campus. In 1920, the YMCA was still, on many campuses, the dominant Christian organization, if not still the only one. By 1930 the college association typically found itself one of a dozen religious agencies working among students. Most were denominational, but some were new interdenominational organizations like the YMCAs.[4]

As the student associations were losing their dominance on the American college campus, the SVM faced the prospect of either being part of the YMCA's decline or cutting itself loose from the associations and forging new relations with the growing number of new campus ministries. Wilder, the founding father, favored greater independence. He had always conceived the SVM as a specialized missionary organization whose alliance with the Y was incidental to its real purpose. That relationship could be changed if the times required. But the SVM had no formal ties with the emerging denominational ministries on campus or with

Figure 9.1

The Decline of the College YMCA, 1920-1930

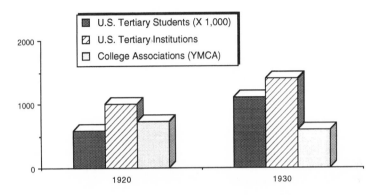

Data from C. Howard Hopkins, *History of the YMCA in North America* (New York, 1951), p. 646.

the new interdenominational ministries that were beginning to challenge the exclusive hegemony of the Y on many campuses. The corporate habits of three decades made it difficult for the SVM to look elsewhere for guidance as to its campus presence. How could the SVM build new alliances? The YMCA and YWCA were the only campus organizations represented on the SVM executive committee. A major restructuring of the SVM would have been required to give voice to the large variety of campus ministries that had emerged since the turn of the century.

Toward the end of the decade there was talk of a united Student Christian Movement and in the 1930s it was vigorously pursued. Had it materialized earlier, it would have both simplified and complicated things for the SVM. A united movement might have made it easier for the volunteer movement to expand its relations beyond the college associations to the growing variety of student organizations. But the loss of the special relationship with the college association movement would have required a new approach to organizing students on campus, new communication networks, and new concepts of student movement representation in SVM decision making. By the time the associations and the SVM were ready to consider such a new entity, the variety of Christian organizations represented on American college campuses and the deepening differences among them made such a united effort impossible.[5]

The YMCA and Missions

A third change in the SVM's relations to the student associations had to do with a shift in the YMCA's attitude toward missions. In spite of vigorous efforts by men like Mott and Speer, the fifteen years after the war saw what Hopkins called "the repudiation of the evangelical position by the American YMCAs." Missions and Bible study groups declined sharply. American leaders who attended a YMCA conference in Europe in 1926, finding it difficult to understand the attitude of the German delegates toward religion, concluded that it was because their approach was more theological, that of the Americans more psychological. Until the war, the YMCA had always maintained a balance between conservative and innovative Christian influences in the movement. After the war, the YMCA movement found its platforms and publications increasingly dominated by liberals. In this, the YMCA followed a broader trend in mainline Protestantism in the 1920s.[6]

Campus leaders attempted to counter declining enrollments in campus Bible classes by experimenting with new approaches. After the war, Bruce Curry combined the traditional, text-centered approach with a more inductive, experience-oriented method of Bible study that he had developed in his work with soldiers. But with students after the war, as with soldiers during the war, there seemed to be little interest in the Bible. In his attempt to relate Scripture to the postwar student, Curry refined his Bible study method still further. Students needed to uncover the "mind and method" of Jesus so they could apply his principles to the problems of contemporary life. The method of Jesus, Curry thought, was reason, goodwill, and nonresistance, and discussion was the "crucible in which both the new and the old ways must be tested." As Curry probed the mind of Jesus in his studies for students, he began to see Jesus as a revolutionary—some might even call him a Communist. And he called for "radicals according to Jesus."[7]

By 1923, Dwight D. Rugh, the student secretary of the college YMCA, could report that most thoughtful association members tended to side with "the truth-seeking processes of science." Since the war, the natural tension between science and religion had been aggravated by the Fundamentalist movement, Rugh said. Fundamentalist attacks on professors and ministers who were admired by students and widely used by the YMCA had caused some of these leaders to lose their jobs. The campus associations were attempting to address the spiritual and intellectual confusion created among students by the Fundamentalist-Modernist controversy, but it was not difficult to tell on which side their sympathies lay. The student associations were in the vanguard in the YMCA's move from a more traditional evangelical approach to one identified solidly with the liberal point of view.

The missionary appeal, the life blood of the SVM, was based on a traditional, and by now conservative, reading of Scripture. By the mid-1920s the SVM was caught between the liberal inclinations of YMCA leaders and association members and the more conservative cast of mission board leaders and of the students who were still volunteering for missionary service. "I believe there is more danger of our movement's losing conservative volunteers than liberal volunteers," Wilder wrote in 1925 to Fay Campbell, of the Yale association. In several schools volunteers had dropped out of the SVM because they believed it had become too liberal theologically. But Wilder was not aware of a single case in which students had left the movement because it was too conservative.[8]

Because of pressure on the SVM from both sides, the movement felt compelled to hold more firmly to its traditional policy of avoiding theological discussion. The leaders believed that the SVM could avoid the polarities of the Fundamentialist-Modernist conflict if they stuck to their last, providing the colleges "a deeply spiritual contribution" free of theological bias. The SVM was caught in a dilemma without a happy medium. It was losing touch with liberal Christian students because the missionary cause was too conservative and restrictive on the social question. Conservative volunteers, on the other hand, were threatening to leave the movement because of its close relations with liberal Protestant churches and the YMCA. "We can continue to hold the allegiance of these volunteers if we continue to render the colleges a deeply spiritual contribution," Wilder wrote to Campbell, "and if we avoid theological discussions."

Increasingly uncomfortable with a postwar YMCA that was losing its appetite for foreign missions, the SVM nevertheless found it difficult to turn its back on the old relationships. The lively struggle between the student YMCA and the SVM over the control of missionary policy, however, did lead after Indianapolis to the articulation of a new campus strategy for the SVM. As a specialized agency, the SVM would work through any general student Christian organization, either interdenominational or denominational, that shared its interests in missions. Wilder quoted

Speer as saying, at the Indianapolis convention, that when unity was
sought at the expense of specialization, the cause of foreign missions suffered. Although Wilder did not say so explicitly, the issue of unity with
which he was concerned had to do with the SVM's relationship with the
Y. In his challenge to the SVM to work with any Christian agency on
campus that shared its vision, Wilder was challenging the YMCA's exclusive sponsorship of the SVM. Wilder was calling for independence.[9]

Attractive as the possibility of independence may have seemed to
Wilder, it was sharply vetoed by a special self-study commissioned by
the SVM in 1925.[10] The volunteer movement "should continue to direct
its own policies and programs as in the past," the Commission of Ten
recommended, but "there should be a closer correlation of its work to the
work of the general organizations at work in the student field." The report was clear on just which general organizations were meant. The
SVM was not, nor should it become, "a duplicate or rival of the Student
Christian Associations." The SVM was related to the associations "not
as a coordinate organization but as a supplementary movement, free and
uncontrolled but not independent; separate but correlated in one comprehensive task."[11]

The commission statement did little to resolve the inherent tensions
between the SVM and the college associations. They firmly squelched
any possible efforts for SVM independence on Wilder's part, however,
by recommending that an "understudy" be appointed to work with
Wilder, in preparation for his "inevitable" retirement. How far Wilder
might have been willing to go in his declaration of independence from
the college associations never became clear. In less than two years after
the Commission of Ten delivered its recommendations, Wilder handed
the leadership of the SVM to Jesse R. Wilson, a young volunteer who
was recalled from a Baptist missionary assignment in Japan to take the
headquarters position.[12]

The End of Foreign Missions?

The college associations gave the SVM its primary link to the campus.
The Protestant mission boards were the volunteer movement's link to the
mission field. In the mainline denominations, the outlook for the SVM
was hardly more promising than with the campus associations. Traditional missionary motives were being openly challenged. Liberal Protestants were changing their minds about the divine judgment that had always stirred the consciences of the complacent. "No longer does the

missionary abroad or the church at home believe that every heathen soul is doomed to everlasting fire," wrote a Protestant leader in 1925. "And thereby is lost what was once a powerful motive for missionary work." As for the urgency of the missionary task, William E. Barton said bluntly, "Jesus is not coming in the flesh, now or ever. The world is not near its end." Any missionary message based on the expectation of Christ's return was mistaken, even if sincere. So why missions at all? The missionary motive, Barton thought, was really no different from that of America's international merchants. The Chinese had a bean oil that served them well before Standard Oil began marketing petroleum fuel in China. "But America had a better oil that gave a better light at less waste of human life and eyesight, and America has the goods and the enterprise to seek a market for her superior products." It was the same with religion. "We have a better religion than the people of China or India," said Barton. "And they need it. Yes, and we need the foreign market for the gospel."[13]

While missionary motivation was being battered—and bartered—by Protestant leaders, the missionary enterprise for which the volunteer movement existed was not getting good press. Tyler Dennett, after an exhaustive review of missionary and diplomatic literature, handed down the verdict that missionaries were often accomplices to imperialism. "It is very difficult," he said, "for an American missionary to resist the conclusion that if only the stars and stripes could be raised over the land of his labors the kingdom of God would thereby be greatly advanced." Dennett argued that Christian missions were "uniformly devastating to the social unity of the people where the missionary makes his converts." In this weakened condition, Dennett believed, the nation or the people were vulnerable to imperialist exploitation.[14]

Not all liberal commentators were negative about missions. China missionary Paul Hutchinson said that the clearest evidence of the church's formative role in the modern world was not in the home churches but in its work abroad. "Its foreign missionary enterprise is the contribution of the Western church in the nineteenth and twentieth centuries to the making of the twenty-first," he wrote in a 1923 article for the *Atlantic Monthly*. Christian missions had not been a failure. If the growth of the church continued at the current rate in India, Hutchinson said, "within one hundred and twenty-five years that empire will be at least nominally Christian." And that would be less time than it took to win the Roman Empire.

Even though missionary work had been well done in the more distant past, Hutchinson was inclined to agree with Tyler Dennett's findings about missions and imperialism during the recent period of missionary history. Hutchinson said that if the West remembered Sir John Bowring at all, it would be as the man who wrote

> In the cross of Christ I glory
> Towering o'er the wrecks of time.

"But the East remembers him as the indefatigable diplomat whose labors contributed so much to the legalization of the opium traffic in China," Hutchinson said. The international sins of Christian nations—political injustice, economic exploitation, racial discrimination, and material standards of success—would have to be addressed if the missionary enterprise was to have integrity in the future. And dealing with these sins would require "an entire change of missionary method," Hutchinson concluded. Although he was vague as to how this new missionary approach would actually work, Hutchinson said it would "locate, describe, and checkmate" international sins, even as they were being committed, and "without regard to nationalistic fetishes." The best example he could give of the new kind of missionary needed was Sherwood Eddy, who was now, after the war, "preaching international conversion to international sinners."[15]

Amidst all the flak, there were still some well-argued defenses of foreign missions from young volunteers. In 1926, Indianapolis convention vice chairman Walter H. Judd, now a medical missionary in China, wrote an article for the *Student Volunteer Movement Bulletin* entitled "Why Leave Non-Christian America for the Orient?" Medical doctor Judd admitted that ten years earlier, Western civilization and Christianity had been practically synonymous for him. The war had changed all that. "If the foreign missionary enterprise is a hopeless one until after a clean-up in America has been completed," Judd wrote, "I surely did not want to throw my life away by going abroad!" The foreign missionary's purpose was really no different from that of any other genuine Christian: to help bring the kingdom of God on earth. "He has gone to work in a foreign land because it is his personal conviction that in that particular place he can best work out this primary purpose," Judd said. The missionary respects the ideas and customs of the people with whom he works, because he knows that they already have many "fruits of the spirit"—more, in fact, than Christians in the West. They have much light, Judd thought, but not yet enough, not until they have learned Christ—"not an eastern or a Western but a *world* Christ."

The reasons behind his original decision to become a missionary seemed to provide justification for his going to China, even under the changed conditions of the postwar world, Judd thought. He felt obligated to go where the needs that he could meet were the greatest and the workers the fewest. The examples of Jesus and Paul compelled him to go. Finally, Judd recalled an illustration that Robert Wilder had given. "Suppose Jesus, the afternoon he fed the multitude on the hillside, had distributed food to the people in the first five rows, and some of them—perhaps even three-fourths of them—had refused to eat. Would he have been justified in spending the rest of the afternoon and evening in trying to persuade those folks that they needed the food and ought to eat it, while he allowed the back rows to go hungry?"

But there were new reasons for leaving non-Christian America for the Orient. Judd was convinced that most of the problems of the West could not be solved unilaterally; international solutions were needed. And that, he thought, was strong justification for "foreign missions of the right sort." On the religious side, the West desperately needed to rediscover how to live the principles of Jesus' religion, and Judd believed that such a rediscovery was most likely to come with help from the Oriental peoples. Western peoples had learned Christ's religion wrongly—or at least poorly. The West had been so long inoculated with a mild form of Christianity that it was practically immune to the real thing. "The great genius of the Oriental peoples is their mysticism," Judd wrote, "their lofty meditation, the depth of their spiritual natures, their intense devotion to the things that they see in vision and that capture their imaginations and loyalties." These gifts, he thought, could bring renewal to Christianity in America and the West. And so a mission to China was also a mission to America![16]

For missionaries and missions advocates like Hutchinson and Judd, the postwar world required a blurring of the borders between the home base and the field. That was a common theme in the Protestant churches that were the volunteer movement's primary constituency. In 1924, the *Christian Century* proclaimed "the end of foreign missions." It was no longer possible, said the editor, to discriminate between "what is to be done 'over there' and what is to be done in other places. The forces that hold back the advance of the kingdom of heaven in Peking and Calcutta and Cairo and Elizabethtown today are not only, nor chiefly, the sins of Peking and Calcutta and Cairo and Elizabethtown. They are as likely to be the sins of Philadelphia and Cleveland and Chicago and Los Angeles." Any distinction between "home" and "foreign" missions was artificial, the editor said, and would "undermine the effectiveness of our total impact."[17]

These could not have been comforting words for a movement dedicated to foreign missions, a movement that had been stoutly resisting efforts to have its mandate enlarged to include recruiting for work at home as well as abroad. There were, to be sure, other voices, more conservative ones. But these, too, often provided slight consolation for the SVM in a time of theological polarization.

Two months after writing his recollections of the SVM's beginnings, Wilder received a letter from a pastor in London, giving him details of the China Inland Mission's decision to withdraw from the British Council of Churches. The last straw for the China Inland Mission had been an article in the official council publication in which Lenin was favorably compared to Jesus. The pastor of St. Paul's (Portman Square) went on to report on the rapid growth of the new Inter-Varsity Movement in Great Britain, largely under the leadership of medical students. If the movement was narrow-minded and ultraconservative and "despised by the leaders of the SCM," it was nonetheless, he believed, a movement of the Spirit and "an unmistakable indication of the swing-back from the unsatisfying and religious generalities of the SCM to the assurances and inspirations of the gospel."[18]

In the United States as in Great Britain, not all students were in step with the new generation. Ruth D. Bailey, a Moody Bible Institute student who had attended the Indianapolis convention, criticized the convention's preoccupation with racism and war. Although these issues were important, Bailey thought them to be wide of the mark set by the watchword. The younger generation wanted to alleviate human suffering by better laws, education, and social reform. "In our optimism we would forget that man is sinful and needs a savior," she wrote, "and that unless men's hearts are changed, other methods fail, no matter how good they may be in themselves." Bailey believed that the new generation would fail in its contribution to world evangelization unless there was a God-inspired return to spiritual understanding of the original leaders of the Student Volunteer Movement. With a new vision of the world and of Christ's saving power, she believed the current generation of students would gladly obey the Great Commission.[19]

By the mid-1920s, conservative students like Bailey were already leaving the volunteer movement. By the end of 1927, the Moody Bible Institute, home of the SVM's first office, was talking about leaving the movement, founded under Dwight L. Moody's patronage, because the

SVM had become too liberal. The SVM executive committee tried to convince institute leaders to change their mind. "We need their point of view decidedly," Fay Campbell wrote to the new general secretary, Jesse R. Wilson. "In fact it would be nothing short of a major tragedy if they were to pull out of the movement now and take with them some of our more conservative group. If there is anything clear about the Modernist movement it is that it lacks some of the great qualities of conservatism. If we had to choose between liberalism and conservatism, I think I should have to join with the Moody group. We cannot afford to lose their convictions and passion for missions from the heart of the movement."[20]

In spite of the efforts of a special committee appointed to try to keep it in the movement, the conservative and nationally influential Moody Bible Institute quietly left. Even after the Moody defection, Wilson was hopeful that the volunteer movement would benefit from a revival of interest among conservative groups and the growing momentum of the "faith mission" societies. These new mission societies, modeled after the China Inland Mission (founded in 1865), involved missionaries directly in the fund-raising process. This had the effect of shifting the financing and administrative control of the society away from denominational structures and into the hands of an independent board. Faith missions could be interdenominational, like the China Inland Mission, or denominational, like the Christian and Missionary Alliance. These faith societies, with their autonomy and a specialized focus on foreign missions, resisted liberal trends that were sapping missionary enthusiasm in the mainline Protestant agencies. By the 1940s, the faith mission boards, together with the more conservative denominational societies, were sending more missionaries abroad than the mainline Protestant societies.

But the SVM was never quite able to fall in step with the new missionary troops. Wilder had tried discreetly to distance the SVM from the YMCA in order to cultivate relations with a wider range of campus groups. But the association bond was too strong to be broken in the crucial postwar years, when new theological alliances were being formed. The SVM policy of avoiding theological discussion did prevent serious theological controversy in the movement, but it had the effect of casting doubt on the SVM's theological loyalties among precisely those churches that would be providing the majority of missionary recruits in the decades ahead. By trying to remain theologically neutral, the volunteer movement forfeited the opportunity to forge new links with the groups that still had sympathy for the watchword and would carry the torch of Protestant foreign missions in the twentieth century.

In the years after the war, the SVM was the subject of a never-ending series of commissions, appointed by the leaders of the movement in an attempt to recapture or reinterpret the old missionary enthusiasm. In the 1930s a new study of the missionary movement appeared, and it included a section on the SVM. The *Laymen's Foreign Missions Inquiry* was one of the many research projects in the period between the two world wars that flourished because of the largesse of John D. Rockefeller Jr. and the considerable research assets of the Interchurch World Movement that he managed to acquire when the movement went bankrupt in 1920. The *Laymen's Report,* as it was popularly known, was as controversial as it was inconclusive. In its multiple volumes it had something for everyone, including some findings for the SVM. The volume that dealt with home base and missionary personnel showed that the Student Volunteer Movement's ability to recruit missionary candidates for the major Protestant boards was declining. In 1918, the volunteer movement had provided 58 percent of the missionaries sailing with these agencies. By 1930, only 32 percent of those sailing were volunteers (see table 9.1).

The *Laymen's Report* also pointed out that the SVM's influence on secular American campuses—"representative centers of American culture"—had declined sharply since the war. The rate of decline was greatest at public universities in the Midwest, while the West Coast institutions had actually increased their share of total sailed volunteers during the first half of the 1920s. The results of the study of volunteers from thirty prominent colleges and universities across the country showed that these schools were providing only half as many sailed volunteers—when taken as a percentage of the total—as they had before the war.[21]

Smaller church colleges had long been the primary source of missionary candidates, and board representatives indicated that these denominational schools were still furnishing a high percentage of the missionaries that they were sending abroad after the war. As to the question of the quality of missionary candidates, mission board spokespersons were near unanimous in saying that the postwar recruits were usually above average and often among the best the colleges had to offer. One leader thought that "not so large a percentage of the highest grade of graduates are now going into Christian service as in former years." On the other hand, a leader from a closely related denomination said that "it is far harder to enter our foreign mission service than to enter West Point or Annapolis" (25–33).

The *Laymen's Report* suggested three reasons for the declining interest in foreign missions among students:

Table 9.1

Declining Influence of the SVM

Year	New Student Volunteers Enlisted	New Missionaries Sailing	Student Volunteers among New Missionaries Sailing	Percentage of Student Volunteers among New Missionaries Sailing
1917	1,376	673	384	57.1
1918	1,413	614	356	58.0
1919	1,789	895	473	52.8
1920	2,783	1,731	595	34.4
1921	2,318	1,620	637	39.3
1922	2,009	1,125	466	41.5
1923	1,471	1,109	527	47.5
1924	1,292	1,052	440	41.8
1925	764	936	406	43.4
1926	506	728	313	43.0
1927	388	558	229	41.0
1928	252	667	269	40.3
1929	570	827	263	31.8
1930	465	713	233	32.7

From *Home Base and Missionary Personnel*, Vol. 7 of the *Laymen's Report*, p. 17.

1. *Uncertainty as to the future of the foreign missionary enterprise.* Some students had been led to believe that the day of foreign missions was past. Others questioned whether the boards would have the financial resources to send them out, even if they volunteered and prepared for missionary service.

2. *Lack of religious conviction.* Many students were uncertain as to their Christian message and had only a vague concept as to the uniqueness of the Christian message. This was attributed in part to a superficial study of comparative religion in the colleges.

3. *Effectiveness of missionary service.* Students were seriously questioning whether they could make their greatest Christian contribution to their generation "through foreign missionary service." There were many new options for international service providing attractive alternatives to traditional missionary work (8–9).

A denominational study of motivation for Christian service in the early 1930s indicated a marked decline in the number of workers who felt a "distinct call from God" as the primary motive for their missionary career. Among senior (three-term) missionaries, 75 percent said God's call was responsible for their decision to serve abroad, while only 25 percent of the younger (one-term) workers gave that reason. The younger missionaries (86 percent) were drawn by the relatively greater need of the foreign field. Two-thirds of missionaries in the field surveyed said that they would remain in the field even if they were offered an attractive position in Christian service at home. Eighty-five percent of the foreign workers said, without qualification, that they would be glad to have one of their children become a missionary.[22]

In spite of such high levels of missionary motivation, by the end of the 1920s foreign mission work in the more liberal denominations was beginning a decline that would continue for most of the century to follow. Representatives of Episcopal, Methodist, and Presbyterian mission boards were beginning, in the early 1930s, to lose their enthusiasm for the SVM. By 1939, Methodist leader H. D. Bollinger stated bluntly that "the SVM is a thing of the past and those who are charged with the responsibility of perpetuating it should realize this fact."[23] The conservatives were still volunteering briskly for traditional missionary service but were increasingly deserting the SVM for safer denominational organizations or for the new interdenominational Student Foreign Missions Fellowship that was founded in 1936. Volunteer bands, once found on the most prestigious college campuses, were by the mid-1930s most often found on small, rural campuses.

The latter half of the 1920s was a difficult time for the volunteer movement. Liberal students did not become volunteers because the foreign missionary cause—or at least the volunteer pledge—no longer appealed to them. Conservative volunteers left the movement because of its "liberal associations." Mainline Protestant churches and even mission boards wondered if the SVM was still needed. And always there were financial difficulties. Meanwhile, in Europe and Australia volunteer movement branches were growing weaker and disappearing. It was time to try something new.

The Search for a New Crusade

With foreign missions losing its old appeal, there were attempts to find a new crusade that could unify the postwar generation of Christian students.

One was an effort to give radical new social content to the old evangelistic campaigns that had been a cornerstone of the association and SVM programs. The second was an attempt, in the first non-SVM national convention, to spark a new movement for social reform that would be a reincarnation of the Mount Hermon Hundred (the students who, in 1886, began the SVM by signing a commitment to become missionaries at a summer conference in Northfield, Massachusetts).

One of the "big four" leaders was able to adjust to the new era of student YMCA work. Three months after the Indianapolis convention, George Sherwood Eddy reported on a meeting in Iowa attended by fifteen hundred church and college representatives. "Before the war I preached a personal gospel," Eddy wrote. "At the close of the war I swung over to the Social Gospel. Today I find the need of presenting a whole gospel, one message integrated, that has both a personal and social application, passionately concerned with the saving of the individual and equally concerned in the application of the gospel to social justice."[24]

Eddy reported on similar meetings at Northwestern College and Northwestern University, with students crowding in large halls to hear Eddy's social challenge. Eddy found "a powerful sentiment against war spreading through the colleges. It is gaining headway as truly as the Abolitionist movement against slavery did a generation ago in these same colleges." At the University of Wisconsin, Eddy dined with "a hundred leading faculty members" before addressing a series of official university convocations, the attendance at which grew from twelve hundred to fifteen hundred. Eddy reported that as many as five hundred students stayed after the meetings for questions. "They continued on the last two nights until after ten and eleven o'clock when the lights in the building were put out." Before the lights were turned off, the students told Eddy, "We'll not go home till morning." American colleges were "wide open," and Eddy saw possibilities for "greater works than these" as he headed east for campaigns at Princeton and the University of Pennsylvania before going on to Harvard and the New England colleges.

A month later Eddy was at the University of Missouri. The auditorium was packed with eighteen hundred people at the opening Sunday night rally. "We began at once by applying Christian principles as the only solution of the industrial, racial, and war problems," Eddy reported in a letter to his brother. "When I spoke on the race question, some began to squirm, and one prominent man walked out." Eddy later learned that this community had recently witnessed the lynching of a Negro for an alleged crime—"without masks, by the will of some of the leading citizens, without allowing anyone to be punished for the deed and without protest from the citizens, clubs, and most of the churches." The next morning, Eddy publicly attacked the Ku Klux Klan, which was reported to have a strong local organization. He charged the entire community with responsibility for the act and asked "how many churches or individuals present had protested or taken any action against it."

In the evening, in a lecture titled "The Faith of Honest Doubt," Eddy outlined five fundamentals on which Christians could agree. Over five hundred students stayed behind to ask questions about Eddy's support for the League of Nations as well as his own personal faith. Students were also concerned about such issues as the relationship between science and the Bible, eternal punishment, war and how it might be abolished, and racism and interracial marriage.[25] Speaking to audiences that were sometimes standing-room-only and whose numbers never fell below eighteen hundred, Eddy finished the week at Missouri with a Social Gospel "altar call." More than two hundred men and one hundred women students signed the decision cards. Student discussion groups were being organized as Eddy left Missouri for the Universities of Colorado, Wyoming, and Nebraska.

"The conversion of Sherwood Eddy into a Social Gospel advocate," Hopkins wrote, "made him a far more influential leader on the American campus than he had been earlier." But his advocacy of missions was less decisive than before. He became deeply involved in helping students to understand the social implications of the gospel at home, to learn how to Christianize the American social order. He devoted less time to the recruiting of ambassadors for the missionary program, and his growing discomfort with capitalism led him in 1922 to give up his extensive fundraising efforts for YMCA missionary work among wealthy Americans. A liberal who by the end of the 1920s was calling himself a socialist, Eddy largely abandoned the traditional approaches to evangelization. A new social order needed to be built at home, and Americans should learn to understand the world before they could hope to evangelize it. More radical than many in the YMCA, his "pilgrimage of ideas" was not unrepresentative of postwar student association thinking.[26]

Eddy's new social and political opinions did not sit well with some of the YMCA's wealthy supporters. One took time to write to John Mott about Eddy's comments at the Indianapolis convention on the distribution of wealth in America. "While I have noticed a tendency on the part of Dr. Eddy lately to discuss social and industrial questions which are, in my judgment, outside the province of the YMCA," he wrote, "I confess I was very much surprised when I read this statement which reads like the utterances of a soapbox agitator or a communist orator. I have always been a great admirer of Dr. Eddy, and esteemed him to be too level-headed to indulge in such claptrap, and I sincerely regret that he has allowed himself to give utterance to such misleading statements as are contained in this extract."[27]

On the other hand, James N. Gamble, of Procter and Gamble, wrote to YMCA leaders in 1922 expressing interest in Eddy's evangelistic campaigns in Asia, Europe, and America. Because they were, he thought, "a most efficient and desirable enterprise for the advancement of Christianity and the welfare of mankind," Gamble gave one hundred shares of Procter and Gamble stock in support of Eddy's work with students.

Eddy refused to soft-pedal his views, even though they generated a lively controversy for the American YMCA. At one point, eager not to rock the YMCA's financial boat, Eddy tendered his resignation to the international committee of the YMCA. The committee did not accept it but instead found ways of using his considerable prowess in communicating with students without alienating the business community that had long been the financial lifeblood of the association movement.[28]

Meanwhile, the college associations were trying to follow American students in a topsy-turvy world where many of the old landmarks had disappeared. Dissatisfied with the SVM's determination to maintain its focus on foreign missionary service at a time when students were more concerned with problems at home, the associations decided after Indianapolis to have their own national convention. In 1926 (three years after the Indianapolis convention) some two thousand five hundred students and leaders gathered in Milwaukee, Wisconsin, in the first National Student Conference.

There was a new watchword—*Ut omnes unum sint* (That all may be one)—and a traditional SVM convention meeting time—the turn of the year. Although there were echoes of the SVM tradition, the new national conference was in tune with the times. Its addresses were built around a Social Gospel focus on the fatherhood of God, and the conference process was an attempt to demonstrate "the spiritual and moral effectiveness of a self-directed student movement." At a time when some students felt the democratic ideal being stifled in American life, the Milwaukee conference deliberately limited plenary addresses in order to give more time for formal and informal discussions among the delegates. Conference leaders took some pride in pointing out that, unlike the two postwar SVM conventions, the Milwaukee conference produced little or no conflict between the conference managers and the delegates.[29]

Reinhold Niebuhr, one of the emerging new leaders in the student movement, spoke about the problem of unbelief. The real enemy of religion, he said, was not skepticism but cynicism. "Our real difficulties are not intellectual difficulties but moral difficulties," he said. "The question is not whether God is intellectually worthy of us, but whether we are morally worthy of God. The question is not whether we can harmonize the concept of a loving God with a ruthless nature, but whether we can harmonize the concept of a loving God with a sort of ruthless civilization which we have built."[30]

American civilization was in some respects the most unethical that the world had ever known, Niebuhr said. Whatever the historical reasons for its being unethical, American society was replacing true religion with a worship of power, comfort, and the nation itself. New York City had just announced the construction of the highest building in the world—eighty-five floors, with forty floors of garage space, all done in the finest Gothic architecture. It was Titanism, Niebuhr thought, "modern civilization preening itself with standards of another age that it did not develop and cannot altogether understand." In the search for physical comfort, America was becoming obsessed with the sensual, the sexual. But the worship of power and comfort was surpassed by the supreme religion of modern people, nationalism.

Christianity was always being born in the college world because students were intelligent enough to be ethical, Niebuhr said. Christianity was always dying on campus because intelligent people became sophisticated. In his distinctive appeal to paradox, Niebuhr told the college students that they needed a critical intelligence, simplemindedness, and the courage to detach themselves from the world. The preceding student generation received its spiritual power from "the great adventure of foreign missions. It was willing to expatriate itself from America in order to build the kingdom of God in the far ends of the earth." But the new student generation faced the dual challenge of evangelizing the nominally non-Christian world and evangelizing the world of nominal Christians. Western civilization had now become a missionary territory.

The slogan of the last generation of students had been "The evangelization of the world in this generation," Niebuhr concluded. The new generation of students must find its slogan in the words of Jesus: "If anyone would come after me, let him deny himself, take up his cross and follow me" (20–21).

A black YMCA leader saw what Niebuhr described as the "missionary adventure" in terms of economic exploitation and political domination. American Christianity had been feeding for the past fifty years "on the enthusiasm and faith and religious experience of missionaries," Mordecai Johnson said, while the faith of American Christians was being kept alive "with continuous hypodermics of apologetics." The major effort for this generation of American Christians must be to capture the national will through "a deliberate and thoroughgoing attempt to emancipate and enlist the Negro in the Christian cause." In 1927 there were twelve million black Americans who were candidates for "somebody's army." Would they become "soldiers in the army of economic and political imperialism, fighting to subdue the world to the United States of America?" Johnson asked. "Or are they going to be soldiers of Christ in the Christian army?" The United States needed a Christian foreign policy toward persons of color, including a commitment to make the League of Nations work. Johnson called for a program of "non-violent non-cooperation" with the imperialistic elements of American life. The state should never be seen as an end in itself, and if moral principle demanded, "the church could absolve the allegiance of its members from the state." Johnson was pleased that, in spite of popular sentiment to the contrary, there was a growing body of American Christians who would not fight in "an imperialistic war."[31]

Timothy T. Lew, a Chinese Christian, had been asked to speak on "how the world has failed to believe in Christ and in his conception of God, the Father of all." He chose instead to speak on how Christians make it difficult for the world to believe in Christ. The failure of Christians to practice what they preach was certainly the largest obstacle to faith. "To us Chinese, Christianity appears to be the most talkative religion," Lew said. When Christians did act—performing the deeds of love and compassion for which missionaries were rightly credited—they failed to provide a program of "thoroughgoing transformation of the nation." Chinese critics did not object to what Christians had done. They insisted that Christians had not done enough. "They have watched as far as we have gone," Lew said, "and they insist that we shall go farther—go the full length of the teachings of Jesus in whom we profess to believe." A third obstacle to belief in Jesus was the sense of superiority with which the "white man's burden" was discharged. "The world is spiritually bleeding today because of the imperialism of the Christian nations," Lew said. How could "loyal Chinese citizens ever forget that China once lost practically all of her most important and valuable harbors to four different Christian powers because of the death of two missionaries?" Chinese people were puzzled, Lew said in his final point, by the innumerable divisions in the Christian church and the lack of tolerance and forgiveness in the West over certain religious issues. "China cries out for a Savior, and the world is waiting in patience with a passionate longing," Lew said in a concluding challenge to the students. "It is said that Christ has come. You and your forefathers have worshiped him for centuries. Have you found him yourselves? Do you understand him?"[32]

By the mid-1920s, the YMCA had developed a radical, crusading spirit. One of the purposes of the campus associations articulated by a 1923 conference of college secretaries was "[to make] revolutionary Christians by stimulating thinking on international, social, industrial, and missionary subjects." Some YMCA secretaries judged the Indianapolis convention to have been successful because it had led participants to voice outspoken objections to military training. These in turn had led to an official reprimand for some students, the expulsion of others, and a request for the resignation of several college YMCA secretaries. In one area of the country alone, five senior YMCA leaders had been fired in 1924 because of their radical views on race relations and ROTC training. The goal of many college secretaries came to be expressed in the statement, "If I can develop one revolutionary Christian this year, I will be satisfied."[33]

One of the major, if unofficial, purposes of the Milwaukee conference was "to furnish spiritual resources for 'tired radicals' " (177). But there was a grander goal. Many association leaders had been planning and praying that this meeting would become another Mount Hermon. They hoped that out of this gathering would emerge "a group of students who, in the realms of economic, racial, international, political, and social relations, would do a work comparable with the achievements of the leaders of the Student Volunteer Movement and the world-wide missionary enterprise in the previous generation." Speakers like Niebuhr and Lew had eloquently described the needs of the postwar world. Johnson had begun sketching the outlines of the crusade to which Christian students in this generation were being called. "You may spend your lives as cannon fodder to support an imperialistic program in the world," Johnson told the students in his parting challenge, "or you may spend them behind the cross of Jesus fighting imperialism on the home ground in behalf of the brotherhood of man."[34] It remained for Kirby Page to fill in the details of the crusade.

"Just as most people in Europe were unconscious of the approaching storm in the early summer of 1914," Page said to the students, "so most Americans today are unaware of the powerful forces which are again driving the nations to the brink of war." As for the United States, it was "rapidly becoming the most feared and most hated of nations." Page quoted a recent editorial suggesting an American response. "With all our neighbors looking for a chance to break into our melon patch, carry off the fruit, and trample the vines, it is time to train a couple of bulldogs and load the shotgun, and not to talk of brotherly love toward those who hate and despitefully use us." If America was to escape the grave danger of such attitudes and the devastation of another war, there needed to be an intelligent, enthusiastic crusade for international understanding, friendship, and cooperation. Page outlined the specific details of the new crusade.

1. *Be intelligent concerning the causes of war.* Economic competition and extreme nationalism were chief.
2. *Help break down the mental and emotional barriers between peoples.* Page supported David Starr Jordan's recent proposal of a Bureau of Conciliation in the Department of State as one practical step forward.
3. *Develop a new technique for handling international disputes.* Page lamented the "arbitrary, insulting decision" by Congress to limit Japanese immigration to the United States as the kind of mistake that could be avoided by the "habit of conference." Page gave the issue of war debts as another international conflict that should be settled in conference rather than by arbitrary and unilateral decisions.
4. *Help create confidence in peaceable agencies and nonviolent sanctions.* There should be no use of armed forces by international bodies, Page thought. International decisions should rely on "the honor of peoples, the power of organized public opinion, diplomatic measures, and in extreme cases, upon economic and financial pressure."
5. *Help destroy the war system.* Page urged students to challenge the campus program of the Reserve Officers' Training Corps (ROTC) as "an organic part of the war system."
6. *Help create a truer type of patriotism.* The truest patriot, Page said, was "the man or woman who most completely reproduces Jesus' way of life, who does most to reconcile the warring factions of God's family."

7. *Take Jesus seriously in international affairs.* Page believed that the teaching of Jesus to love the enemy could be applied in international affairs. If it sometimes led to suffering, it would point to the cross as "God's way and Jesus' way of overcoming evil."[35]

Page warned the students that the nations of the world, including the United States, were engaged in a dangerous replay of the attitudes and behavior that had led to the world war and were "rushing surely and swiftly on toward another great disaster, if left unchecked." What the world needed now, Page said, was a great new liberating movement that would unite students around these tasks—a Student Volunteer Movement for peace and social justice.

The Milwaukee conference had minimized the platform and placed great hope in its discussion groups—that they would play a large part "in stimulating creative thinking." But the discussion groups were a disappointment. They were neither as carefully planned nor as democratically structured as similar ones had been at Indianapolis. They were built around the lectures, the first ones of which did not capture the attention or interest of the students. Recently retired professor George A. Coe thought that the program had given too much time to the "mysticism" of the Bible studies and had further postponed the engagement with reality by a Modernist exercise of trying "to reach the present through the past." Whatever the cause of the slow beginning, Coe observed that when Johnson and Page came on, three days into the conference, with their "analysis of concrete situations that are not yet mastered by our religion," "there was an instant response from students, and from that moment their languid discussion groups became eager and alert, as if the Spirit of God were then and there struggling in and through them to create a new world." Some of the devotional periods, Coe thought, encouraged "an introversion that amounts to a flight from reality." The next conference, Coe thought, should "start the program where students are." And it should provide more of what Coe described as the religion of ethical creativity—"finding God by doing the will of God in unprecedented ways in the spirit of Jesus"—as proclaimed by Niebuhr, Page, and Johnson.[36]

In spite of Coe's delight in what the religion of ethical creativity had done for the discussion groups, it did not produce much in the way of concrete results after the convention. The new Mount Hermon Hundred had failed to materialize. Overall, the momentum of the conference, which had been planned to emerge from the groups, never quite came together. It was a convention that came, ironically, to depend on several good platform presentations for its impact. The new student movement that was hoped would emerge from the discussion groups died in the lethargy produced by speakers who did not connect with the students and for want of student leaders to carry the radical vision of the older generation. The postwar generation were hardly more inclined to join a crusade for radical reform at home than they were to take up the banner of world evangelization. They had fought their last crusade.

Eddy's Social Gospel crusades and Milwaukee's "religion of ethical creativity" both suffered from a fatal flaw. They lacked a motivated, organized movement to help students put into practice the radical social vision of crusade or convention. The genius of the Student Volunteer Movement was that it took students from the decision of the volunteer pledge to engagement in ongoing Bible and missions study groups on campus, regional missionary conferences, and national conventions, all focused on helping the student to become a foreign missionary. The students and their elders in the 1920s were unable to put together the kind of cross-generational coalition that had made the volunteer movement a reality in the 1890s. The Student Volunteer Movement for Peace and Social Justice never came to be.

Was it the alienation of young from old produced by the war? Was it simply a weariness among the young of crusades—of any kind? Or was there at a deeper level a lack of spiritual power, of religious reality, in the new cause of social justice?

Chapter 10

An End and a Beginning

When I think of the fifty years of the Student Volunteer Movement, I remember that these are just the fifty years from 1885 to the present in which we gave ourselves in America to a false dream of the possibilities of a Christian nation, imagining that it would be an easy thing to achieve a Christian social order and a Christian world order, that it was only necessary to preach love a little more charmingly than we had previously done and we would enter into the kingdom of God.

—Reinhold Niebuhr, 1936

So ruthless have been the events during these years [1915–34] that no movement is as it was before 1915.

It now seems incredible that universities and churches together could have accepted the naïve assumptions of 1870–1915 and, in the name of culture and religion, "blessed" the slaughter of the world's finest youth with no seeming sense of sin or shame.

—Clarence P. Shedd, 1934

By the mid-1920s, the war's shadow seemed to fall darker than ever across the missionary enterprise. What had Christians to carry to other peoples that can justify missionary work today, student volunteer R. C. Hutchison, wondered in 1925 as he sailed to Iran for his first missionary assignment. The recent war was a grim heritage—"Christian nations engaged in the most frightful carnage of history. No human device of cruelty and murder was too terrible for use. No human ingenuity was unappropriated for the purpose of destroying life. Nominal and real Christians fought other nominal and real Christians. Pulpits behind both trenches preached the crusade, held the cross before armed regiments and called down upon the carnage the blessing of God." Hutchison lamented the dark years that followed the war, years in which Christians scratched among the ashes of destruction to find some good, "eager to proclaim with conviction that these dead have not died in vain."[1]

This blessing upon arms and war was certainly not worth carrying across sea and desert. But it was a legacy that could not be left at home, even if the postwar volunteer had wished to do so. It was already in the international "public domain," as was that earlier chapter in Christian history, the Crusades. Richard the Lion-Hearted, once Hutchison's boyhood hero, had fallen from grace. History had repudiated the medieval Crusade with its legacy of "righteous rancor" and continuing vengeance. The church that had once blessed holy war was now beginning to question whether any crusade could claim Christ's name that "seeks its end through hacked and maimed bodies, through burnt and pillaged cities." But was the modern missionary enterprise just another wrong-headed crusade—"one of those strange human movements in which men frantically pour out their lives, and leave nothing for the world but the glory of their blind heroism?"—volunteer Hutchison wondered as his ship lay at anchor off Acre in Palestine, site of one of the Crusade camps of Richard the Lion-Hearted.

A few days later the Hutchisons were in Galilee, their last stop before the laborious trek across desert and mountain to Teheran. They had spent Easter in Jerusalem. They had gone to Golgotha, and, early on Sunday morning, to the tomb. "The stone was rolled away," Hutchison wrote. "The tomb was empty. Christ was risen again in our hearts." But still the young volunteer grappled with questions about his missionary vocation, questions that would not have been asked before the war.

> There was no doubt then. The couriers of the cross carried a flaming gospel of redemption and salvation. To a world lost in heathendom and sin they brought the only name under heaven whereby men might be saved. There was one final and absolute faith. They were its bearers. They needed no apologetic. The absoluteness, the utter uniqueness of Christian salvation gave them every justification for the most relentless missionary endeavors, the most penetrating and persistent campaigns of spiritual aggression, and inspired them for the most appalling personal hardships.[2]

There was a note of wistfulness in Hutchison's words, written on a Sabbath by the Sea of Galilee. But he did not dwell on the past. That earlier rock-hard assurance had cracked, and the young Presbyterian missionary bound for one of the toughest, least responsive of all mission fields felt intuitively the crumbling of the old verities. This was a new

shed. The war marked the end of its great successes and the beginning of a long decline that led to its eventual dissolution. For two decades the volunteers had been the avant-garde of the student Christian movement. They were the role models for students throughout North America and the United Kingdom and, to a lesser extent, in Europe. From 1890 until the war, the missionary idea and the volunteer movement had been at the creative edge of the student Christian movements, both intellectually and in student organization and activities. In its shattering of the Protestant missionary crusade, the war marked the end of the SVM dominance of the student movement. The volunteer movement stood for missionary outreach to the non-Christian world, and the war made that mission seem hypocritical. No longer holding the moral high ground, the volunteers and their leaders were never able to recapture the leadership of the student Christian movement, either in North America or in other countries where the movement was active.

Although the Detroit convention in 1928 brought a renewed focus on foreign missions, the watchword never again appeared above convention platforms after the 1924 quadrennial. When Robert Wilder suggested to Jesse Wilson in the early 1930s that it might still be revived, Wilson contended that such an effort would be futile. "The Evangelization of the World in This Generation was used of God to challenge a full generation, and perhaps no similar number of words has been more fruitful in the whole history of the world. Nevertheless, not by legislation or edict of any individual or group, the watchword did lose its grip and power to compel, and my judgment all along has been that no amount of bolstering or promulgation will ever bring it back again."[3] Evangelization no longer encompassed the enlarged task of the modern missionary movement. If there was to be a watchword at all, Wilson thought, it would have to grow out of the genius of a new generation of missionary-minded people.

But Wilder did not give up. If the watchword could not be revived in the SVM, perhaps it would catch on with the new evangelical student movements in Europe. At the time he received Wilson's letter, Wilder was in contact with the new Inter-Varsity Fellowship[4] in Britain and spoke at a 1934 conference in High Leigh in Hertfordshire. Wilder made a profound impression on the young British evangelicals and encouraged their consideration of the watchword. After vigorous discussion, the recently formed Inter-Varsity Missionary Fellowship coined a new watchword and adopted it officially in 1935: "Evangelize to a finish to bring back the king." Although it had the urgency of the old watchword, its millennial overtones made it less immediately understandable to students. Nor did it gain a currency beyond the student world, as had the earlier volunteer movement slogan.[5]

The British Inter-Varsity Fellowship eventually came to the United States by way of Canada. In 1938 a group of evangelical students at the University of Michigan organized, with help from the Canadians, the first American chapter of the IVF. The American movement merged with the Student Foreign Missions Fellowship (founded in 1936) as its missionary department and began, after World War II, to organize triennial missions conventions modeled after the student volunteer quadrennials. These conventions, held on the University of Illinois campus at Urbana, grew from six hundred students in 1946 to nearly twenty thousand participants in the 1980s, three times the size of the largest SVM quadrennial. When considered as a percentage of total student population, however, attendance at the Urbana conventions never grew beyond two students per thousand—about the level of the last SVM quadrennial in 1936. Nor did the IVF program provide as vigorous a missionary educational program for students who signed the declaration card (indicating their willingness to become foreign missionaries) as had the volunteer bands and the regional unions.

The Inter-Varsity Fellowship was not another SVM. It was a new interdenominational student Christian movement with an active missionary program, a conservative, evangelical alternative to the older and now more liberal campus movements. The Associations and the WSCF were very much aware of the growth of the Inter-Varsity movement in the United States, especially in the years following World War II. But in spite of cautious contacts, the two groups were never able to connect. The federation viewed this disunity as a tragedy and made some efforts to build bridges with the new evangelical movement and its international expression, the International Fellowship of Evangelical Students. But WSCF leaders admitted in 1947 that the federation "passion for Christian unity" was simply not shared by the Inter-Varsity Fellowship.

There was a rueful acknowledgment that Robert P. Wilder had "played a far more important part in the development of the IVF than we have thought." "There is no doubt," the WSCF report stated, "that in the last decade before the [Second World] War, Mr. Wilder had drawn away from the movements within the federation, and closer to the IVF movements." Wilder was able to delay the formation of the International Fellowship of Evangelical Students—a parallel structure to the WSCF—in hopes that the federation would repent.[6] Although deeply disappointed in the loss of the personal membership criteria in the WSCF, Wilder remained a loyal friend of the federation and the SVM until his death in 1938.

WSCF leaders recognized that they could no longer write off the IVF as a Fundamentalist movement but found it difficult to understand or categorize the new evangelicals. They admired the deep religious earnestness of the new movement but were repelled by a "strangely rigid position" that made the evangelicals uncomfortable even with the neo-orthodoxy of Karl Barth or C. H. Dodd. Federation observers at the Inter-Varsity Fellowship's first missionary conference in 1946 (held in Toronto at the traditional quadrennial time, between Christmas and New Year) seemed embarrassed by talk of an imminent judgment day and graphic descriptions of the heathen but were moved "at seeing some two hundred and sixty students respond to the declaration to go to the foreign field." There was a note of condescension toward the anticommunist spirit of one of the speakers and toward the authoritarian view of the Bible. The federation observers kept asking themselves, "Why do these students attend the university?"[7]

But it was these new evangelicals who would have the most lively Christian fellowship and witness in American and British colleges and universities in the second half of the century, and their international outreach would eventually eclipse the old Protestant ecumenicity of the WSCF. The missionary vigor of the SVM was reborn in the Inter-Varsity Fellowship, and in another campus movement that began after World War II, the Campus Crusade for Christ. These movements, while lacking organic relations with mission boards, cultivated a network of informal links with the new mission agencies that proliferated after 1950. Although the new volunteers would fly rather than sail, and their numbers could not be tracked with the same precision as in the SVM, the student missionary enterprise had, by the centenary of the birth of the SVM, recaptured much of the vigor of that earlier incarnation.

The End of the SVM

The Student Volunteer Movement, as a crusade, was stopped by the Great War. But student volunteers continued to step forward for foreign missionary service—although in sharply decreasing numbers—for another decade. By 1938 the number of new volunteers dwindled to twenty-five; the records for sailed volunteers were incomplete from that year onward (see fig. 10.1). No systematic record of volunteers was kept after the 1930s. The number of active student volunteer unions declined from forty-one in 1925 to only six in 1940. Headquarters staffing went from a high of twenty-nine in the early 1920s to only four by the end of the 1930s, and the budget fell from $94,000 in 1924 to $14,000 in 1937. The national program of the SVM virtually collapsed after Jesse Wilson left the movement in 1936, although the SVM lived on for a quarter of a century longer.

The 1936 convention, with an attendance of about two thousand students, was the last quadrennial to be planned solely by the SVM. After that the college Associations, the Canadian Student Christian Movement, and denominational student organizations shared sponsorship of the conventions. For a time they became more consultative, and attendance was limited. After World War II, however, there was a return to the large missionary convention format, and some twenty-five hundred students turned out for the 1948 convention in Lawrence, Kansas. In the opening address, Walter H. Judd, student vice chairman of the 1924 convention, missionary doctor to China, and now congressman from Minnesota, urged U.S.

Figure 10.1

Student Volunteers, 1930-1938

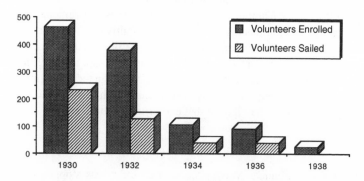

Based on data from William H. Beahm, "Factors in the Development of the Student Volunteer Movement for Foreign Missions," p. 234.

support for the Chinese government of Chiang Kai-shek. A group of students protested "the note of international power politics" and the "apparent identification of the Christian church with one side in such politics." It was reminiscent of Des Moines. In planning its 1960 convention, the last to be held before the SVM ceased to be an autonomous movement, the Student Volunteer Movement was still well enough in tune with domestic and international trends to recruit Martin Luther King Jr. and Bishop Lesslie Newbigin as speakers.

At a 1939 North American student conference sponsored by the National Intercollegiate Christian Council (the College YMCAs and YWCAs), the Council of Church Boards of Education, and the SVM, it was recommended that the volunteer movement be continued as the mission arm of the cooperating student Christian movements, to provide education and recruits for the Christian world mission of the student movements, at home as well as overseas. The SVM was reluctant to lose its autonomy at a time when it saw itself as more broadly ecumenical than the mainstream Protestant groups represented at that Toronto conference. Five years later, however, when the United Student Christian Council was formed as a federation of mainstream Protestant campus ministries, the volunteer movement consented to serve as its Missionary Committee and in 1954, as its Commission on World Mission. The SVM still retained its financial and administrative autonomy in the new ecumenical structure.

During the 1940s and 1950s, the SVM had largely given over to the various campus ministries the responsibility for missionary education on the campus. After World War II there was some effort to reestablish an SVM campus presence in the form of missionary fellowship groups. These were intended to remain informal interest groups and not to evolve into a separate organization structure. But there was no longer any threat that the SVM could become a rival campus organization—as the old volunteer bands and regional SVM unions had seemed capable of doing in the mid-1920s.

In 1959, the SVM merged with the United Student Christian Council and the Interseminary Committee to form the National Student Christian Federation (NSCF), becoming the Commission on World Mission of the new federation. Its tasks were to be the same as in the past: missionary education, fellowship, and recruitment. The new commission helped to plan the Ecumenical Student Conference on the Christian World Mission in 1964. Two years later, when the NSCF was reconstituted as the University Christian Movement, the Commission on World Mission voted itself out of existence. The commitment to world mission was now so well embodied in the student Christian movement, the Commission on World Mission believed, that its services were no longer needed.[8]

By 1945, after which there were few recruits added to the ranks, a total of 20,745 SVM members were reckoned to have "sailed" for missionary service abroad (see fig. 10.2). Three-quarters of these came from the United States, and more than 97 percent were from the Anglo-Saxon world. The volunteer movement was essentially an English-speaking movement, although it could be argued that its recruits, especially after World War I, were no longer exclusively Anglo-Saxon.[9]

Reasons for the Decline

Why did the SVM decline so rapidly after the Great War? There are many obvious causes. There were leadership problems, constant reorganizations, and endemic financial problems, provoked in part and then aggravated by the crisis of a waning student interest in foreign missions. The college associations of which the movement was an integral part were losing their traditional evangelical moorings, their sense of spiritual direction. College life in general was becoming more secular as state universities replaced the denominational colleges as the new cornerstone of American higher education. And the war produced a general loss of faith, especially among the young.

Figure 10.2

Volunteers Sailed, 1886-1945

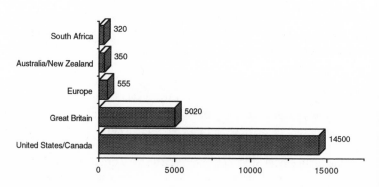

Based on data from an unpublished document in the WSCF archives.

Without a robust religious faith, missionary zeal languished. The churches fell into their own postwar conflict. Students were often drawn into the theological controversies that erupted in force after the war. There were battles for the Bible, for the gospel, and for religious real estate. The missionary enterprise took its share of the flak and also suffered from the cultural introversion of the Fundamentalist-Modernist controversy. After an initial postwar surge, mainline Protestant missions experienced a more-or-less steady decline until after the Depression.

But, as we have seen, there were deeper reasons for the SVM decline. The war severely tarnished the moral luster of the missionary idea. The missionary crusade and the volunteer movement became tainted by their association with a military crusade that required enormous human sacrifice but yielded little progress toward a safer world. The ideals of international Christian fellowship were fractured by the war among Christians, and the supposed moral superiority of Western civilization was impugned.

In the ethical rubble left by the war, the Student Volunteer Movement searched in vain for the vision to reconstruct the student crusade for world evangelization. At least for the young, Christian conquest seemed out of place in the postwar world. The military metaphors of the missionary crusade served poorly the postwar quest for peace and social justice. Foreign missions had become less attractive to the young precisely at the moment when leadership for the SVM needed to be passed into their hands. Either the SVM would become a student movement again or it would cease being a movement.

The problem was as old as the voluntary association that has always been a defining feature of American life and peculiar to the relationship between ethics and democracy. In a democracy the majority rules, even when it is wrong—as in the case of slavery before the Civil War. The tendency of a democracy toward chauvinism has been corrected again and again by minority religious or ethical movements (e.g. abolition, women's suffrage, prohibition, civil rights, nuclear disarmament, antiabortion) that often reshape the will of the majority. A movement survives, however, only as long as people continue joining it and working for the accomplishment of its goals and the public is persuaded by the justice of its critique. When the majority endorses the views of the movement, it no longer needs to exist. On the other hand, if the movement is drawn away from its convictions toward the majority point of view, it may lose the independence and finally the integrity of its critique.

During the nineteenth century, the foreign missions movement represented the dominant, continuing, unofficial statement about America's relations to the world, a kind of religious foreign policy. It sometimes acted as a corrective to U.S. foreign policy and sometimes as a rubber stamp. As the century came to a close, the American missionary message became more closely identified with the nation's own expansionist foreign policy. By the time of the Great War, the missionary message was virtually submerged in the public rhetoric of the military crusade. The war was an expression of the spirit of foreign missions. Soldiers were missionaries of democracy.

In the 1920s the SVM paid the price for this wartime intimacy of religious and military causes. As the American public became aware of the failures of the war and disillusioned with the failures of peace, they looked for a guiding alternative, a moral reference point in a disappointing world. But the churches and the missionary movement were so intimately associated with the war effort that they no longer provided that alternative moral reference. Protestant missionary leaders in America had been willing to sacrifice the independence of their crusade in order to save Western civilization. But in doing so, they compromised the integrity of their cause. When the Great War was over, their hands were too bloody to carry the flag of internationalism.

The war was a powerful engine of change, but it was not the only force acting to reshape the missionary cause in the 1920s. There were other changes taking place in American—and European—culture that contributed to the "disestablishment" of the missionary cause. Darwinism and the rise of the social sciences seemed to challenge the central role of religion in society. In the Scopes "Monkey Trial," the scientist challenged the preacher for leadership in American culture. The scientist won. The preacher would continue to preach, but the Protestant Bible was no longer guaranteed the last word in the public square. That loss of authority did not leave the missionary gospel untouched.

As the preacher lost ground at home, the missionary voice competed with new experts on the subject of exotic peoples. In the new science of anthropology, religion was seen as but one part of a larger cultural whole. Religious change was historical and evolutionary, shaped by the culture. Religious ideas, like biological organisms, were engaged in a struggle for survival in which the strongest would gradually emerge. Scientific ideas of struggle for survival, whether in the biological or the social sphere, were a dominant part of the Western intellectual furniture by the turn of the century. And these notions of the "survival of the fittest," on the broadest cultural and political level, certainly shaped the clash of

Anglo-Saxon and Teutonic worlds in the two great wars of this century, even as they shaped the rhetoric and practice of the Protestant foreign missions crusade. Democracy may have won the world wars, but Christian and missionary ideals suffered huge losses.

The Great War did not settle the hegemonic questions for the West. But it did render a telling historical judgment against the religious crusade to evangelize the world. And it severed finally, for the missionary movement, the Constantinian connection between church and state. When the language of crusade was employed again by evangelicals after the Great War, it was without the blessing of a Christian civilization. Christendom died in the trenches of Flanders. If the holocaust of the following war could still be charged by some historians to the account of a decadent European Christianity, it was only to put the final nail in the coffin that the earlier war had constructed. And it ensured that those who carried the missionary torch in the second half of the twentieth century would the more cautiously invoke the memory or metaphors of Christendom in the effort to win the world to Christ.

Of course, there were continuing domestic and missionary efforts to civilize after 1918, the Sherwood Eddy evangelistic campaigns of the 1920s and the Social Gospel of the 1927 Milwaukee convention being the most outstanding student examples. But the postwar world demanded a more subdued gospel. After Versailles, the Social Gospel could never muster the same optimism, the same certainty of victory, that had enthused its preachers before 1914. Once an assurance of inevitable progress in the arrival of the kingdom, it provided for students in the 1920s a context for criticizing the American and Western status quo, if it did not always lead to a call to repentance. The coming of the kingdom of God had been set back for hundreds of years, and now, after the Great War, it seemed that the evangelization of the world would take many generations.

Persons like Reinhold Niebuhr brought a more modest gospel to the Student Volunteer Movement in the early 1930s. It was a gospel more willing than the Social Gospel had been to confront the bad news of evil, both in the individual and in society. "It is a world of sin," Niebuhr told the students at the 1936 SVM convention in Indianapolis, "a world of anarchy." "We have gone through a world war. We had dreams that that war would teach us such lessons that we would never have another war; and now, only a little more than a decade after that terrible calamity, we face another war. Have you ever had a more perfect symbol of human impotence and the tragedy of human sin than the way in which the nations are drifting toward this next war, everybody hoping that it can be avoided and nobody seeming to know how it can be done?"[10]

Neoorthodoxy called students back to the cross, a cross that meant death rather than conquest. Its dialectic between God and the world, between the word of God and the voice of men and women, between the eternal and the time-bound, often ending in paradox—this was hardly the stuff of slogan and crusade. But it was a crisis theology that fit the more subdued mood of the 1930s. If it failed, in the land of its birth, to exorcise the demons of National Socialism, it could claim that it had a hand elsewhere in keeping the church judiciously distant from the propaganda of the state. The American church in World War II did not lose her distinctive voice as much as she had in the first. The Student Volunteer Movement was drawn, in the years of decline, to the probing dialectic of neoorthodoxy. It was a retreat from the liberalism of the 1920s, but it stopped well short of the other theological polarity of that decade of extremes.

Student volunteer Hutchison, in a concluding defense of his mid-1920s decision to become a missionary in the Middle East, told a story from Constantinople, where a YMCA leader was describing the advantages of a Christian association. The senior secretary was interrupted by a Turk: "We appreciate these splendid ideals and teachings. But we have good ones in our religion. It is something more than ideals which we need. We need that which will make a man live up to his ideals. We have nothing which will grip the young man who does not want to be good and so change him that he will want to obey the high ideals of our or any other religion. What have you in Christianity?"

There was, young Hutchison thought as he stood beside the Galilee, an answer to that question in Christianity—in its power to grip a heart and turn it toward God, its power to touch and transform a life. "Unless we can be used as channels of that power as well as that teaching, we had better not go," he wrote. "Unless such be its message, the Christian church should withdraw from its foreign field and leave to education, commerce and philanthropy the task of propagating civilization and ethics. But we do carry a unique contribution, a living, supreme and divine Christ who will call and change human hearts. Galilee means living power—or nothing."[11]

The encounter of Christianity with the great world religions was the theme of the 1928 meeting of the International Missionary Council. By the time of the Jerusalem conclave, "missions" had become "mission" as the focus shifted from geography to theology, from human action to divine initiative. For some, the change signified a divine mission larger even than Christianity, in which Christian witness was one among many tributaries to the "ultimate truth."

Senior volunteer John R. Mott could admit by the late 1920s that past missionary attitudes toward other religions had been far from exemplary. "We have doubtless been prone to fix attention on their weaknesses, shortcomings, even errors and stains," Mott wrote in a book reporting on the Jerusalem conference. The International Missionary Council meeting had been designed, Mott said, to redress the injustices done by Christians in the past, by dealing especially with "the values of the various non-Christian systems." Christ, after all, had come not to destroy but to fulfill. And Jesus himself had insisted that the one who did not oppose was in fact an ally. "Sharing" and "values" were catchwords of the new interreligious ecumenism that emerged after the war.[12]

Some Europeans worried that the absolute uniqueness of Christ would be compromised and that syncretism was in the wind. They recognized that the challenge of other religions struck at the heart of the Christian message. "We quite understand that when Christ is set in contrast over against the failures and sins of other faiths," Mott wrote, "they suffer by comparison; but, if we only knew all that is noble, true, beautiful, and helpful in them, it might be shown that, while Christ would still be seen to be desirable, he would not appear absolutely essential."

While the conference presented Christ as the ultimate reality, a final and yet ever unfolding revelation of "what God is and of what man through him may become," there was a new note. Instead of the triumphant Christ of the Protestant crusade, there was a crucified God, "suffering with men in their struggle against sin and evil, bearing with them and for them the burden of sin." In place of clamorous cries of an imminent victory, there was an acknowledgment that all were far from God. None was worthy of his love. Yet the crucified Christ who had identified with human weakness and tragedy gave also the assurance of restoration and pardon to all who believed.[13] The crusade was gone, but the cross had not disappeared.

The word crusade carried an overtone of meaning from its pre-English roots, "marked with a cross." The cross was, for the SVM founders, a symbol of conquest. The older generation followed a triumphant Christ who seemed to bless their expansive civilization and its gospel of spiritual conquest. The postwar generation, chastened by a tragic and unfinished war, lived in the shadows of a more somber cross. Christian civilization, perhaps even Christianity itself, had been weighed in the balance and found wanting. Theirs was a cross not of triumph but of shame.

Although it was not clear who should shoulder responsibility for the Great War, it did not seem possible in the 1920s that the Christian church could be excused from a measure of guilt. And yet the nation in the twentieth century was changing from what it had been when kings and queens wielded scepters that combined political and religious authority. The emergence of an omnipotent state challenged the rule and the role of the church—indeed, of religious institutions of any kind. After World War II, questions about the power of the modern state, and about the role of religion in the public square, loomed larger than ever before. And the missionary movement found itself challenged by a secularism that increasingly restricted the influence of the church at home just as other religions resisted its missionary claims abroad. But even in such an unlikely environment, the cause of missions continued to flourish.

In the summer of 1919, a young college student named Donald McGavran had led a delegation of students to an association conference in Lake Geneva, New York. One night he returned to the tent where his delegation were staying. "I was talking with Wilder about India," he said, "and he got me." McGavran was waving an SVM declaration card that he had signed "off in the woods somewhere."[14] After Des Moines and some further study, he left for India, where he served as a missionary for more than a quarter of a century. He returned to the United States in the 1950s to do a comparative study of why some mission work is more effective than others. In subsequent years at the Fuller School of World Mission in California, student volunteer McGavran led a renaissance in missiological research that combined the best insights of theology and the social sciences to provide Christian workers from every continent the tools for effective missionary witness. His work was a continuation, with significant revisions, of the SVM's crusade for "the evangelization of the world in this generation."

If the Student Volunteer Movement had died, the missionary movement itself was alive and well. William R. Hutchison points out that the fourteen thousand career missionaries of the late 1920s declined by several thousand during the Depression but then soared—from eleven thousand in 1935 to thirty-five thousand in 1980. In many ways this was a new crusade, with "32,000 of the foot soldiers in this new missionary army [representing] agencies not related to the churches that had earlier dominated the mission enterprise." More than 90 percent of Protestant missionaries in 1980 came from the faith missions and from the conservative denominations, groups that had begun to turn their back on the Student Volunteer Movement in the late 1920s.[15] And not a few of the missionaries of the 1980s had attended Inter-Varsity conventions where they had signed a pledge to serve in the foreign field.

As far as the global mission of Christianity—as it was now more modestly described—those who looked after numbers in the 1980s estimated that the percentage of the world population who had heard the Good News of Jesus Christ was still growing toward that goal set by the Student Volunteer Movement one hundred years earlier. In the 1920s about half of the world was evangelized. By the centenary of the volunteer movement in 1986, that number had grown to nearly three-quarters of the world's five billion people. The number of Christians, however, when taken as a share of the world's population, stood at about one-third in 1986, slightly less than it had been calculated to be in 1900, the year that John R. Mott published *The Evangelization of the World in This Generation*.[16]

Anticipating the Millennium

Although there were relatively few volunteers around to witness, the 1980s and 1990s brought a renewal of the effort to evangelize the world—this time by the year 2000. The AD 2000 Movement was organized, with Chinese missions leader Thomas Wang as chairman, in an attempt to coordinate some of the more than two hundred active plans for world evangelization, many with a strategic focus on the year 2000. American Protestant missions leaders were busy analyzing the active movements for world evangelization, attempting to build networks that could lead to effective cooperation among the various Christian groups engaged in the massive task of reaching the one-quarter of the world's population who still lived beyond the reach of any Christian witness. It was an effort that would have seemed familiar to volunteers like Robert P. Wilder and John R. Mott, had they been around to see it. The vast majority of these evangelization plans, however, appeared unlikely candidates for cooperation. Conservative Protestants seemed more fiercely independent than they had been a century earlier. As the decade of the 1990s draws to a close it seems probable that this latest movement will not reach its goal by the year 2000, and its watchword has already been adjusted to reflect that likelihood: "AD 2000 and Beyond."[17]

Whatever the outcome of this latest international campaign, the growth of the church in the non-Western world was one of the most important facts of the twentieth century. By the 1990s, several of the world's largest Protestant congregations were to be found in Korea. Less visible, but more important as a concluding footnote to the story of the Student Volunteer Movement, was the growth of non-Western missions. The most striking change that seemed likely to occur by the year 2000 was a decisive shift of the Protestant missionary center of gravity—from North America and the West, to Africa, Asia, and Latin America. In 1988 Protestant missionaries worldwide were reckoned to number 121,000, about 30 percent of whom came from the non-Western world. By the year 2000, given current trends, the home base of Protestant missions would be in the non-Western world.[18]

A legacy of the Student Volunteer Movement could be seen in the remarkable ecumenical achievements of the World's Student Christian Federation and later in those of the World Council of Churches, founded in 1948 with volunteer John R. Mott as honorary chairman. The missionary impulse that gave the early and definitive shape to this ongoing ecumenical program was to no small extent influenced by the vision and the federation program of the movement that began in Northfield, Massachusetts, in 1886. When student response to the Great War demanded that the ecumenical program for the federation replace, in priority, the evangelistic cause, the student missionary campaign was taken up by others. A legacy of the volunteer movement could also be seen, one hundred years after its founding, in the triennial missions conventions of the Inter-Varsity Fellowship, and in the continuing Christian mission—now more widely based than ever before—to share the gospel of Jesus Christ with those who had not heard. In the ecumenical and missionary vocations of the church at the end of the twentieth century, the student volunteers still spoke.

Notes

Introduction

1. Arthur T. Pierson may have been the author of the watchword, but it was John R. Mott and the leaders of the Student Volunteer Movement who gave it wide currency throughout the English-speaking world and, to a lesser extent, in Europe and in the "mission lands."

2. The most complete accounts of the Anglo-American student movements in the eighteenth and nineteenth centuries are Clarence P. Shedd, *Two Centuries of Student Christian Movements: Their Origin and Intercollegiate Life* (New York: Association Press, 1934), and Tissington Tatlow, *The Story of the Student Christian Movement of Great Britain and Ireland* (London: SCM Press, 1933). The best history of the SVM is the William H. Beahm thesis, "Factors in the Development of the Student Volunteer Movement for Foreign Missions" (Ph.D. diss., University of Chicago, 1949).

3. "Association" was often used as shorthand for the YMCA and YWCA, which were active on most campuses in North America during this period. "Association" as used in this book refers to either the YMCA or the YWCA or both.

4. The pledge read: "It is my purpose, if God permit, to become a foreign missionary."

5. John King Fairbank, "Assignment for the '70s," *American Historical Review* 74 (February 1969), pp. 877–78. Fairbank notes that "the early twentieth century saw a concentration on China as the principal overseas extension of the American frontier" (p. 878).

6. William R. Hutchison, *Errand to the World* (Chicago: University of Chicago Press, 1987), pp. 5–9.

7. When Australia, New Zealand, and South Africa are added, the

picture becomes one of an almost exclusively English-language movement. European volunteers made up less than 2 percent of the total.

8. The Mount Hermon Hundred were the students who at the Northfield, Massachusetts, conference in 1886 signed a declaration that they
were "willing and desirous, God permitting, to become foreign missionaries." From these one hundred students came the founders and leaders
of the SVM. John R. Mott, *Five Decades and a Forward View* (New
York: Harper and Brothers, 1939), pp. 4–5.

9. John R. Mott, *The World's Student Christian Federation: Origin,
Achievements, Forecast* (WSCF, 1920), p. 57.

10. In 1902, SVM founder and missions leader Robert E. Speer reckoned that there were 18,682 Protestant missionaries serving in 558 missionary societies (American and European) worldwide. There were
7,319 mission stations, 14,364 churches, 94 colleges and universities,
20,458 schools, 379 hospitals, 782 dispensaries, 152 publishing houses,
and 64 ships. The Bible had been translated into 452 languages in countries where local churches employed some 79,396 native workers.
Hutchison, *Errand to the World,* p. 100.

11. There were various understandings during this period of just
what was meant by "the evangelization of the world," but by any standard of the period the goal was not achieved. Nineteenth-century mission enthusiasts and strategists had not reckoned with the complexity
of the task of evangelizing the world, and the end of the century saw
barely more than half of the world evangelized and only one-third of
the world's population even nominally Christian. See *World Christian Encyclopedia,* ed. David B. Barrett (Nairobi: Oxford University
Press, 1982).

12. Mark A. Noll, introduction to *The Christian College,* by William
C. Ringenberg (Grand Rapids: Eerdmans, 1984), p. 25.

13. Woody Allen, in the movie *Zelig.*

14. Sydney E. Ahlstrom, *A Religious History of the American Peo-
ple,* 2 vols. (Garden City, N.Y.: Image Books, 1975) 2:367, 369;
Shailer Mathews, *Patriotism and Religion* (New York: Macmillan,
1918), pp. 100–103; George M. Marsden, "The Era of Crisis: From
Christendom to Pluralism," in *Eerdmans' Handbook to Christianity in
America,* eds. Mark A. Noll, Nathan O. Hatch, George M. Marsden,
David F. Wells, and John D. Woodbridge (Grand Rapids: Eerdmans,
1983), p. 369.

15. Randolph H. McKim, quoted in Ahlstrom, *Religious History,* p.
367.

Chapter One

1. Ruth Rouse, *The World's Student Christian Federation: A History of the First Thirty Years* (London: SCM Press, 1948), pp. 176–77.

2. Sherwood Eddy, *The Re-Education of Sherwood Eddy* (New York, 1934), p. 162.

3. "The Sino-Japanese War, which closed only four months before the [WSCF] Vadstena Conference; the Venezuela incident between Britain and the United States at the very time of the first Liverpool Quadrennial, 1896; the Italian-Abyssinian War, 1896; the Greco-Turkish War, 1897; the Spanish-American War, 1897–8, and continued trouble after it in the Philippines; the Boer War, 1899–1902, overshadowing the London Quadrennial and the Versailles federation conference in 1900, to which the Netherlands movement refused to send delegates as they felt they could not meet the British; the Boxer troubles in China, 1901; the Russo-Japanese War, 1904–5; trouble over the separation of Norway and Sweden, 1905"; Rouse, *WSCF,* pp. 176–77. Tatlow, *Story of SCM,* p. 506. Eddy, *Re-Education,* p. 162.

4. John R. Mott, *The Decisive Hour of Christian Missions* (New York: SVM, 1910), pp. 230–31, 239.

5. Mott, *The Present World Situation* (New York: SVM, 1915), pp. 112, 118. "What a record against the fair name of a great Christian power has been its complicity in helping to fasten the opium curse upon China," Mott wrote. "In the whole history of moral reform there can be found no more inspiring example than that of the heroic and apparently remarkably successful effort of the Chinese reformers to shake off this terrible evil." The greatest resistance to these reforms came from British government representatives, Mott alleged—though Mott steadfastly avoided mentioning Great Britain by name at any point in his exposé. Mott noted that in 1911 three West African countries imported 6.5 million gallons of European hard liquor, while in China, Western firms were marketing cigarettes aggressively, giving away free samples even to small boys. Christian nations would always bear the responsibility, Mott said, for introducing alcohol into normally abstinent Muslim and Hindu countries.

6. Mott, *Decisive Hour,* p. 236; *Present World Situation,* pp. 13, 123.

7. John R. Mott, "The World Situation," typescript of an address to the national YMCA convention, 1913; in the John R. Mott Papers, pp. 16–17.

8. John R. Mott, "The Present World Conflict and Its Relation to Christian Missions," *Outlook of Missions* 7 (December 1915), p. 579 (a copy in the Mott Papers).

9. John R. Mott, "Modern World Movements: God's Challenge to the Church," an address delivered in the Royal Albert Hall, London, November 21, 1908, published as a pamphlet by the SVM (n.d.), p. 17, in the SVM archives. "The missionary is the great mediator between the East and the West," Mott said. "They are bringing about a larger understanding and sympathy between races radically different and in some cases bitterly antagonistic." Two of the five founding objectives of the WSCF were: (1) to influence students to devote themselves to the extension of the kingdom of God in their own nation and throughout the world, and (2) to bring students of all countries into mutual understanding and sympathy, to lead them to realize that the principles of Jesus Christ should rule in international relations, and to endeavor by so doing to draw the nations together.

At the 1897 WSCF conference in Williamstown, New York, Mott praised as characteristic of the federation the pacific spirit which, soon after the Sino-Japanese War, allowed Ding Ming Wong of China to nominate Japan student Christian movement president Ibuka as vice-president of the federation. "The Relation of the Student Federation to the Peace and Arbitration Movements," a 1908 pamphlet in the Mott Papers, p. 11.

10. D. Willard Lyon, *The Christian Equivalent of War* (New York: Association Press, 1915), p. 83

Chapter Two

1. B. H. Liddell Hart, *History of the First World War* (London: Pan Books, 1972), p. 28.

2. WSCF, *Reports of Student Christian Movements, 1917–1918* (1919), pp. 19–21.

3. Rouse, *WSCF*, p. 186–89

4. Eldon G. Ernst, *Moment of Truth for Protestant America* (Missoula, Mont.: Scholars' Press, 1972), p. 25

5. Robert E. Speer, "The War Aims and Foreign Missions," *Intercollegian* 36, no. 1 (October 1918), pp. 2–5.

6. Walter Rauschenbusch, in the Nathaniel W. Taylor Lectures at Yale in 1917, *A Theology for the Social Gospel* (New York: Macmillan, 1918), p. 226. "The Great War is in truth a discussion of the future of the race on this planet, but a discussion with both reason and religion left out," p. 223.

7. Matthew 28:19–20, a text frequently quoted as Jesus' mandate for

foreign missions: "Go therefore and make disciples of all nations, baptizing them in the name of the Father and of the Son and of the Holy Spirit, and teaching them to obey everything that I have commanded you. And remember, I am with you always, to the end of the age." (NRSV)

8. Eddy, *Re-Education,* p. 182; Robert E. Speer, *The New Opportunity of the Church* (New York: Macmillan, 1919), p. 89.

9. Tatlow, *Story of SCM,* p. 510.

10. "The Student Movements and the War," *Student World* 9 (January 1916), p. 35.

11. Tatlow, *Story of SCM,* p. 540.

12. H. C. Rutgers, "The Christian Student Union and the War," *Student World* 10 (October 1917), p. 285 (translated from the May-June 1917 issue of *Eltheto,* the journal of the Christian Student Union of the Netherlands).

13. Ruth Rouse, "Notes on work amongst Students in Europe in Wartime," an unpublished document in the WSCF archives, p. 1; *WSCF,* p. 182.

14. Quoted in Rutgers, "Christian Student Union and the War," p. 282.

15. Suzanne de Dietrich to John R. Mott, May 17, 1915; French original and English translation in the Mott Papers.

16. Beahm, "Factors," p. 238.

17. As tracked by the SVM from mainline Protestant sources. See Beahm, "Factors," p. 211.

18. Tissington Tatlow, "The British Student Movement in War Time," *Student World* 8 (April 1915), p. 132; WSCF, *Reports, 1919–1920* (1920), p. 27.

19. WSCF, *Reports 1916–1917* (1918), pp. 83–85. The British SCM leaders did not submit an annual report to the WSCF in 1918. The WSCF reprinted the previous year's report in order to maintain a "record of the movement."

20. "The Student Movements and the War," *Student World* 9 (January 1916), pp. 31–34; E. O. Jacob, "Ministry to Soldiers and War Prisoners in Germany," *Student World* 10 (January 1917), pp. 250–59. The former head of the German Student Volunteer Movement took charge of the German student movement work among German soldiers in Turkey.

21. H. C. Rutgers, "A Visit to Central Europe," *Student Movement* 18 (March 1916), pp. 129–31.

22. "The Missionary Retreat," *Student Movement* 18 (November 1915), pp. 38–39; Editorial, *Student Movement* 18 (February 1916), p.

13; "The Unsearchable Riches of Christ," *Student Movement* 18 (February 1916), pp. 98–100.

23. The SVM agreed before the meeting that the Northfield conference would not be a regular quadrennial. The 1913–14 convention in Kansas City was the seventh quadrennial. Northfield, had it been so considered, would have been the eighth. Instead, the 1919–20 convention in Des Moines was entitled the eighth quadrennial. Two decades later, however, when John R. Mott reflected back on the Student Volunteer Movement, he did include Northfield in his list of quadrennial conventions. Mott, *Five Decades,* p. 16.

24. "The Message of Northfield, 1918," by Professor Hallam (no first name given), *Association Outlook* 17 (February 1918), p. 27.

25. Winnifred F. Thomas, "North American Students Mobilizing for Christian World Democracy," *Association Outlook* 17 (February 1918), pp. 21–22.

26. "The Northfield Volunteer Conference," *North American Student* 6 (February 1918), pp. 189–90.

27. The campaign was a united program of work among soldiers and prisoners of war in which the Associations were deeply involved, both in fundraising in North America and in the wartime work in Europe.

28. "Following Northfield," *North American Student* 6 (February 1918), p. 191.

29. J. Lovell Murray, *The Call of a World Task in War Time* (New York: Association Press, 1918), pp. 2–3. Another American estimate claimed that two-thirds of the human race were directly involved in the conflict, "and every other human being indirectly." S. Earl Taylor and Halford E. Luccock, *The Christian Crusade for World Democracy* (New York, 1918), p. 13.

30. Murray, *Call of a World Task,* pp. 5–6

Chapter Three

1. Tatlow, *Story of SCM,* p. 519.

2. Ibid., p. 519–20. The letter contained a note saying that it had been written "with the entire approval of the President of the Committee of Management of the *Deutsche Christliche Studenten Vereinigung,* Dr. G. Michaelis."

3. "The German Student Movement on the South African War," *Student Movement* 18 (October 1915), pp. 20–21.

4. Tissington Tatlow, "The British Movement in War Time," *Student World* 8 (April 1915), p. 133.

5. George Irving, "The Student Movement and the War," *North American Student* 3 (October 1914), pp. 22–24.

6. Rutgers, "Visit to Central Europe," pp. 129–31.

7. Bengt Sundkler, *Nathan Söderblom, His Life and Work* (London: Lutterworth Press, 1968), pp. 174–75. "The Swedish title of the SCM volume was *Kampen bakom fronterna*. The correspondence for it had been carried on by K. B. Westman and P. Hasselrot. It is a volume of 184 pages; the first part of the book contains the letters, the second part certain representative statements, such as war sermons. K. B. Westman had a concluding interpretation of the material thus collected, under the characteristic title: 'The unity and dividedness of Christendom with reference to the present world situation'" (p. 175).

8. "At War," *North American Student* 5 (May 1917), p. 324.

9. Murray, *Call of a World Task,* pp. 7–10.

10. Harry F. Ward, "Tell Your Church People That!" *North American Student* 6 (March 1918), pp. 262–63.

11. Edward I. Bosworth, "The Christian Witness in War," *North American Student* 5 (April 1917), pp. 328–29.

12. *New York Times,* February 19, 1918, p. 3. On the Northfield conference, see chapter 2 above.

13. *New York Times,* February 23, 1918, p. 12

14. John F. Piper Jr., "Robert E. Speer: Christian Statesman in War and Peace," *Journal of Presbyterian History* 47 (September 1969), pp. 201–25.

15. *New York Times,* February 26, 1918, p. 8.

16. See Piper, "Christian Statesman," p. 209. "During the entire controversy," Piper notes, "the *Times* published only one pro-Speer letter."

17. Ibid., pp. 209–10.

18. Robert E. Speer, "The War and the Nation's Larger Call to World Evangelism," *Christian Century* 34 (July 12, 1917), pp. 10–12.

19. Ruth Rouse, "Notes on Work amongst Students," p. 11. Harry Emerson Fosdick, *The Challenge of the Present Crisis* (New York: Association Press, 1918), pp. 54–55.

Chapter Four

1. J. H. Oldham to John R. Mott, August 5, 1914, in the SVM archives.

2. J. H. Oldham to Herbert Anderson, Calcutta, August 11, 1914,

with an attached statement, "The War and Missions: British Appeal for German Missions," in the John R. Mott Papers.

3. John R. Mott, "The Foreign Missionary Situation as Affected by the European War," a typescript copy of an address given to the Foreign Missionary Conference of North America (1917), in the John R. Mott Papers, pp. 160–63.

4. Mott, "Foreign Missionary Situation," p. 165.

5. Foreign Missions Conference of North America, *Report of the Twenty-sixth Conference of Foreign Missions Boards in the United States and Canada, January 14–17, 1919* (New York: Foreign Missions Conference, 1919), pp. 116–27.

6. There were, of course, criticisms of the watchword before the war, especially from the Germans. William R. Hutchison describes controversy on the Continent about American and British missionary "activism" and complaints about the watchword brought by German missions historian Gustav Warneck in a paper prepared for the Ecumenical Missionary Conference in New York (1900). *Errand to the World,* pp. 132–36.

7. Jeremiah W. Jenks, *The Political and Social Significance of the Life and Teachings of Jesus* (New York: International Committee of the YMCA, 1906), pp. 137, 138.

8. Walter Rauschenbusch, *The Social Principles of Jesus* (New York, 1916), pp. 190, 191, 196.

9. William H. Morgan, *Student Religion during Fifty Years* (New York: Association Press, 1935), pp. 96–101.

10. William Adams Brown, "Developing the Missionary Consciousness in the Modern Man," *International Review of Missions* 6 (October 1917), pp. 501–2.

11. Robert E. Speer, *The War and the Religious Outlook* (Boston: Pilgrim Press, 1919), pp. 22–26.

12. Hopkins estimated that thirty thousand students studied Weatherford's book during the five or six years after its publication in 1909. Hopkins, *History of the YMCA,* p. 636.

13. A slightly abbreviated and uncorrected stenographic report of an address by W. D. Weatherford, "Promoting the Spirit of Evangelism," *North American Student* 6 (February 1918), pp. 223–26.

14. Channing H. Tobias, "The Student Movement among American Negroes," *Student World* 9 (July 1916), pp. 111–16; Hopkins, *History of the YMCA,* pp. 540–43, 580–82, 636–37.

15. Clifton J. Phillips, "The Student Volunteer Movement and Its

Role in China Missions, 1886–1920," in *The Missionary Enterprise in China and America,* ed. John K. Fairbank (Cambridge 1974), p. 102.

16. Hutchison, *Errand to the World,* p. 136; "War Year Objectives," *North American Student* 6 (October 1917), p. 29. German students, on the other hand, believed they were defending the faith and the fatherland against the perversities of Anglo-Saxon imperialism. Their mission was the preservation of a genuine "Christian civilization."

17. Robert E. Speer, *The Christian Man, the Church, and the War* (New York: Macmillan, 1918), pp. 70–71.

18. Murray, *Call of a World Task,* pp. 17–18.

19. Fosdick, *Challenge of the Present Crisis,* pp. 4–12.

20. John R. Mott, "American and Canadian Students in Relation to the World-wide Expansion of Christianity," a report of the executive committee to the Kansas City quadrennial, 1914, in SVM archives, p. 10; *Decisive Hour,* p. 236.

21. Mott, "Foreign Missionary Situation," pp. 161, 164, 175–76.

22. Tissington Tatlow, "Missionary Study in War Time" (London: Lay Reader Headquarters, 1916), a pamphlet in the SVM archives, p. 8.

23. Quoted in Mott, "The Present World Conflict," p. 578.

24. Foreign Missions Conference of North America, *Report, 1919,* p. 119.

25. SVM, "Mission Study Courses: Prospectus for 1918–1919" (New York: SVM, n.d.), in the SVM archives, p. 4.

26. Ward, "Tell Your Church People That!" pp. 259–63.

27. Channing H. Tobias, "Shall America Be Made Safe for Black Men?" *North American Student* 6 (March 1918), pp. 266–67.

28. Weatherford, "Spirit of Evangelism," p. 225.

29. "Students and Christianity Today: A Symposium of Statements by Leaders in Many Lands," *Student World* 14 (April 1921), pp. 72–73.

30. WSCF, *Reports of Student Christian Movements, 1916–1917* (1918), p. 83.

31. *The Student Christian Movement in 1919–20* (London: SCM Press, 1920), p. 23.

32. Mott, "Foreign Missionary Situation," p. 164.

33. Mott, *Decisive Hour,* pp. 227, 229.

34. J. H. Oldham to John R. Mott, August 5, 1914, in the Mott Papers.

35. Translated excerpt of an article in the *Kirchenzeitung* (1917), p. 86, in the Mott Papers; John R. Mott to G. Haussleiter, July 3, 1915, in the Mott Papers; typescript of D. Karl Axenfeld's comments to John R. Mott, Berlin, June 29, 1916, in the Mott Papers.

36. Typescript translation of a declaration that appeared in the *Missions-Zeitschrift* (n.d.), in the Mott Papers.

37. D. Karl Axenfeld to John R. Mott, June 17, 1920, in the Mott Papers, pp. 4–6.

38. Ibid., pp. 7–16.

39. Hutchison, *Errand to the World,* p. 129.

40. Emerging nationalistic movements in the European colonies were a political parallel to what missionaries had been encouraging—at least in theory—for nearly a century. Movements for national independence, though often supported by missionaries, usually needed to distance themselves from foreigners and, insofar as it was viewed as an exotic religion, from Christianity.

41. Edwyn Bevan, "Missions and the New Situation in Asia," *International Review of Missions* 9 (1920), p. 322.

42. G. A. Gollock, "A Survey of the Effect of the War upon Missions: The Church in the Mission Field," *International Review of Missions* 9 (1920), p. 29.

43. Bevan, "New Situation in Asia," p. 328.

44. "Students and Christianity Today," pp. 71–73.

45. The findings of an informal conference of Indian and missionary leaders in Allahabad in April 1919, reported in Gollock, "Church in the Mission Field," pp. 30–31.

46. Latourette, *World Service* (New York: Association Press, 1957), pp. 128–29; K. T. Paul, "Indian Leadership in Mission and Church," *Young Men of India* 29 (August 1918), 449–60.

47. In Great Britain, the watchword had suffered decline even before the war. Wilder, who had worked for the SCM as secretary for foreign students until midway through the war, noted that no British leader had even made reference to the watchword at the Liverpool Conference in 1912. After that, the executive committee and the traveling secretaries of the British movement had done nothing to keep the watchword before the British students, Wilder said. Although the watchword was not seriously questioned in the United States until after the war, William H. Beahm noted that "after 1900 the watchword was seldom used as the title of addresses," and "after 1914 the appeals to it or from it had greatly declined." The watchword continued to be printed in the SVM *Bulletin* and set as a banner across quadrennial convention platforms through the Indianapolis quadrennial of 1924. Robert Wilder to John Mott, September 22, 1921, in the SVM archives. Beahm, "Factors," p. 314.

48. Tyler Dennett, "Democracy and the Backward Races," *Intercollegian* 36 (January 1919), pp. 6–8.

49. Kenneth Scott Latourette, *The Christian Basis of World Democracy* (New York: Association Press, 1919), p. viii.

50. Latourette, *World Democracy,* pp. 189–92.

51. Speer did not name any of the respondents quoted in his address. Robert E. Speer, "Is a Restatement of the Christian Message to the Non-Christian Peoples and a Reinterpretation of the Missionary Objective for the Church at Home Necessary?" in Foreign Missions Conference of North America, *Report, 1919,* pp. 141–42.

Chapter Five

1. *Intercollegian* 36 (December 1918), p. 2.

2. These enrollment statistics were based on a survey of 210 colleges and universities immediately after the war. These institutions, which had 87,000 students enrolled in 1914, reported enrollments of 294,000 during the 1918–19 school year. In some fields, of course, the increase was far more dramatic. There were nearly ten times as many engineering students in 1918 as in 1910. WSCF, *Reports of Student Christian Movements,* 1919–1920 (1921), pp. 80–81.

3. Of the sixty-nine pamphlets issued by the SVM before 1920, eleven were first published before 1900, forty-seven between 1900 and 1910. Only eleven were issued between 1910 and 1920. The ten pamphlets that had the longest usage were:

1. Speer, "Prayer and Missions," 1893–1922 (30 years)
2. Schauffler, "Money: Its Nature and Power," 1897–1924 (28 years)
3. Eddy, "The Supreme Decision of the Christian Student," 1900–24 (25 years)
4. Eddy, "The Opportunity of the Hour," 1900–24 (25 years)
5. Eddy, "Cycle of Prayer of the SVM," 1900–24 (25 years)
6. Speer, "What Constitutes a Missionary Call," 1902–26 (25 years)
7. Mott, "Bible Study for Personal Growth," 1901–23 (24 years)
8. Wilder, "The Bible and Foreign Missions," 1893–1915 (23 years)
9. Lyon, "The Volunteer Declaration," 1894–1915 (23 years)
10. Brockman, "If God Permit," 1903–24 (22 years)

Beahm, "Factors," p. 217.

4. The SVM "Mission Study Courses: Prospectus for 1918–1919"

listed one significant addition to the usual missions titles: *The Call of a World Task in War Time,* by J. Lovell Murray, educational secretary of the SVM. As noted in chapter 2, this book was prepared for the Student Volunteer Conference held in Northfield, Massachusetts, January 3–6, 1918, in place of the usual quadrennial convention.

5. The general secretary of the SVM at the end of the war was Fennell P. Turner. He had served in that position for twenty-two years. J. Lovell Murray was educational secretary, a position he had held since 1906. Another headquarters veteran was William P. McCullogh, business secretary. John R. Mott continued as chairman of the SVM executive committee, a position he had held since the founding of the movement in 1890. Serving as vice chairman was J. Ross Stevenson, president of Princeton Theological Seminary and moderator of the Presbyterian Church in the United States of America, a twenty-year veteran of the movement.

6. Robert P. Wilder to John R. Mott, March 8, 1919, in the SVM archives. Perhaps in anticipation of possible controversy over the future direction of the movement, Wilder, in his letter of acceptance, specifically asked Mott and the executive committee for the freedom to choose his own associates and helpers.

7. Robert P. Wilder to friends, August 1, 1919, in the Robert P. Wilder Papers.

8. John R. Mott, "The Present Advantageous Position of Christian Missions," in *Report of the Twenty-seventh Conference of Foreign Missions Boards in the United States and Canada, January 13–15, 1920* (New York: Foreign Missions Conference, 1920), p. 95.

9. "The Present Advantageous Position of the Worldwide Christian Movement," a document in the SVM archives. This address seems to be a revision of the text Mott had used two years earlier when addressing the Foreign Missions Conference of North America.

10. W. H. P. Faunce, "The Church and Social Reconstruction," *Standard* (May 31, 1919), p. 989, quoted in Ernst, *Moment of Truth,* p. 40.

11. Ernst, *Moment of Truth,* p. 38.

12. Taylor and Luccock, *Christian Crusade,* p. 11.

13. Ibid., pp. 22–26.

14. Tyler Dennett, "Democracy and the Backward Races," *The Intercollegian* 36 (January 1919), pp. 6–8; Taylor and Luccock, *Christian Crusade,* p. 181.

15. A common phrase in John Mott's speaking and writing, he took it as a chapter title in one of his books: "How the Impact of Our Western

Civilization May Be Christianized." Mott, *Present World Situation,* pp. 127–50.

16. Hutchison, *Errand to the World,* p. 92, 146.

17. An editorial in the *Watchman-Examiner* 7 (January 2, 1919), p. 5.

18. John R. Mott, typescript of an address given to the Foreign Missionary Conference of North America, January 1920, in the SVM archives.

19. Daniel Johnson Fleming, *Marks of a World Christian* (New York: Association Press, 1919), p. 126. In the same way, Fleming defended American action in the Philippines as wise and proper treatment of a weaker nation by a stronger one and as a laudable expression of the national missionary spirit. "Individuals and groups and private corporations may have fallen short of the nation's high ideal, and through their selfish exploitation marred the clearness of the national missionary spirit, but the American people as a whole have never wished the unexpected relationship with these islands to be other than an unselfish service for humanity" (127).

20. "The Reconstruction of Loyalty," *Intercollegian* 36 (December 1918), pp. 1–2.

21. John R. Mott, "Why a Student Volunteer Convention at This Time?" *Intercollegian* 39 (November 1919), p. 1.

22. The readiness of SVM members to fight was a prominent theme in the annual SVM reports from the various national movements from the beginning of the conflict. Actual statistics were given at the beginning of the war—on how many students were enlisted and in what percentages—from the student missions movement in Germany as well as those from the Allied countries. Later in the war, such specific reports were not published, presumably because the information had become classified.

23. Murray, *Call of a World Task,* p. 125.

24. *Watchman-Examiner* 7 (January 2, 1919), p. 6.

25. Murray, *Call of a World Task,* pp. 132–33.

26. "Many a time in the future the American people will be called upon to give," Mott concluded with his usual extravagance, "but never will they be summoned to associate themselves in furthering a greater cause in the midst of greater days." Mott here succumbed to that blurring of the distinction between national and religious causes for which he was severely criticized by the Germans in the international student movement after the war. "Above all, as we remind ourselves of the difficulties, humanly speaking insuperable, which have attended this great

undertaking and as we recall the wonderful miracle which has been wrought in ushering in the worldwide and, as we trust, enduring peace which synchronized with the launching of the Campaign, let us reverently and gratefully acknowledge Almighty God as the great and only efficient Cause of this great victory of peace, as He was of the great victory of the War." John R. Mott, "The Largest Voluntary Offering in History (n.d.), p. 9, copy of a pamphlet in the Mott Papers.

27. Murray, *Call of a World Task,* pp. 128–29.

28. Taylor and Luccock, *Christian Crusade,* p. 186.

29. Ernst, *Moment of Truth,* p. 41.

30. William Adams Brown, *The Church in America: A Study of the Present and Future Prospects of American Protestantism* (New York: Macmillan, 1922), p. 119.

31. Ernst, *Moment of Truth,* p. 58.

32. Editorial, *World Call* 2 (May 1920), p. 3, quoted in Ernst, *Moment of Truth,* p. 140.

Chapter Six

1. John R. Mott, "The World Opportunity," an address to the eighth international convention of the Student Volunteer Movement for Foreign Missions, Des Moines, Iowa, December 31, 1919, to January 4, 1920; in SVM, *North American Students and World Advance,* ed. Burton St. John (New York: SVM, 1920), p. 17.

2. John F. Carter Jr., "'These Wild Young People'—By One of Them," *Atlantic Monthly* 126 (September 1920), p. 303.

3. Mott, "World Opportunity," pp. 17–23.

4. December 2, 1919, letter to John R. Mott, quoted in Beahm, "Factors," pp. 309–10.

5. David R. Porter, "The Des Moines Convention," *Student World* 13 (April 1920), p. 59.

6. Minutes of the executive committee of the Student Volunteer Movement (September 30, 1919), p. 4, in the SVM archives. The first SVM convention, held in Cleveland, Ohio, in 1891, had the following objectives: to discuss the problems facing the SVM; to provide opportunities for contact among volunteers, mission board secretaries, and returned foreign missionaries; to inform mission board leaders about the purpose and methods of the SVM; and to give renewed unity and impetus to the cause of world evangelization.

The broadening of the base of participation was not a sudden thing, of course, and was related at least partly to a growing diversity in the larger collegiate YMCA program with which the SVM was closely identified. Just before the end of the war, John D. Rockefeller Jr. had written to Mott, quoting a Baptist leader and friend of the association who was concerned about the future of the YMCA movement. He noted that the war had compelled the YMCA to accept and work overseas with people of a wide range of religious confessions. Now that the war was over, would the movement be able to accept at home the Catholics, Jews, Christian Scientists, and Unitarians with whom it had worked so amicably overseas during the war and from whom it had received contributions? In the past, the YMCA had defined the word Christian, and qualification for membership, in terms of church affiliation and theology. The "emergencies of the war" had caused the YMCA to set aside these "limitations" of denomination and theology. What was needed now after the war, Rockefeller believed, was a far simpler creed, one that could be accepted by Catholic, Protestant, or Jew. "I know you feel as I do about the matter," concluded Rockefeller to Mott, "and am simply sending this quotation to show you how other leaders are viewing the situation." (John D. Rockefeller Jr. to John R. Mott, July 18, 1918, in the Mott Papers.)

7. Robert P. Wilder to Francis Miller, May 21, 1919, in the Wilder Papers. "Of the eleven million graves due to the war, less than one hundred thousand are American graves," Wilder wrote to Miller. Because the United States had suffered relatively little damage during the war, Wilder said, "our land is under obligation to make a much larger contribution to the work of foreign missions than any other country."

8. John R. Mott, "Address on the War," circa 1914, in the SVM archives, p. 12. The appeal to the heroic in students is pervasive in most of Mott's writings. In a 1917 address: "Some have seen in this awful slaughter of the multitudes a call for the use of their full capacities for heroism and adventure, for self-denial and for devotion to high and holy causes, and a call which in turn has given them new boldness of faith in laying hold upon the latent sources of Christendom so that wherever I move among the colleges now I find men and women are ready to respond to difficult and impossible tasks in the way that they were not before this struggle." "Foreign Missionary Situation," p. 162.

9. Porter, "Des Moines Convention," p. 58.

10. *World Advance,* pp. 159, 172.

11. Robert E. Speer, convention address, "The Personal Worth or Failure of Christianity," *World Advance,* pp. 176–77.

12. Speer, "Worth or Failure," pp. 178–79.

13. Sherwood Eddy, convention address, "The Gospel Indispensable to North American Students," *World Advance*, pp. 196, 191. David Porter wrote, "It was estimated by one who talked with many of the speakers that fully one-half of the addresses were either prepared after reaching Des Moines or else were radically revised after the convention started." David R. Porter, "Des Moines Convention," p. 63.

14. Eddy, "Gospel Indispensable," pp. 191–92.

15. *The Achievements of the Student Volunteer Movement for Foreign Missions during the First Generation of Its History, 1886–1919*, report of the executive committee to the Des Moines convention (New York, n.d.), in the SVM archives, pp. 23, 84.

16. Harvard *Crimson* (January 7, 1920), a clipping in the SVM archives.

17. Ahlstrom, *Religious History of the American People*, vol. 2, p. 378.

18. Stan R. Pier to Jesse R. Wilson, August 20, 1926, in the SVM archives.

19. WSCF, *Reports, 1919–1920* (1921), pp. 82–83.

20. Kenneth Scott Latourette, "The Postwar Student Mind," *Intercollegian* 37 (May 1919), p. 4.

21. Quoted in Ernst, *Moment of Truth*, p. 139.

22. Frederick Lewis Allen, *Only Yesterday* (New York: Harper, 1931) p. 31.

23. Ernst, *Moment of Truth*, pp. 140–41.

24. Charles E. Harvey, "John D. Rockefeller, Jr., and the Interchurch World Movement of 1919–1920: A Different Angle on the Ecumenical Movement," *Church History* 51 (1982): 198–209. Harvey says that Raymond B. Fosdick, brother of Harry Emerson Fosdick and close associate of Rockefeller, conspired with Rockefeller to cover up the ecumenical financier's responsibility "for pushing the Interchurch World Movement beyond the denominations' willingness to back the campaign." He believes that Rockefeller did not want the public to know of his "crucial role in financing many church, missionary, and research organizations, including the Federal Council of Churches" (p. 205). The Student Volunteer Movement was one of the beneficiaries of Rockefeller's largesse during the period after the war.

25. Ernst, *Moment of Truth*, p. 151.

26. Department of the Interior, U.S. Bureau of Education, *Biennial Sur-*

vey of Education, 1918–1920 (Washington, D.C.: Government Printing Office, 1923), pp. 290–92. Volunteers were Christian, of course, and were naturally found in higher proportions on Christian college campuses.

27. Rollo LaPorte, "Report of the First Student Council of Student Volunteers," an unpublished document in the SVM archives.

28. Robert P. Wilder to John R. Mott, May 13, 1920, in the Wilder Papers.

29. Sherwood Eddy to the SVM executive committee, July 17, 1922, in the SVM archives.

30. Ibid.

31. Quoted in the minutes of the executive committee of the SVM, September 23, 1922, p. 7; in the SVM archives.

32. Minutes of the standing committee of the SVM, November 21, 1922, p. 5, a document in the SVM archives.

Chapter Seven

1. Walter H. Judd, "The Purpose of the Convention," in SVM, *Christian Students and World Problems,* ed. Milton T. Stauffer (New York: SVM, 1924), pp. 1–9.

2. Sherwood Eddy, "Present Day Social and Intellectual Unrest," in SVM, *Christian Students and World Problems,* pp. 113–29.

3. Robert. E. Speer, "The Relation of the Foreign Missionary Enterprise to the World Situation Today," in SVM, *Christian Students and World Problems,* pp. 132–33.

4. F. Eugene Corbie, "The Open Session," *SVM Bulletin* 5 (February 1924), pp. 102–4.

5. Goodwin B. Watson, "How the Discussion Groups Worked Out," *SVM Bulletin* 5 (February 1924), pp. 97–101; Charles E. Rugh, "The Open Session," *SVM Bulletin* 5 (February 1924), pp. 101–2.

6. Corbie, "The Open Session"; Ruth E. Bowles, "Student Impressions of Indianapolis," *SVM Bulletin* 5 (February 1924), pp. 90–91.

7. "Student Addresses" in SVM, *Christian Students and World Problems,* pp. 253–54.

8. Based on estimates (no count was made) of a floor vote as reported in "Student Addresses," SVM, *North American Students and World Advance,* p. 261.

9. T. T. Brumbaugh, "The Open Forum," *SVM Bulletin* 5 (February 1924), pp. 122–24.

10. T. T. Brumbaugh, "Convention Mistakes," a document in the

SVM archives, part of which was published in the *SVM Bulletin* in February 1924.

11. T. H. Sailer, "A Study in Contrasts," *SVM Bulletin* 5 (February 1924), pp. 119–22; James G. Endicott, "Student Impressions of Indianapolis," *SVM Bulletin* 5 (February 1924), pp. 91–92.

12. Robert E. Speer, "The Relation of the Foreign Missionary Enterprise to the World Situation Today," in *Christian Students and World Problems,* pp. 131–46.

13. Sailer, "A Study in Contrasts," p. 121.

14. "Student Addresses," SVM, *Christian Students and World Problems,* pp. 268–73; Henry P. Van Dusen, "The Spiritual Tone of Indianapolis," *SVM Bulletin* 5 (February 1924), pp. 104–7.

15. Paul A. Varg, *Missionaries, Chinese and Diplomats* (Princeton: Princeton University Press, 1958), p. 157.

16. Minutes of the SVM executive committee, January 19, 1924, in the SVM archives, pp. 3–4.

17. Statistics in Beahm, "Factors," pp. 222, 234. By 1930, the SVM was apparently still supplying about one-third of the mainline Protestant missionaries, but after the Depression when the number of mainline missionaries began to increase again, the SVM seemed to have stopped keeping records on "sailed volunteers." See also table 9.1, p. 161.

18. Arthur Jorgensen, "Foreign Missions and National Consciousness," *Christian Century* 40 (May 3, 1923), pp. 553–55.

19. Robert W. Wilder to John R. Mott, September 11, 1923, in the SVM archives.

20. Robert P. Wilder, "A Retrospect: Five-Year Report by the General Secretary to the Executive Committee," September 27, 1924, an unpublished document in the SVM archives.

21. Wilder, "A Retrospect.

Chapter Eight

1. Rouse, *WSCF,* p. 217.

2. Adolph Keller, "Moral and Spiritual Conditions in Europe," in SVM, *Christian Students and World Problems,* p. 157.

3. *Student Movement* 23 (December, 1920), p. 5.

4. *Christianity and the Colleges 1921–1922* (London: SCM Press, 1922), pp. 32–33; *Our Work in the Colleges* (London: SCM Press, 1923), pp. 27–28.

5. Tatlow, *Story of SCM,* p. 614.

6. Robert Wilder and John Mott tried their best to keep the watchword alive in Great Britain, even after the commission report. At the end of a meeting in 1921, Tatlow expressed to Wilder the hope that the American SVM would not give up the watchword. But the British general secretary feared that nothing would save it in Britain, since British students were different from Americans: "British students think!" he said. "However," Tatlow concluded, "your representatives *may* be able to convince us to continue the watchword." Robert Wilder to John Mott, September 22, 1921, in the SVM archives.

7. Tatlow, *Story of SCM,* pp. 613–17.

8. Douglas Johnson, *Contending for the Faith* (Leicester, Eng.: Inter-Varsity Press, 1979), pp. 74, 77–78.

9. The heated response to conference posters implying that the gospel was not being preached faithfully at Oxford led to the evangelicals being satirized in student shows. Johnson writes that "members of one of the college rugby football clubs let it be clearly known that, if they persisted in the open-air meetings (which had been commenced in the broad space by the Martyrs' Memorial in St. Giles), 'the preachers' would be carried off and dumped in the river. It is said that some of the hefty forwards did set out, but on the way came upon a Communists' strike meeting and exhausted their energies there." *Contending for the Faith,* p. 99.

10. Johnson, *Contending for the Faith,* pp. 115–48, 187–96.

11. WSCF, *Reports of Student Christian Movements, 1922–1923* (1924), p. 67; "Students and Christianity Today," pp. 60–61.

12. "Students and Christianity Today," p. 62.

13. WSCF, *Reports, 1919–1920* (1921), pp. 40–41.

14. In the 1919–20 report, the German movement stated that about sixty members of the Student Missionary Union had gone to the field since the beginning of the movement. In 1921, nine were reported sailing. Later records of the American SVM indicate that the number increased very little after the early 1920s.

15. "Students and Christianity Today," pp. 58–59; *Christ and the Student World: A Review of the WSCF, 1920–1921* (Letchworth, Eng.: Garden City Press, 1921), p. 34.

16. *Christ and the Student World,* p. 34; Margaret Holmes (headquarters secretary of the Australian Student Christian Movement) to Robert P. Wilder, June 22, 1932, in the SVM archives; Margaret Holmes, in WSCF, *Reports, 1919–1920* (1921), p. 9. The disbanding of

the Australian SVM apparently came to be seen by some Australian student leaders as a mistake, in that "the claims of Christian work abroad need special emphasis if they are to be kept adequately before the minds of students, and that such work needs special training and preparation." In 1926, after a visit of John Mott, a Foreign Student Fellowship was formed, with a similar purpose to that of the discontinued SVM. Margaret Holmes to Robert P. Wilder, June 22, 1932.

17. Quoted in a letter, Robert P. Wilder to John R. Mott, November 22, 1921, in the John Mott Papers.

18. John K. Fairbank, *The Great Chinese Revolution, 1800–1985* (New York: Harper and Row, 1986), pp. 182–203.

19. Fairbank, *Chinese Revolution,* pp. 192, 199–200; also Hopkins, *History of the YMCA,* p. 696. Fairbank writes that "Protestant missions in China had learned to walk with two supports—medicine and education" (p. 193). Just how much influence the mission schools had on national movements of the period is a matter of considerable debate. "The exact influence of Christian missions on the rise of the New Culture movement is still obscure and fraught with difficulty," Fairbank writes. "Foreigners, being better informed about the missionary movement, may tend to exaggerate its influence, while Chinese patriots, being more aware of the New Culture's indigenous roots and protagonists, may give the missionaries short shrift. This will make for ongoing Chinese-foreign contention" (p. 190).

20. Paul Hutchinson, "The Future of Religion in China," *Atlantic Monthly* 127 (January 1921), pp. 119–25.

21. Chang Hsin-hai, "The Religious Outlook in China: A Reply," *Atlantic Monthly* 127 (June 1921), pp. 840–48.

22. R. C. Hutchison to an unidentified publication, August 4, 1921, in Hutchison's personal papers.

23. Rouse, *WSCF,* p. 280.

24. A YMCA worker's description in John Hersey, *The Call* (New York: Alfred A. Knopf, 1985) pp. 334–35. See also Fairbank, *Chinese Revolution,* pp. 200–201.

25. Rouse, *WSCF,* p. 280.

26. David R. Porter, "The Peking Conference," *Student World* 15 (July 1922), p. 87; Rouse, *WSCF,* pp. 283–84. See also Hersey, *The Call,* pp. 350–55.

27. Jonathan T'ien-en Chao, "The Chinese Indigenous Church Movement, 1919–1927: A Protestant Response to the Anti-Christian Movements in Modern China," Ph.D. diss., University of Pennsylvania, 1986,

pp. 135–45. In the Anti-Christian Student Federation declaration, the YMCA was singled out, along with Christian churches, as a tool of capitalist exploitation (p. 140).

28. C. H. Tobias, "The Young Men's Christian Associations in American Negro Colleges," *Student World* 17 (January 1924), pp. 58–62.

29. Minutes of the WSCF general committee meeting, Peking, March 29–April 2, April 11–12, 1922; in the WSCF archives, p. 28. Peking minutes, p. 28. When the actions of a non-Western country were under review, the federation was less reserved in its call for political action on the part of delegates. The Peking delegates made a formal statement on the "slaughter of helpless men, women and children" going on in Turkey, urging "the whole membership of our Federation to take immediate steps so to arouse the public conscience of their fellow countrymen that effective national and international action will speedily result" (p. 22).

30. It was said that it took a delegate from West China longer to get to Peking than it would take a Brazilian to travel to Peking via London, New York, and San Francisco. Porter, "Peking Conference," p. 88.

31. R. O. Hall, "The Price of World Federation, Peking, 1922," *Student World* 15 (July 1922), pp. 140–41; R. O. Hall, "Under Heaven One Family," *Student Movement* 25 (October 1922), pp. 11–13.

32. Rouse, *WSCF,* pp. 274–75; Peking minutes, p. 25

33. Peking minutes, p. 28.

34. Karl Heim, "The Federation after Twenty Years," *Student World* 15 (July 1922), p. 122.

35. H. C. Rutgers, "The Meeting of the General Committee," *Student World* 15 (July 1922), p. 128

36. Hall, "Price of World Federation," pp. 142–45.

37. Chao, "Chinese Indigenous Church," pp. 245, 267–73.

38. "The More Immediate Policy of the WSCF," a document in the WSCF archives. Those who drafted the paper were F. A. Cockin, Zoë Fairfield, R. O. Hall, Dorothy Steven, along with SCM general secretary Tissington Tatlow who wrote the cover letter to John Mott dated December 19, 1923.

39. Rouse, *WSCF,* pp. 302–14. Minutes of the WSCF general committee meeting, High Leigh, England, August 7–20, 1924; in the WSCF archives, pp. 29–32.

40. Minutes of the WSCF general committee meeting, Nyborg Strand, Denmark, August 11–24, 1926; in the WSCF archives, pp. 13–15.

41. "Evangelization of the Universities," *Student World* 19 (October 1926), pp. 175–95.

42. "Evangelization of the Universities," p. 182.

43. Nyborg Strand minutes, pp. 33–36.

44. Nyborg Strand minutes, quoting from the High Leigh conference, p. 34.

45. J. H. Oldham, "The World's Student Christian Federation Past and Future," *Student World* 18 (October 1925), p. 171.

46. Nyborg Strand minutes, p. 35.

47. Minutes of the WSCF general committee meeting, Constantinople, April 20–27, 1911; in the WSCF archives, p. 9.

48. Minutes of the WSCF general committee meeting, St. Beatenberg, Switzerland, July 30-August 7, 1920, in the WSCF archives, pp. 6–9. In 1900 John Mott recalled that "when the Federation was formed the 'basis question' was not a serious matter in the British movement because practically all its members were either Volunteers for foreign missions or other thoroughly evangelical men; that in the German movement it was not a practical question because all of its members were, to use the phrase of the German leaders, 'converted men'; that in the American and Canadian movement all the unions had a satisfactory personal basis; and that the Scandinavian movement in those days was . . . simply a series of conferences." Minutes of the WSCF general committee meeting, Versailles, France, August 1900; in the WSCF archives, p. 10.

49. Robert P. Wilder to John R. Mott, Norway, August 18, 1920, in the Robert Wilder Papers; incomplete letter, apparently from a Volunteer *en route* to India, to Thomas Sharp at SVM headquarters, written on board the S.S. *Massilia*, April 17, 1924, in the Wilder Papers.

50. Gerard Brom, "Report on the World's Student Christian Federation," *Pax Romana*, January 1922; a translation in the WSCF archives, pp. 8–10.

51. John 17:21, Latin translation. Already in 1915 the slogan "Ut omnes unum sint" was described in the *Student World* as "the hope and the watchword of Christian students in many lands." George W. Nasmyth, "Christian and Social Reconstruction," *Student World* 8 (January 1915), p. 58.

52. Nyborg Strand minutes, pp. 35–36

Chapter Nine

1. Robert P. Wilder to D. Friedrich Würz, June 11, 1926, in the SVM archives.

2. "Report of the Student YMCA of the United States, 1920–1921," document in the WSCF archives, p. 6.

3. WSCF, *Reports, 1922–1923* (1924), pp. 193–94; 223.

4. Denominational "student centers" on state university campuses began with the Presbyterians (PCUSA) in 1905 at the University of Michigan. "Other denominations quickly followed the Presbyterian example, and by the 1930s denominational student centers operated on the campuses of at least 100 state and independent universities." Ringenberg, *Christian College,* p. 154.

5. A plan submitted to the SVM in 1933 proposed a Student Christian Movement that would have as cochairmen a Roman Catholic cardinal and the chairman of the Federal Council of Churches. The general secretary of the SVM would be one of a number of vice chairmen, all executive officers of student Christian organizations. In this plan, the SVM was asked—while maintaining its independence and organization—to take a subsidiary position in the SCM for a trial period of five years. It would furthermore provide salary and office services for a transitional SCM "organizing secretary" and offer the SVM headquarters for use by the SCM for the first five years. "A Recommendation for the Organization of the Student Christian Movement in America, Being the report of Newton T. Peck on thoughts supplied to the SVM Commission by Mission Board representatives, YWCA Staff, YMCA Staff and friends, and other interested friends." A document in the SVM archives.

6. Hopkins, *History of the YMCA,* p. 518.

7. Morgan, *Student Religion during Fifty Years,* pp. 159–61.

8. Robert W. Wilder to Fay Campbell, November 17, 1925, in the SVM archives.

9. In the early days of the SVM, when the YMCA was working to channel the nascent movement into becoming the missionary department of the college associations, Y leaders found Wilder's independent spirit difficult to control. The head of the college association work reported that, when Wilder was visiting colleges on behalf of the movement in 1886–87, "he talked Mission Band all year and never to my knowledge did he try to retain the work in the association and never did he try to aid any other department of the association work. As a result of his method the College Associations are conducting fewer missionary meetings." Luther Wishard to C. K. Ober, August 6, 1888, in the Mott Papers. In 1889 the SVM became the official missionary arm of the College YMCA and YWCA.

10. The Commission of Ten included India missionary E. D. Lucas, Daniel J. Fleming of Union Theological Seminary, Ralph Harlow of Smith College, and Robert E. Speer. Student representatives were Fay Campbell of Yale, Virginia Prichard of Richmond, Virginia, and Wade Bryant of the Southern Baptist Theological Seminary in Louisville.

11. "Report of Commission of Ten on the Student Volunteer Movement," a document in the SVM archives.

12. Wilder's retirement seemed to have been hastened as much by of his lack of administrative skills as by his age and his inability to adapt to the new student mood. William H. Beahm noted that Wilder was not as strong an administrator as Mott, yet he was called to lead the SVM "in a period marked by religious revolt." Wilder told Beahm, in an interview at the Indianapolis convention, that "he felt it was as natural for Mott to handle political matters with finesse as it was for him to breathe, but that he himself had to be content with simpler methods and greater risk of blundering." Beahm, "Factors," p. 285.

13. William E. Barton, "Missionary Motive and Message," *Christian Century* 42 (June 11, 1925), pp. 758–60.

14. Tyler Dennett, "Christian Missions and Imperialism," *Christian Century* 39 (December 21, 1922), pp. 1584–86; a further elaboration of Dennett's views is found in a response to a critic in a letter to the editor, *Christian Century* 40 (April 12, 1923), pp. 464–65.

15. Paul Hutchinson, "Christian Missions: An Attempt at Reappraisal," *Atlantic Monthly* 132 (September 1923), pp. 389–93.

16. Walter N. Judd, "Why Leave Non-Christian America for the Orient?" *SVM Bulletin* 6 (January 1926), pp. 5–8; (February 1926), pp. 4–10.

17. "The End of Foreign Missions," an editorial in *Christian Century* 41 (November 6, 1924), pp. 1433–34.

18. J. Stuart Holden to Robert P. Wilder, August 21, 1926, in the Wilder Papers.

19. Ruth D. Bailey, "Student Views of the Indianapolis Convention," *Missionary Review of the World* 47 (February 1924), p. 174.

20. Fay Campbell to Jesse R. Wilson, January 31, 1928, in the SVM archives.

21. *Home Base and Missionary Personnel,* ed. Orville A. Petty, vol. 7 of *Laymen's Foreign Missions Inquiry* (New York: Harper and Row, 1933), p. 21. The thirty colleges included ten from New England, ten from the Midwest, five from the Pacific Coast, and five from the South.

22. "A Methodist Study of Motivation" (1931) in Petty, *Home Base and Missionary Personnel,* pp. 37–39.

23. H. D. Bollinger to Fay Campbell, November 29, 1939, in the SVM archives.

24. Sherwood Eddy to friends, March 5, 1924, in the Sherwood Eddy Papers.

25. Sherwood Eddy to D. Brewer Eddy, April 8, 1924, in the Eddy Papers.

26. WSCF, *Reports, 1922–1923* (1924), pp. 186–87; Hopkins, *History of the YMCA,* p. 644; Eddy, *Re-Education,* pp. 155, 249–59.

27. T. J. Gillespie to John R. Mott, May 9, 1924, in the SVM archives.

28. It required no financial commitment to keep Eddy on board, since he was supported throughout his career by income from a family trust, the capital of which was not allowed to increase—on principle. "After about 1922," Eddy wrote, "when I felt called upon to make the demands for social justice imperative, I found I could not logically ask men to give their wealth while at the same time criticizing them for the way in which they made it, or the conditions existing in their industries. Accordingly, I permanently dropped this financial work." Eddy, *Re-Education,* p. 155.

29. Introduction, in *Religion on the Campus,* ed. Francis P. Miller (New York: SVM, 1927), pp. vii–x.

30. Reinhold Niebuhr, "The Practical Unbelief of Modern Civilization," in Miller, *Religion on the Campus,* pp. 11–12.

31. Mordecai Johnson, "The Meaning of God's Universal Fatherhood in the Relations of the Races," in Miller, *Religion on the Campus,* pp. 80–94.

32. Timothy T. Lew, "How Christians Make It Difficult for the World to Believe in Christ," in Miller, *Religion on the Campus,* pp. 62–79.

33. Morgan, *Student Religion during Fifty Years,* p. 165.

34. Johnson, "God's Universal Fatherhood," p. 93.

35. Kirby Page, "International Relations and the Religion of Jesus," in Miller, *Religion on the Campus,* pp. 95–114.

36. George A. Coe, "What Ails Our Conference?" *Intercollegian* 44 (March 1927), pp. 159–60.

Chapter Ten

1. R. C. Hutchison, "Can I Give My Life to Christian Missions?" *International Review of Missions* 16 (January 1927), p. 118.

2. Hutchison, "Can I Give My Life?" p. 114.

3. Jesse R. Wilson to Robert P. Wilder, May 18, 1932, in the SVM archives.

4. Founded in 1924 as the Inter-Varsity Conference of Evangelical Student Unions, it was usually called the Inter-Varsity Fellowship in Britain or the Inter-Varsity Christian Fellowship in the United States. We will use Inter-Varsity or IVF for convenience.

5. Johnson, *Contending for the Faith,* p. 192. Wilder was the only founding leader of the SVM who worked with the new generation of evangelical student movements that emerged after the war.

6. "The Relationships of National Student Christian Movements and the WSCF to the Inter-Varsity Fellowship of Evangelical Unions and the International Fellowship of Evangelical Students," Memorandum 2 (Geneva, August 1947; no author given), an unpublished document in the WSCF archives, pp. 3–4.

7. "Relationships of National SCMs and the WSCF to the IVF," pp. 10–11.

8. Martha Lund Smalley, "Historical Sketch of the Student Volunteer Movement for Foreign Missions," an essay in the Register of the Archives of the Student Volunteer Movement for Foreign Missions (October 1980), pp. 32–36, 169–71, an unpublished manuscript in the SVM archives.

9. The 1945 figures seem to have been collected by John R. Mott and Ruth Rouse, as part of their work on the WSCF history. The further breakdown of countries not shown on the graph: Germany: 180; Switzerland: 25; Sweden: 100; 50 each from Holland, France, Norway, Denmark, and Finland; Australia: 250; New Zealand: 100; from a document in the WSCF archives.

10. Reinhold Niebuhr, "Our World," in *Students and the Christian World Mission,* ed. Jesse R. Wilson (New York, 1936), pp. 7–8.

11. Hutchison, "Can I Give My Life?" pp. 119–20.

12. John R. Mott, *The Present-Day Summons to the World Mission of Christianity* (London: SCM Press, 1932), p. 163.

13. Documents from the Jerusalem conference quoted in Mott, *Present-Day Summons,* p. 164.

14. Lyman Hoover to Robert P. Wilder, July 18, 1927, in the SVM archives.

15. Hutchison, *Errand to the World,* pp. 176–77.

16. Barrett, *World Christian Encyclopedia,* pp. 119, 798; "Status of Global Mission, 1987, in Context of the 20th Century," *International Bulletin of Missionary Research* 11 (January 1987), p. 25.

17. David B. Barrett and James W. Reapsome, *Seven Hundred Plans to Evangelize the World* (Birmingham, Ala.: Foreign Mission Board of the Southern Baptist Convention, 1988); *AD 2000 and Beyond* 1 (January/February 1990), pp. 3–4.

18. Larry D. Pate, *From Every People* (Monrovia, Calif.: MARC, 1989), pp. 50–52.

Bibliography

Unpublished Sources

The Yale University Divinity School Library holds the archives of the Student Volunteer Movement as well as the papers of Robert P. Wilder, its founder and general secretary (1920–27); longtime chairman John R. Mott (1888–1920); volunteer and committee member Kenneth Scott Latourette; and other supporters including George Sherwood Eddy. There is also a significant volume of archival material from the early years of the collegiate YMCA and from the World's Student Christian Federation through about 1925. The materials are well organized and are professionally catalogued and managed for convenient access and review by researchers.

Archives of the Student Volunteer Movement for Foreign Missions. Record Group 42. Yale University Divinity School Library.

Archives of the World's Student Christian Federation (1895–1925). Record Group 46. Yale University Divinity School Library.

Archives of the YMCA, Student Division. Record Group 58. Yale University Divinity School Library.

Beahm, William H. "Factors in the Development of the Student Volunteer Movement for Foreign Missions." Ph.D. diss., University of Chicago, 1949.

Chao, Jonathan T'ien-en. "The Chinese Indigenous Church Movement, 1919–1927: A Protestant Response to the Anti-Christian Movements in Modern China." Ph.D. diss., University of Pennsylvania, 1986.

Eddy, George Sherwood. Papers. Record Group 32. Yale University Divinity School Library.

Huckabee, Weyman C. "History and Significance of the Student Volunteer Movement for Foreign Missions." Master's thesis, Duke University, 1932.

Mott, John R. "Address on the War." Typescript of an address given in
      1914. Mott Papers.
———— "American and Canadian Students in Relation to the World-wide
      Expansion of Christianity," a report of the executive committee to the
      Kansas City quadrennial, 1914, in SVM archives (box 450, folder 5274).
———— "The Foreign Missionary Situation as Affected by the European
      War." Typescript of an address given in 1917. Mott Papers.
———— *Modern World Movements: God's Challenge to the Church.* An
      address given in London in 1908. SVM archives.
———— Papers. Record Group 45. Yale University Divinity School Li-
      brary.
———— *The Relation of the Student Federation to Peace and Arbitration
      Movements.* WSCF archives.
———— "The World Situation." Typescript of an address to the national
      YMCA convention, 1913. Mott Papers.
———— *The World's Student Christian Federation: Origin, Achieve-
      ments, Forecast.* WSCF archives.
Rugh, Dwight D. "A Study of the Foreign Missionary Enterprise in the
      Life of the Student Christian Movement of the United States." Mas-
      ter's thesis, Yale University, 1929.
SCM (Student Christian Movement). *Christianity and the War: Sugges-
      tions for United Study.* WSCF archives.
Speer, Robert E. *What Constitutes a Missionary Call.* SVM archives.
SVM (Student Volunteer Movement). Annual reports of the general sec-
      retary published in pamphlet form during the period 1910–25. SVM
      archives.
———— *Mission Study Courses: Prospectus for 1918–1919.*
      SVM archives.
———— *The Student Volunteer Movement after Twenty-Five Years,
      1886–1911.* SVM archives.
———— *Studies in the World Enterprise of Christianity, 1921–1922.*
      SVM archives.
Tatlow, Tissington. *Missionary Study in War Time.* WSCF archives.
Wilder, Robert Parmelee. Papers. Record Group 38. Yale University Di-
      vinity School Library.
———— "A Retrospect: Five-Year Report by the General Secretary to the
      Executive Committee." September 27, 1924. SVM archives.
———— *The Student Volunteer Movement for Foreign Missions: Some
      Personal Reminiscences of Its Origin and Early History.* SVM
      archives.

Published Sources

In addition to the journal articles cited below, I have also cited numerous articles from the following student and missions periodicals: *Association Outlook* (published by the City and College YWCA of Canada); *Association Men* (published by the YMCA thoroughout the period of this study); *Intercollegian* (published monthly by the YMCA during the school year from 1912 to 1940); *International Review of Missions* (published quarterly after 1912); *Missionary Review of the World* (published annually from 1888 to 1939); *North American Student* (published jointly by the SVM and the college YMCA, monthly from March 1913 to June 1918); *Student Movement* (published monthly during the school year by the SCM of Great Britain and Ireland); *Student World* (published quarterly by the WSCF after 1908); *SVM Bulletin* (published quarterly, and later monthly, during the school year, from 1920 to 1930); *SVM Record* (annual bulletin published from 1910 to 1919); *Young Men of India* (published throughout the period of this study by the YMCA of India).

Abrams, Ray H. *Preachers Present Arms*. New York: Round Table Press, 1933.

Ahlstrom, Sydney E. *A Religious History of the American People*. 2 vols. Garden City, N.Y.: Image Books, 1975.

Allen, Frederick Lewis. *Only Yesterday*. New York: Harper and Brothers, 1931.

"American Youth Movement and Missions." Editorial. *Missionary Review of the World* 47 (February 1924): 85–88.

Bailey, Ruth D. "Student Views of the Indianapolis Convention." *Missionary Review of the World* 47 (February 1924): 174.

Barrett, David B., and James W. Reapsome. *Seven Hundred Plans to Evangelize the World*. Birmingham, Ala.: Foreign Mission Board of the Southern Baptist Convention, 1988.

———— "Status of Global Mission, 1987, in Context of the 20th Century." *International Bulletin of Missionary Research* 11 (January 1987): 25.

———— Ed. *World Christian Encyclopedia*. Nairobi: Oxford University Press, 1982.

Barton, James L. "The Modern Missionary." *Harvard Theological Review* 8 (January 1915): 1–17.

Barton, William E. "Missionary Motive and Message." *Christian Century* 42 (June 11, 1925): 758–60.

Beach, Harlan P. "Students at Detroit Seeking Truth." *Missionary Review of the World* 51 (February 1928): 134–36.

Beach, Harlan P., and Charles H. Fahs, eds. *World Missionary Atlas*. New York: Institute of Social and Religious Research, 1925.

Beaver, R. Pierce. "Missionary Motivation through Three Centuries." *Reinterpretation in American Church History*. Ed. J. C. Brauer. Chicago: University of Chicago Press, 1968: 113–51.

——— Ed. *American Missions in Bicentennial Perspective*. South Pasadena, Calif.: William Carey Library, 1977.

Bevan, Edwyn. "Missions and the New Situation in Asia." *International Review of Missions* 9 (1920): 321–39.

Bosworth, Edward I. "The Christian Witness in War." *North American Student* 5 (April 1917): 325–30.

Braisted, Ruth Wilder. *In This Generation: The Story of Robert P. Wilder*. New York: Friendship Press, 1941.

Brown, William Adams. *The Church in America: A Study of the Present Condition and Future Prospects of American Protestantism*. New York: Macmillan, 1922.

——— "Developing the Missionary Consciousness in the Modern Man." *International Review of Missions* 6 (October 1917): 497–510.

Brumbaugh, T. T. "Convention Mistakes" in "The Open Forum." *SVM Bulletin* 5 (February 1924): 122–24.

Cairns, David S. "The War and the Student Christian Federation." *Student World* 12 (July 1919): 85–90.

Capen, Samuel B. *Foreign Missions and World Peace*. World Peace Foundation Pamphlet Series, Number 7, Part III. Boston: World Peace Foundation, October 1912.

Carter, John F., Jr. "'These Wild Young People' — By One of Them." *Atlantic Monthly* 126 (September 1920): 301–4.

Carter, Paul A. *The Decline and Revival of the Social Gospel: Social and Political Liberalism in American Protestant Churches, 1920–1940*. Ithaca, N.Y.: Cornell University Press, 1954.

——— *The Uncertain World of Normalcy: The 1920s*. New York: Pitman, 1971.

Caution, Ethel. "The Young Women's Christian Association among Colored Women Students." *Student World* 17 (January 1924): 51–62.

Chang Hsin-hai. "The Religious Outlook in China: A Reply." *Atlantic Monthly* 127 (June 1921): 840–48.

"Changes in the Leadership of the Movement." Editorial. *SVM Bulletin* 1 (May 1920): 3–5.

Coe, George A. "What Ails Our Conference?" *Intercollegian* 44 (March 1927): 159–60.

"The Colleges and World Reconstruction." An editorial. *Intercollegian* 36 (December 1918): 2.

Committee on the War and the Religious Outlook. *The Missionary Outlook in Light of the War*. New York: Association Press, 1920.

Corbie, F. Eugene. "The Open Session." *SVM Bulletin* 5 (February 1924): 102–4.

Dennett, Tyler. "Christian Missions and Imperialism." *Christian Century* 39 (December 21, 1922): 1584–86.

———— "Democracy and the Backward Races." *Intercollegian* 36 (January 1919): 6–8.

Department of the Interior, U.S. Bureau of Education, *Biennial Survey of Education, 1918–1920* (Washington, D.C.: Government Printing Office, 1923).

Eddy, Sherwood. *Eighty Adventurous Years, An Autobiography*. New York: 1955.

———— *Everybody's World*. New York: George H. Doran, 1920.

———— *A Pilgrimage of Ideas, or, the Re-Education of Sherwood Eddy*. New York: Farrar and Rinehart, 1934.

———— *Religion and Social Justice*. New York: George H. Doran, 1927.

———— *Suffering and the War*. London: Longmans, Green, 1916.

———— "A Whole Gospel." *Student World* 17 (April 1924): 78–83.

"The End of Foreign Missions." Editorial. *Christian Century* 41 (November 6, 1924): 1433–34.

"Evangelization of the Universities." *Student World* 19 (October 1926): 175–95.

Ernst, Eldon G. *Moment of Truth for Protestant America*. Missoula, Mont.: Scholars' Press, 1972.

Fahs, Charles Harvey. *America's Stake in the Far East*. New York: Association Press, 1920.

———— *Trends in Protestant Giving*. New York: Institute of Social and Religious Research, 1929.

Fairbank, John K. "Assignment for the 70s." *American Historical Review* 74 (February 1969): 861–79.

———— *The Great Chinese Revolution, 1800–1985*. New York: Harper and Row, 1986.

Faunce, William Herbert Perry. *Christian Principle Essential to a New World Order*. New York: Association Press, 1919.

—— *Religion and War*. New York: Abingdon Press, 1918.

—— *Social Aspects of Foreign Missions*. New York: Missionary Education Movement of the United States and Canada, 1914.

Fleming, Daniel J. *International Survey of YMCA and YWCA*. New York: International Survey Committee, 1932.

—— *Marks of a World Christian*. New York: Association Press, 1919.

—— *Whither Bound in Missions*. New York: Association Press, 1925.

"Following Northfield." An editorial report. *North American Student* 6 (February 1918): 191–92.

Foreign Missions Conference of North America. *Report of the Twenty-sixth Conference of Foreign Missions Boards in the United States and Canada, January 14–17, 1919*. New York: Foreign Missions Conference, 1919.

—— *Report of the Twenty-seventh Conference of Foreign Missions Boards in the United States and Canada, January 13–15, 1920*. New York: Foreign Missions Conference, 1920.

Fosdick, Harry Emerson. "Are Christian Missions in the Far East Worth While?" *Christian Century* 38 (November 10, 1921): 14–18.

—— *The Challenge of the Present Crisis*. New York: Association Press, 1918.

—— *The Church's Message to the Nation*. New York: Association Press, 1919.

Fussell, Paul. *The Great War and Modern Memory*. London: Oxford University Press, 1975.

"The German Student Movement on the South African War." *Student Movement* 18 (October 1915): 20–21.

Gollock, G. A. "A Survey of the Effect of the War upon Missions: The Church in the Mission Field," *International Review of Missions* 9 (1920): 19–36.

Grose, Howard B. "Youth and the Missionary Enterprise Fifty Years Ago and Now." *Missionary Review of the World* 51 (February 1928): 137–42.

Hall, R. O. "The Price of World Federation, Peking, 1922." *Student World* 15 (July 1922): 139–45.

—— "Under Heaven One Family." *Student Movement* 25 (October 1922): 11–13.

Handy, Robert T. "The American Religious Depression, 1925–1935." *Church History* 29 (1960): 3–16.

——— *A Christian America: Protestant Hopes and Historical Realities.* 2d ed. New York: Oxford University Press, 1984.

Harris, Frederick, ed. *Service with Fighting Men.* 2 vols. New York: Association Press, 1922.

Harvey, Charles E. "John D. Rockefeller, Jr., and the Interchurch World Movement of 1919–1920: A Different Angle on the Ecumenical Movement." *Church History* 51 (1982): 198–209.

Heim, Karl. "The Federation after Twenty Years." *Student World* 15 (July 1922): 120–23.

Hersey, John. *The Call.* New York: Alfred A. Knopf, 1985.

Hocking, William Ernest. *Human Nature and Its Remaking.* New Haven: Yale University Press, 1918.

Hogg, William R. *Ecumenical Foundations: A History of the International Missionary Council and Its Nineteenth-Century Background.* New York: Harper and Brothers, 1952.

Hopkins, C. Howard. *History of the YMCA in North America.* New York: Association Press, 1951.

——— *John R. Mott, 1865–1955.* Grand Rapids: William B. Eerdmans, 1979.

——— *Rise of the Social Gospel in American Protestantism.* New Haven: Yale University Press, 1940.

Hutchinson, Paul. "Christian Missions: An Attempt at Reappraisal," *Atlantic Monthly* 132 (September 1923): 389–93.

——— "The Future of Religion in China," *Atlantic Monthly* 127 (January 1921): 119–25.

Hutchison, R. C. "Can I Give My Life to Christian Missions?" *International Review of Missions* 16 (1927): 109–20.

Hutchison, William R. *Errand to the World.* Chicago: University of Chicago Press, 1987.

——— *The Modernist Impulse in American Protestantism.* Cambridge: Harvard University Press, 1976.

Irving, George. "Our Present and Our Future." *North American Student* 6 (June 1918): 408–10.

——— "The Student Movement and the War." *North American Student* 3 (October 1914): 22–24.

Jenks, Jeremiah W. *The Political and Social Significance of the Life and Teachings of Jesus.* New York: International Committee of the YMCA, 1906.

Johnson, Douglas. *Contending for the Faith.* Leicester, Eng.: Inter-Varsity Press, 1979.

Jones, E. Stanley. "The Aim and Motive of Foreign Missions." *SVM Bulletin* 6 (March 1925): 3–8.

Jorgensen, Arthur. "Foreign Missions and National Consciousness." *Christian Century* 40 (May 3, 1923): 553–55.

Judd, Walter. "Why Leave Non-Christian America for the Orient?" 2 parts. *SVM Bulletin* 6 (January 1926): 5–8; (February 1926): 4–10.

Latourette, Kenneth Scott. *The Christian Basis of World Democracy.* New York: Association Press, 1919.

——— *A History of the Expansion of Christianity,* Vol. 7: *Advance Through Storm.* Grand Rapids, Mich.: Zondervan, 1970.

——— *Christianity in a Revolutionary Age: A History of Christianity in the Nineteenth and Twentieth Centuries,* 5 vols. New York: Harper and Brothers, 1958.

——— *World Service.* New York: Association Press, 1957.

"Let Gratitude Fill Our Hearts." Editorial. *Watchman-Examiner* 7 (January 1919): 5–6.

Leuchtenburg, William E. *The Perils of Prosperity, 1914–1932.* Chicago: University of Chicago Press, 1958.

Liddell, Hart B. H. *History of the First World War.* London: Pan Books, 1972.

Lotz, Denton. "The Watchword for World Evangelization." *International Review of Missions* 68 (1979): 177–89.

Lyon, D. Willard. *The Christian Equivalent of War.* New York: Association Press, 1915.

Marsden, George M. "The Era of Crisis: From Christendom to Pluralism," in *Eerdmans' Handbook to Christianity in America,* eds. Mark A. Noll, Nathan O. Hatch, George M. Marsden, David F. Wells, and John D. Woodbridge (Grand Rapids: Eerdmans, 1983): 277–391.

Mathews, Basil. *John R. Mott, World Citizen.* New York: Harper and Brothers, 1934.

Mathews, Shailer. *Patriotism and Religion.* New York: Macmillan, 1918.

May, Henry F. *The End of American Innocence: A Study of the First Years of Our Own Time, 1912–1917.* New York: Knopf, 1959.

Meyer, Donald B. *The Protestant Search for Political Realism, 1919–1941.* Westport, Conn.: Greenwood Press, 1960.

Miller, Francis P., ed. *Religion on the Campus.* The report of the National Student Conference, Milwaukee, Wis., December 28, 1926–January 1, 1927. New York: Association Press, 1927.

"Missionary Forces in 1914 and 1918," *International Review of Missions* 8 (1919): 479–90.

"The Missionary Retreat." *Student Movement* 18 (November 1915): 38–39.

Morgan, William H. *Student Religion during Fifty Years*. New York: Association Press, 1935.

Mott, John R. *Addresses and Papers of John R. Mott*. 6 vols. New York: Association Press, 1947.

———— "Christian Missions: Forward Together!" *Christian Century* 42 (March 19, 1925): 375–77.

———— *The Decisive Hour of Christian Missions*. New York: Student Volunteer Movement, 1910.

———— *The Evangelization of the World in This Generation*. New York: Student Volunteer Movement, 1900.

———— *Five Decades and a Forward View*. New York: Harper and Brothers, 1939.

———— "The Present World Conflict and Its Relation to Christian Missions." *Outlook of Missions* 7 (December 1915): 573–80.

———— *The Present World Situation*. New York: Student Volunteer Movement, 1915.

———— *The Present-Day Summons to the World Mission of Christianity*. London: SCM Press, 1932.

———— Why a Student Volunteer Convention at This Time?" *Intercollegian* 39 (November 1919): 1–2.

Murray, J. Lovell. *The Call of a World Task in War Time*. New York: Association Press, 1918.

Noll, Mark A. Introduction to *The Christian College*, by William C. Ringenberg. Grand Rapids, Mich.: Eerdmans, 1984.

"The Northfield Volunteer Conference." Editorial report. *North American Student* 6 (February 1918): 189–90.

Oldham, J. H., ed. "A Survey of the Effect of the War upon Missions." A series of reports over a two-year period in the *International Review of Missions* 9 (1919) and 10 (1920).

———— "The World's Student Christian Federation: Past and Future." *Student World* 18 (October 1925): 167–72.

Pate, Larry D. *From Every People*. Monrovia, Calif.: MARC, 1989.

Petty, Orville A., ed. *Home Base and Missionary Personnel*, Vol. 7 of *The Laymen's Foreign Missions Inquiry*. New York: Harper and Row, 1933.

Phildius, Eberhard. "Work During War in Austria." *Student World* 9 (January 1916): 1–9.

Phillips, Clifton J. "Changing Attitudes in the Student Volunteer Movement of Great Britain and North America, 1886–1928." In *Missionary Ideologies in the Imperialist Era: 1880–1920*, ed. Torben Christensen and William R. Hutchison, 131–45. Struer, Den.: Aros, 1982.

———— "The Student Volunteer Movement and Its Role in China Missions, 1886–1920." *The Missionary Enterprise in China and America,* ed. John K. Fairbank, 91–109. Cambridge: Harvard University Press, 1974.

Pierard, Richard V. "John R. Mott and the Rift in the Ecumenical Movement during World War I." *Journal of Ecumenical Studies* 23 (Fall 1986): 601–20.

Piper, John F., Jr. "Robert E. Speer: Christian Statesman in War and Peace." *Journal of Presbyterian History* 47 (September 1969): 201–25.

Porter, David R. "The Des Moines Convention." *Student World* 13 (April 1920): 58–69.

———— "Maintaining Christian Ideals in War Time." *North American Student* 6 (February 1918): 227–31.

———— "The Peking Conference." *Student World* 15 (July 1922): 86–92.

Rauschenbusch, Walter. *Christianizing the Social Order.* New York: Macmillan, 1912.

———— *The Social Principles of Jesus.* New York: Association Press, 1916.

———— *A Theology for the Social Gospel.* New York: Macmillan, 1918.

"The Reconstruction of Loyalty." An editorial. *Intercollegian* 36 (December 1918): 1.

Ringenberg, William C. *The Christian College.* Grand Rapids, Mich.: Eerdmans, 1984.

Rouse, Ruth. *The World's Student Christian Federation: A History of the First Thirty Years.* London: SCM Press, 1948.

Rugh, Charles E. "The Open Session." *SVM Bulletin* 5 (February 1924): 101–2.

Rutgers, H. C. "The Christian Student Union and the War." *Student World* 10 (October 1917): 281–87.

———— "The Meeting of the General Committee." *Student World* 15 (July 1922): 128–39.

———— "A Visit to Central Europe." *Student Movement* 18 (March 1916): 129–31.

Sailer, T. H. P. "A Study in Contrasts." *SVM Bulletin* 5 (February 1924): 119–22.

SCM (Student Christian Movement). *Student Christian Movement of Great Britain and Ireland.* Annual reports published in book form by the SCM Press (London) during the period 1910–34. The reports include a section on the Student Volunteer Missionary Union.

Shedd, Clarence P. *The Church Follows Its Students.* New Haven: Yale University Press, 1938.

———— *Two Centuries of Student Christian Movements: Their Origin and Intercollegiate Life.* New York: Association Press, 1934.

Speer, Robert E. *The Christian Man, the Church, and the War.* New York: Macmillan, 1918.

———— "Christian Missions: An Enterprise of Hope." *Missionary Review of the World* 46 (1923): 195–99.

———— *The Gospel and the New World.* New York: Fleming H. Revell, 1919.

———— *The New Opportunity of the Church.* New York: Macmillan, 1919.

———— "The War Aims and Foreign Missions." *Intercollegian* 36 (October 1918): 2–5.

———— "The War and the Nation's Larger Call to World Evangelism." *Christian Century* 34 (July 12, 1917): 10–12.

———— *The War and the Religious Outlook.* Boston: Pilgrim Press, 1919.

"The Student Movements and the War." Various authors. *Student World* 9 (January 1916): 27–43; 10 (January 1917): 161–273.

"Student Views of the Indianapolis Convention." Editorial comments. *Missionary Review of the World* 47 (March 1924): 173–74.

"The Student Volunteers in Des Moines." No author given. *Missionary Review of the World* 43 (February 1920): 82–85.

"Students and Christianity Today: A Symposium of Statements by Leaders in Many Lands." *Student World* 14 (April 1921): 57–92.

Sundkler, Bengt. *Nathan Söderblom, His Life and Work.* London: Lutterworth Press, 1968.

SVM (Student Volunteer Movement). Ed. Milton T. Stauffer. *Christian Students and World Problems.* Report of the Ninth International Convention of the SVM, Indianapolis, Ind., Dec. 28, 1923 to Jan. 1, 1924. New York: Student Volunteer Movement, 1924.

———— *North American Students and World Advance.* Ed. Burton St. John. Addresses Delivered at the Eighth International Convention of the SVM. Des Moines, Iowa, Dec. 31, 1919 to Jan. 4, 1920. New York: Student Volunteer Movement, 1920.

———— *Students and the Christian World Mission.* Ed. Jesse R. Wilson. Report of the Twelfth Quadrennial Convention of the Student Volunteer Movement for Foreign Missions. New York: Student Volunteer Movement, 1936.

────── *Students and the Future of Christian Missions*. Ed. Jesse R. Wilson. Report of the Tenth Quadrennial Convention of the SVM, Detroit, Mich., Dec. 23, 1927 to Jan. 1, 1928. New York: Student Volunteer Movement, 1928.

────── *Students and the Present Missionary Crisis*. Addresses Delivered Before the Sixth International Convention of the SVM. Rochester, N.Y., Dec. 29, 1909 to Jan. 2, 1910. New York: Student Volunteer Movement, 1910.

────── *Students and the World-Wide Expansion of Christianity*. Ed. Fennell P. Turner. Addresses Delivered Before the Seventh International Convention of the SVM. Kansas City, Kans., Dec. 31, 1913 to Jan. 4, 1914. New York: Student Volunteer Movement, 1914.

Tatlow, Tissington. "The British Student Movement in War Time." *Student World* 8 (April 1915): 129–33.

────── *The Story of the Student Christian Movement of Great Britain and Ireland*. London: SCM Press, 1933.

Taylor, S. Earl, and Halford E. Luccock. *The Christian Crusade for World Democracy*. New York: Methodist Book Concern, 1918.

Thomas, Winnifred F. "North American Students Mobilizing for Christian World Democracy." *Association Outlook* 17 (February 1918): 21–23.

Tobias, Channing. "Shall America Be Made Safe for Black Men?" *North American Student* 6 (February 1918): 266–67.

────── "The Student Movement among American Negroes." *Student World* 9 (July 1916): 111–16.

────── "The Young Men's Christian Associations in American Negro Colleges." *Student World* 17 (January 1924): 58–62.

"The Unsearchable Riches of Christ." *Student Movement* 18 (February 1916): 98–100.

Van Dusen, Henry P. "The Spiritual Tone of Indianapolis." *SVM Bulletin* 5 (February 1924): 104–7.

Varg, Paul A. *Missionaries, Chinese, and Diplomats: The American Protestant Missionary Movement in China, 1890–1952*. Princeton: Princeton University Press, 1958.

────── "Motives in Protestant Missions, 1890–1917." *Church History* 23 (1954): 68–82.

"War Year Objectives." *North American Student* 6 (October 1917): 29.

Ward, Harry F. "Missions and Social Evangelism." *North American Student* 6 (February 1918): 233–34.

────── "Social Duties in War Time." *North American Student* 6 (October 1917): 16–23.

———— "Tell Your Church People That!" *North American Student* 6 (March 1918): 259–63.

Watson, Goodwin B. "How the Discussion Groups Worked Out." *SVM Bulletin* 5 (February 1924): 97–101.

Weatherford, W.D. "Promoting the Spirit of Evangelism." *North American Student* 6 (February 1918): 223–26.

Wheeler, Reginald W. *A Man Sent from God: A Biography of Robert E. Speer*. Westwood, N.J.: Fleming H. Revell, 1956.

Wilder, Robert P. *The Great Commission: The Missionary Response of the Student Volunteer Movements in North America and Europe*. London: Oliphants, 1936.

———— "The Governing Aims of Foreign Missionary Effort." *SVM Bulletin* 1 (March 1920): 1–3.

———— "Has the Missionary Motive Changed?" *Missionary Review of the World* 48 (1925): 931–35.

Wiley, S. Wirt. *History of YMCA-Church Relations in the United States*. New York: Association Press, 1944.

Wilson, E. Raymond. "What Shall We Do with the Student Volunteer Movement?" *SVM Bulletin* 5 (March 1924): 143–46.

Wilson, Jesse R. "Students and Foreign Missions Today." *International Review of Missions* 51 (1928): 885–91.

Index

About the Author

Nathan D. Showalter has worked with churches and Christian organizations in Kenya, Germany, Hong Kong, Indonesia, Taiwan, and the United States. A specialist in cross-cultural communication, he worked for six years with World Vision International, traveling to several dozen countries on six continents. A Mennonite who trained at Fuller Seminary and Harvard Divinity School (Th.D.), he currently serves as senior pastor of Taipei International Church in Taiwan. He and his wife, Christina, are parents of Eli (named after his Amish Mennonite great-grandfather) who is receiving a bilingual education in Chinese and English.